Preachers
·A·PECULIAR·PEOPLE·

OYEZ!
OYEZ!
HEAR YE!

by Albert Preston Whitaker, Jr.
with Stephen L. Robbins

North Wind Publishing
Brewer, Maine

2021

Copyright ©2021 Albert P. Whitaker, Junior.

ISBN: 978-1-7329319-7-8

LCCN: 2021939299

All rights reserved. No part of this publication may be reproduced, stored in a retrieval system, or transmitted in any form or by any means, electronic, mechanical, recording or otherwise, without the prior written permission of the author.

Published by North Wind Publishing, Brewer, Maine.
Printed in the United States of America.

Table of Contents

Dedication and Acknowledgments iv
Chapter 1 All Rise 1
Chapter 2 This Court Is Now In Session 7
Chapter 3 Son Of Ahaz 11
Chapter 4 Men Of The Cloth 17
Chapter 5 Reverend Rolla Lee Utley Junior 29
Chapter 6 Reverend Doctor Eugene Sumner Philbrook . 45
Chapter 7 Reverend Doctor Clifford Earl Jones 165
Chapter 8 Reverend Howard Burton Higgins Junior . . . 213
Chapter 9 Reverend Barry Lowell Grahl 243
Chapter 10 Reverend William Howard Stone Junior 277
Chapter 11 Reverend Harvey Lee Cossaboom 325
Chapter 12 Doctor Haddon William Robinson 355
Chapter 13 Doctor Hudson Taylor Armerding 365
Chapter 14 Pastor Stanley Harland Griffin 375
Chapter 15 Amen! 391
Chapter 16 Epilog 397
Appendices
    A. How To Be King Of Your Castle, *by Polly Utley* . . 403
    B. Memories Of My Church, *by Polly Utley* 408
    C. The Sunday Stone, *by Rev. Eugene S. Philbrook* 412
    D. Our Pastor, *by Mrs. Edwin Stetson* 417
    E. "Plus Ultra," *by Albert P. Whitaker, Jr.* 419
    F. The Uppertaker, *by Polly Utley* 426
    G. Tribute to Barry Grahl, *by Christopher Berchelmann* 427
    H. Tribute to Rolla Utley, *by Albert P. Whitaker, Jr.* . . 429
About the Authors 433

Dedication

To all PREACHERS of the Gospel who toil daily with matters most of us would never understand, and who work tirelessly proclaiming the "Word of the Lord," and who do far more in ministering to their communities.

Acknowledgments

Special appreciation to:

Polly (Bunker) (King) Utley, wife of Rev. Rolla Utley. Polly walked the authors through the extensive details of her husband's long life and fruitful ministry. Polly also shares her own poetry which compliments Rolla's and Rev. Grahl's stories in this book.

JoAnn Randall and her cousin **Carl Philbrook,** grandchildren of the late Rev. Dr. Eugene Philbrook. JoAnn and Carl helped locate much information and pictures, which greatly assisted our writing about their beloved grandfather.

Lillie (Stokes) Jones, wife of Rev. Dr. Clifford Jones. Lillie reviewed the manuscript of the chapter about her husband, made helpful suggestions, amended and clarified information.

Robert "Bob" Howard Higgins of Meridian, Mississippi, son of the late Rev. Howard B. Higgins. Bob provided much of the information on his father: photographs, "This is your life" manuscripts and the like – an invaluable contribution to a detailed life story.

Faith (Grahl) Spivey of Fayette, Georgia, daughter of the late Rev. Barry Grahl. Faith enthusiastically contributed extensive information on her father, enhancing his legacy.

Betty (LaTour) Stone of St. Cloud, Florida and Vassalboro, Maine, wife of Rev. William Stone. Betty's pages of detail tell the story of Bill and his long ministry in the rural areas of northern New England. Betty also provided many photographs, and encouragement for our effort.

Dorothy (Emery) (Cossaboom) Meldrum, of Farmington, Maine, widow of the late Rev. Harvey Cossaboom. Dorothy helpfully critiqued the authors' words and has added so much more to Harvey's story.

Steve Robbins, son-in-law of author Al Whitaker. With patience and dedication, Steve edited the author's rough drafts into a more acceptable final form. Steve put in many tiresome hours doing detailed research on Rev. Dr. Eugene Philbrook and others. And his skills in locating appropriate images have also enhanced the final product. Steve also edited our two previous books, <u>This is My Story: From Where I Sit</u> (2015) and <u>This Is OLIO</u> (2020).

Janet Robbins, cousin of the editor and publisher of our two previous titles as well as this volume. Each time when our projects' technical requirements reached the limit of our abilities, Janet has carried our work through to completion with her professional publishing expertise. We are grateful for Janet's kind assistance.

PREACHER (English) = EKKLESIASTES (Greek) = QOHELETH (Hebrew)

The Old Testament book of *Ecclesiastes* in our English Bible is *Ekklesiastes* in the Greek Septuagint translation.

Its original Hebrew title is *Qoheleth* (from the root word *qahal*, meaning "one who addresses an assembly, a preacher").

A rural church without a preacher, Limington, Maine.

(Highsmith, Carol M, photographer. This old church, high above the old highway known as the Ossipee Trail, near Limington, Maine, is abandoned and unmarked [photograph]. Taken 15 Sep. 2017. Library of Congress, <www.loc.gov/item/2017882630/>. Edited.)

Chapter 1

All Rise!

In 1978, Dr. Walter L. Cook was *field education director* at the Bangor Theological Seminary in Bangor, Maine. This position placed seminary students into the pulpits of rural Maine churches, as a part of their training to become pastors. Requests for a short-term preacher usually came into Dr. Cook's office from the smaller churches, and often at the last minute. These churches were often near desperation because their regular pastor was incapacitated, or maybe had just left.

Dr. Cook responded by sending out a student to a requesting church. But sometimes the student sent had no previous public speaking experience. Some seminary students were older, coming from unrelated vocations, and had never before filled a pulpit or publicly expounded the Scriptures.

Dr. Cook noted that his task was a rewarding, and sometimes exciting, experience. He sent out "wet behind the ears" people to do often-big assignments. His notes about these experiences he compiled into a little book: *Send Us A Minister: . . . Any Minister Will Do.*[1] (Dr. Cook adds, "Surely a church should be more selective when asking for a pastor."[2]) His book relates what happened when students were dispatched to the small rural churches tucked away in the almost-unknown hamlets of northern Maine. Dr Cook's humorous (if not disastrous) accounts relate the students' unusual experiences as well as the "patience on the part of church people with these fledging ministers."³

We have known several pastors who possessed unique approaches to ministry. While they usually served larger congregations than did Dr. Cook's students, some may have begun their ministries in such humble places, "in the woods" – sparsely-populated rural areas. Along the way, each had a unique, imaginative ministry which left a distinctive mark.

These preachers were much more than the "any minister will do" type. Because of their impacts upon their congregations and communities, they are worthy to be remembered as "giants in the ministry". May their stories, presented here and gleaned from our personal encounters with them, be an encouragement and inspiration for generations far beyond theirs.

In the mid-1950s I joined "The Gideons." Gideons International is an organization of laymen who adopt a ministry of personal evangelism. Our mission is accomplished largely by placing Scriptures amidst the world's traffic lanes. Most commonly, copies of the printed Bible are placed in nearly every hotel or motel room. Gideons is typically a missionary extension of sympathetic local churches. Gideons members periodically report the organization's successes to their supporting church congregations.

The organization took its name from Gideon of the Bible, who, with only few men, liberated an entire nation (Israel) from the oppression of its enemy neighbors.⁴

Gideon was, much to his surprise, called by the angel of the LORD a "mighty man of valour."[5] He is also listed in the New Testament among the great heroes of the faith.[6] Although Gideon began with a very reserved and humble attitude, he accepted God's challenge and stepped up to accomplish great things for God. Gideon, like us, was not a perfect man. In fact, he did not finish life as well as we may have preferred. It's tough – impossible really – to try being a perfect example.

Many of the pastors we have known and present here began life with simple, reserved, and maybe even shy personalities. But, with God's leading and their dedicated effort, they became instruments fit for the Lord's use, doing His sometimes-difficult work of ministry. Like Gideon, they stepped up to do great things for God.

In the past there was a distinct difference between a "minister" and a "preacher." Most churches, especially in rural America, desired a "minister" – one who would minister. That meant becoming involved – not just in the lives of church members, but also with the entire community.

A minister's duties were expected to include:

(a) a message from the pulpit expounding how people could improve themselves by following Biblical principles;

(b) teaching the Bible;

(c) participation and leadership in church events; and

(d) innovation and encouragement for living a Holy life.

A minister was also expected to extend his sphere of influence beyond the church and into the local community. There, he would be respected for his strong Christian values, and his wisdom and leadership in various town organizations.

A minister's expected participation in "extra-curricular" (not church-related) events might include diversified lectures, assistance in humane and charitable meetings, performing weddings and funerals, visiting the ill and aged, and counseling – all were a part of "ministering."

"Preaching" was left to the circuit rider who, on an occasional basis, visited a church and its local community. The itinerant preacher loudly proclaimed the Gospel in "revival" meetings, which often changed residents' and church members' lives for the better. He was not there to minister, but to "preach" and cause a change in one's life.

In present times, we have confused the matter by calling pastors and ministers – as preachers. Regrettably, many called to "minister" to a congregation become just "preachers," and leave the ministering to "associates" or "assistants."

Not "any minister will do." Only the dedicated will be considered, with expectations for their long hours and hard work.

With all this in mind, we have lumped together all ministers, pastors, evangelists, and preachers. Their legacies will speak of their accomplishments. Let us tell you about some whom we have known.

The court is now in session.
PLEASE ALL RISE !

"Old Church, Medford, Maine, internal view."
[DrStew82 (https://commons.wikimedia.org/wiki/File:Old_Church,_Medford,_Maine,_internal_view_image_1.jpg), edited by Stephen Robbins, (https://creativecommons.org/licenses/by-sa/4.0/legalcode).]

ENDNOTES

[1] Cook, Walter L. *Send Us a Minister: ... Any Minister Will Do*. (Rockland, Me: Courier-Gazette, ©1978). No pagination.
[2] Ibid., [from "Introduction"].
[3] Ibid., [from "Preface"].
[4] Judges 6:1-10.
[5] Judges 6:12 (King James Version).
[6] Hebrews 11:32.

Hear ye, hear ye!

Preacher is about to speak!

Church bells traditionally call villagers to come hear a Sunday morning sermon. *(circa 1900. Up: Library of Congress; Down: ebay.com)*

Chapter 2

THIS COURT IS NOW IN SESSION

"**1 Shout for joy** . . . . **4 Enter** . . . **his courts with praise;** . . ."
—*Psalm 100:1, 4 [partial] (New International Version)*

Modern technology has progressed rapidly in the last fifty years to where NEWS is disseminated almost instantly to the public – that is, to those toting iPhones or other handheld information devices. Times have rapidly changed.

When radio was introduced less than one hundred years ago, people marveled at hearing a voice relay the war news and such.

Before radio, news traveled chiefly in crudely-printed newspapers or leaflets, which were not accessible to everyone.

Preceding printed news, a settlement's primary method of communication (other than *by word-of-mouth*) was through its TOWN CRIER. The crier's job was to first get the inhabitants' attention, then tell them the news or make public announcements.

A town crier usually dressed in elaborate, colorful attire and swung a large, monotone brass bell. His loud voice, already well above the twelve-decibels level of chainsaws, often reached an ear-piercing ninety-seven decibels. His thunderous voice first captured the public's attention, then introduced public announcements, bringing "life to our history." Such a crier worked without salary and had to obtain his own attire. He must have public speaking skills, a sense of humor, a love of people (especially children), and a keen knowledge of his locality. He indeed enlivened his area. The crier's only reward was the satisfaction of having relayed important news and having delighted his audience.

"Oyez, oyez! Welcome, one and all," a crier bellowed. Any nearby persons could hear and be challenged to listen, whether just out of curiosity or wanting to understand the soon-to-be-revealed news.

Oyez is said to be a French interjection meaning "pay attention and listen," or an Anglo-Saxon word for *listen*. Others believe this simply means "O yes, O yes!"

"Oyez, oyez! Hear ye, hear ye!" was a clarion call to listen and pay attention.

One recognizes that these words are often spoken when a court session opens, to announce the judge's entrance. They are an alert to *listen* because important things are about to be said, acted upon, and adjudicated.

Court Is Now In Session !

Preachers are about to speak!

Oyez! Hear ye, hear ye!

O yes, O yes!

A humble and impoverished pastor, on his way to preach to his congregation. *(Caldecott, Randolph, illustrator, in: Irving, Washington, <u>Old Christmas</u>, (1875); archive.org)*

Pastoral Vignette
Middleboro, Massachusetts

Nicholas Medberry was the first pastor at Central Baptist Church, preaching there from 1828 to 1832.

> Rev. Medberry was paid the munificent sum of $475 per year as his salary and he received it but once a year. The story is told that in prayer meeting, while thinking of good Pastor Medberry, one worthy deacon prayed, "Lord, you keep him humble and we will keep him poor." [1]

The local church's lay leadership prays for its pastor.
(Detail from: Lorimer, John Henry, Ordination of elders in a Scottish kirk. *1891; wikimedia.org)*

ENDNOTE

[1] Maddigan, Michael J., "Central Baptist Church History," *Recollecting Nemasket: Writing About the History of Middleborough & Lakeville, Massachusetts* [online blog]. Posted Wed. 25 Aug. 2010; <http://nemasket.blogspot.com/2010/08/central-baptist-church-history.html>; © 2009-2020. Citing: Stetson, G. Ward, *Central Baptist Church, Middleboro, Massachusetts: History*. [manuscript], Apr.1966.

Hezekiah [stained glass], in East Window at York Minster, England.
By Coventry glazier John Thornton circa 1405-1408. *(wikimedia.org)*

Chapter 3

SON OF AHAZ

**"O come, let us worship and bow down:
let us kneel before the Lord our maker."**
—Psalm 95:6 (King James Version)

When my children were of college age, one of my best arguments for them to obey our house rules, or carry out my wishes and instructions, was: "Because *Hezekiah* 1:9 says so!" Sometimes I posited this reason to others, in support of some idea or desire. Of course, there is no such book as *Hezekiah* in the Old Testament. This often-quoted verse must be a long and comprehensive one, because it has addressed an endless variety of matters. The irony was that sometimes a person agreed with me; but later, whether out of conviction or curiosity, when they tried looking-up my citation's "book and page" – they were only confounded. And my integrity and authority were no more!

Perhaps you recall the story about a preacher who announced that his sermon for the upcoming Sunday was based on Hebrews, chapter fourteen, suggesting that congregants should read it before then. When sermon time arrived, the pastor asked for those who read Hebrews fourteen to raise hands. Half of the congregation did this. Pastor then announced the morning's subject: "Lying." Of course, there's no chapter fourteen in Hebrews!

But now, with a more serious approach, let's examine a real Bible person named Hezekiah.

Hezekiah was a young, twenty-five-year-old King of Judah who trusted the Lord and was a strong spiritual leader. His activities were often unexpected and certainly controversial.[1] Among his directives was the destruction of the serpent-of-brass-upon-a-pole which Moses had made.[2]

(wikimedia.org)

The Israelites had preserved that item as an ongoing reminder of how God provided them a way of escape from danger. Over time, however, the people had turned that memento into an object of worship.

The lesson for us today should be clear and understandable. Churches often preserve their own "idols." Begun as reminders of their Christian experiences, the objects fast became idols. In many cases, these things were worshipped by those who should know better.

Past

The first of these idols could be <u>the past</u>. Oh, how we love what has been done in the past and long to return to those times. Really? The past would mean dirt roads, horse and buggy, hard labor, no air conditioning, no iPhone and, of course, no microphone amplification, just to note a few realities. We long for the past and how things used to be done, falsely believing that times were better then. We could truthfully be accused of longing for the past, instead of longing for the Lord and his future return. Does this need to be changed?

Building

Secondly, we often worship <u>the church building itself</u>. We have been so involved and appreciate the structure for its varied usages that we expound upon it, rather than the Lord, to our neighbors and friends. Often, we forget that the true church is not a building but the people, without whom there would be no church. Whenever a disaster does away with a church building, the real "church" remains. Was God or Hezekiah the one responsible?

Programs

Thirdly, we may worship <u>programs and activities</u> within the church as ends in themselves. These may be fine endeavors, but we should recognize they are not to be held up and worshipped. Sure, we used to have a *Training Union*, a *Christian Endeavor* and maybe a *Lady's Tea* as regular organizations. Although they once served a purpose "back when," have they become a *serpent-of-brass-upon-a-pole* which now needs to be broken?

Preacher

Here's a big area for concern – <u>the worship of a preacher</u>. While our preacher may be endeared and chosen by the Lord, there is a problem if our esteem approaches adoration and even becomes worship. The Lord probably blessed him (or her?), and we fully appreciate him and his ministry, but he must not be made the object of our worship. Like with the Israelites, it is right to appreciate a pastor and remember how the Lord has used him in our lives – a reminder, perhaps, of the time he led us to Jesus so that now we are truly alive. But some folks appear to worship their former pastors, even those of long, long ago.

In this book we investigate the lives and times of some preachers from "long ago." Their examples and successes ever remind us of the Lord's ongoing, unending work. These men are not to be worshipped, but we can appreciate and learn from their efforts to further the ever-timeless Gospel message. Many churches and ministries have become what they are today because of these dedicated, hard-working, ambassadors of the Lord who occupied the past.

The Lord instructed Moses to make the serpent-of-brass-upon-a-pole for a purpose: to point people to the Lord, who alone could *save* them. This was a *type* of Christ and the work He completed on the Cross. The serpent-of-brass-upon-a-pole artifact was retained solely as a reminder to people who so easily forget. We must not worship any pastor, memento, or even the old wooden Cross itself; they are only to remind us of the Lord and His work for us.

But the Lord also sanctioned the destruction of this serpent-of-brass-upon-a-pole, because the people began to worship it instead of Him.

Let these preachers remind us of the Lord's work. Profit by their stories, but do not worship them. Worship Our Savior only! These preachers would agree.

Hezekiah 1:9 says so!

Oh, and Hezekiah was the son of King Ahaz.

𝔓astoral 𝔙ignette[3]
Yarmouth, Massachusetts

REV. TIMOTHY ALDEN.
BORN 1736–DIED 1828.

Mr. Alden was a good sermonizer, peculiarly happy in the choice of texts. One of his parishioners, complaining that she was not profited by his preaching, he selected for her especial benefit the next Sabbath, Heb. IV: 2—"The word preached did not profit them, not being mixed with faith in them that heard it."

Another instance is well remembered, when the customary day for supplying the parsonage with wood having passed, he preached the following Sabbath from Proverbs XXVI: 20—"Where no wood is, there the fire goeth out." The wood was forthcoming the next day.

ENDNOTES

[1] Second Kings 18.
[2] Numbers 21:9.
[3] Swift, Charles Francis. *History of Old Yarmouth: Comprising the Present Towns of Yarmouth and Dennis: From the Settlement to the Division in 1794 With the History of Both Towns to These Times*. (Yarmouth Port, [Massachusetts]: Published by the Author, 1884), [image:] facing p. 190, [text:] p. 191. Web: <https://www.google.com/books/edition/History_of_Old_Yarmouth/eq1qzgjQqqkC>.

FROM: The Apostle, Paul ...
TO: Titus ... the preacher in Crete
DATE: AD 63
SUBJECT: How to do church right

Speak, with full authority, the things which become sound doctrine;

Do all things showing yourself a pattern of *Good Works*;

Teaching with integrity, seriousness and soundness of speech;

Encouraging young men, *Train* young women;

Looking for the glorious appearing of our great God and our Savior;

Let no one despise you;

Allow Jesus to purify you as one of *His Peculiar People*.

Adapted from Titus 2

Chapter 4

MEN OF THE CLOTH

"And He Himself gave some *to be* apostles, some prophets, some evangelists, and some pastors and teachers"
—*Ephesians 4:11 (New King James Version)*

Pastors, ministers, preachers, . . . whatever. Today they must be entertainers. They have changed the church program from its traditional reverent liturgy, which included reciting the *Lord's Prayer*, reading the *Apostles' Creed*, listening to *Scripture* being read and hearing a *Pastoral prayer*. These are no longer a part of worship.

Also gone, in most churches, is the scholarly, well-prepared, skillfully-crafted and professionally-delivered sermon. Not only was the sermon Scripture-based and taught Bible doctrine, it also presented us with a practical application – how to live by it. The sermon then concluded with a challenge that sent one away enthused and encouraged. The address avoided repetition and didn't waste words – it was to the point.

Today's "worship" service, however, presents a far different picture. It has "progressed" out of the quiet, meditative and reverent traditional mode into a style that almost appears to be a celebration – even entertainment.

The music has also been revised. The calm, meaningful and uplifting hymnology has been abandoned and replaced by very loud (even noisy) renditions which employ often-meaningless words. It is now known as "praise." Regrettably, today's concluding musical number fails to dismiss one from the service with head held high, marching at an upbeat pace as once was practiced. But this new norm is widely appreciated and accepted. Maybe that is good.

One must take a historical look at the American church and how it has worshipped. For English immigrants seeking religious freedom, "music" was mainly reciting the Psalms *without* music, except for voice modulation. At some point thereafter, some instrumentation began to creep in. When the organ was introduced, this made singing (and listening) much more enjoyable. To many, however, including the minister, this was irreverent and not pleasing to God. Perhaps this was even the "sin" of entertaining, because the people enjoyed it so much. Little is recorded about the method or content of the preaching.

The sermon message has also been altered to fit the transition from worship to praise. The preacher's role as minister is diminished; he is now more of a motivational speaker. Content is less important than rhetoric – one's ability to maintain audience attention by using speaking gifts and a delightful voice. Such orations often lose connection with the outside world, politics, local events and concerns. Scripture passages, previously a vital part of Bible book expositions, are now merely "jumping off" points for a flow of words. The original intended meaning or lesson of a chapter or verse is sometimes ignored. This change, from a serious, thoughtful challenge and in-depth Bible study to entertainment speaking, follows the younger generation's current expectations interest.

Seminaries long encouraged homiletics pupils (preachers-in-training) to craft a structured three-point message. Although this method was possibly overused at times, it granted the hearer some remembrance of what had been said. Often today, though, no apparent outline is expected.

A person's attention span for hearing a sermon with understanding is about twenty minutes; this has long been recognized. Today's speaker who exceeds this norm faces the danger of losing his audience. What more can be preached with emphasis beyond twenty minutes? A minister who disrespects time – perhaps going on for forty-five minutes – can make his audience uneasy and fidgety for any number of reasons. Rare is the deliverer who can keep a crowd actively interested for an extended period, to make a specific emphasis. Billy Graham may have been that exception.

Many have considered Aristotle an expert on the practice of speaking. He noted that public speaking was an art. Further, he suggested ethics, politics, psychology and the law needed to be included, but cautioned that excess, too little or too much, negatively influences the argument presented. Importantly, he was convinced that effective speaking could be taught and would improve both knowledge of the subject and the application thereof.

Many others addressed the need for formal instruction in homiletics. By careful study, a student-preacher could learn how to improve his ability in effective oratory.[1]

Currently, public speaking could be more effectively taught, even in colleges where people are preparing for ministry. When a minister is expected to become a church's sole chief operating executive (COE), the seminary offers them no courses in business management or finance. In this same vein, how often do pastoral students study Quintilian's <u>Institutes of Oratory</u>,[2] a classic in the subject?

In the early 1800s, Boston clergyman Henry Ware advanced his belief in the practicality of extemporaneous preaching and the importance of obtaining an audience response.[3] He emphasized the delivery primarily through voice and bodily action. Ware might have been encouraged by today's "preachers."

In times past, a sermon would hopefully instill Biblical truth, then conclude by requesting listeners to respond – heed Christ's call to repent of wrongdoings, moral failures, and inaction; and accept His free gift of salvation. Hopefully, as the congregation exited, each was mindful that a response was required and, ideally, would be implemented.

In the absence of voluntary persuasion, the sermon in many evangelistic protestant churches today is followed by a drawn-out *altar call* sometimes lasting fifteen-to-twenty minutes (or even longer). What used to be a discrete *invitation* for a specific purpose on a particular Sunday has often become a call to "accept Christ" plus some commitment such as joining that church. Many times, this has detracted from a well-presented and challenging sermon. In my younger days, after a specific address or emphasis, we often heard the opportunity for young people to dedicate themselves to full-time Christian ministry, including missionary work. This important response is no longer suggested.

It is believed the *invitation* was first used by evangelist Dwight L. Moody in 1871, after he had addressed an overflow crowd in Chicago. Others have attributed this type of *altar call* to Charles Finney. Initially, such an invitation was at the discretion of the preacher, who could discern the Holy Spirit's direction in the response to his just-preached message. Altar calls are not necessarily Scriptural, but Jesus' words are clear: "Come unto me" – in Luke 14:23 and other places.

Frankly, if a preacher's message, in and of itself, does not initiate a response, all the pleading in the world will not move the uninspired. This is the position taken by the famous Bible expositor, J. Vernon McGee, who notes that more decisions are made on a one-to-one basis, often at the prayer meeting, a mid-week service. Many decisions are made during a conversation that is not prolonged or begging for a positive response. Although many pastors feel an altar call is necessary, it can be a more dignified and meaningful experience when presenting the opportunity briefly and without extended pleading.

The COVID-19 pandemic[4] has revised the methods by which the *invitation* is utilized. Time constraints dictate that a broadcast exposition must fit within allotted air time. The sermon itself should now provoke the viewer-hearer to action. "Hits" on local church broadcasts verify that "attendance" at virtual Sunday services far exceeds a church's physical seating capacity in many instances. This phenomenon will no doubt continue post-pandemic, even after "normal" in-person services resume. Once the "preaching" has concluded, a viewer may immediately opt out the broadcast – possibly to "take the roast out of the oven" – thus missing any concluding matters. Therefore, any hope a preacher may have for inducing affirmative action must be built into his sermon presentation.

Regrettably, the art of *public speaking* has deteriorated over the years. Its aspects of style and delivery, along with scholarly, colorful, and vibrant rhetoric may have succumbed to recent trends in the teaching of English language. Public schools are less concerned now with misspelled words, vocabulary, grammar, and cursive writing – those particulars do not seem as important for communicating with today's world. The "proper" expression of one's self is simply unnecessary, even undesired. Is it any wonder when a pastor's best rhetorical and oratorical efforts go unheeded?

The importance of a pastor's personal appearance has been discussed in detail in our previous book.[5] There was such a high regard for Scripture that anybody who read it publicly was expected to be properly-attired. This held true even in the 1790s in the wilderness frontier of eastern Maine. The dozen families[6] in the new settlement called Robbinston could afford neither a church edifice nor a pastor's salary.[7]

> Meetings were held in each other's houses until a large log school house was built [in 1795] which answered for a school and meeting house. Mr. Jones and Mr. Bugbee continued to read for us for some years. They used to read Doddridge, Baxter's and Whitefield's sermons . . . . [The proprietor, Edward H.] Robbins sent both readers, Samuel Jones and William Bugbee, a suit of black broadcloth and a military hat, so that on Sunday they might appear in clothing appropriate to their ministerial duties."[8]

Robbinston folks built this church 1841 (burned 4 July 1910; replaced 1911). After the Civil War, this congregation often could not afford a minister nor keep one very long. (1907; Robbinston Historical Society)

Does the appearance, including the dress, of a preacher, ever go unnoticed?

For many years all ministers displayed the title of *Reverend* before their name. Such a designation usually became valid and was used after their *ordination*. One expecting to become a minister within a denomination had to pass an ordinance council's questioning and receive its positive recommendation.

Ordination was an identification and acknowledgement that one was qualified and trusted as an effective and educated representative of his denomination. It would be a title of respect for a spiritual leader, and would authorize one to perform religious rites and ceremonies. He was a *voice* and one to be looked up to for decency, guidance, moral counsel, advice and direction – even in local government.

Today in the more *evangelical* circles, the title *Reverend* has been minimized because it possibly connotes a *Reverend* is better than his peers. The title *Brother* is a less offensive substitute. However, the title *Doctor* is acceptable – even expected of many senior pastors who have earned that degree – without implications of superiority or pride. Although *Reverend* means more to the community than *Doctor*, probably both titles are less respected now than in earlier days.

And, speaking of respect . . . When I was growing up, my parents insisted that we never address the minister by his given name or "nickname," as is normal and in use today. We were to call him *Pastor* alone, or *Reverend* when using his surname. I also remember that when addressing one's elders, it was considered inappropriate to use a nickname or first name.

There was a time, in the not too distant past, when there were differences in the duties and practices expected of the minister, the pastor, the preacher, or just a clergyman. Each of these *men of the cloth* could be defined by their different duties and responsibilities.

A church would *call* a minister (or, in the case of some denominations, a minister would be assigned to a church). The minister oversaw the congregation's spiritual welfare and delivered the Sunday sermon. Thus, he "ministered" to the people.

A minister became a *pastor* when his duties expanded to include counseling parishioners, attending to the welfare of widows and, in many cases, taking on administrative responsibilities for the organization. In *the olden days* a minister had to tend the wood-burning furnace and sweep the floors. When someone else could assume these duties, the minister was then promoted to pastor.

Along the way, a minister might assume the designation of *clergyman* as he became involved in the local community. This involvement generated a wider respect, but also could disturb those locals whose practices bordered upon the unethical. A clergyman would often offer an *invocation* or a *benediction* to a civic meeting (probably as a courtesy to him, and meaningless to others).

Then came the *preacher*. In earlier times he was a horseback rider, servicing various and sundry parishes, often speaking at more than one church each Sunday. He seldom was the "resident minister" at any, but filled pulpits on a random basis, such as when a minister was ill, had left, or was just lazy. Maybe the congregation needed a different voice to enthuse them. This *circuit rider* was sometimes an evangelist, expounding "hell fire and brimstone" and even enlarging a congregation. He was typically an enthusiastic, capable and motivating speaker. He was always on the move, with an old Bible in one hand and the horse reins in the other. He was not a minister or a pastor, but a fast-moving, dynamic *preacher* who could revive any assembly. He had no other duties or responsibilities at any church beyond that exercise.

Today, we have abandoned all of these titles, and maybe for good and proper reasons. The one who is now called to, or assigned to, a church is characteristically labeled a *preacher*. And that is his primary activity. Others (assistant pastor, associate pastor, minister of education) are hired to perform the varied church duties of minister and pastor.

Otherwise, the titles of pastor, minister and clergyman have been removed into the dustbin of history. So, now we write about *preachers*, because that is how people have come to understand the profession. Our biographies of these people define the qualities of men who performed exceptionally well in all areas of their calling. Each was once called *The Minister*. But today they would be, and are, classified by us as PREACHERS. Or, possibly consider them APOSTLES?   ~ Hear Ye! ~

Robbinston Village, Maine. *(circa 1910; Robbinston Historical Society)*

ENDNOTES

[1] Wiersbe, Warren W., and Lloyd M. Perry. *The Wycliffe Handbook of Preaching and Preachers*. (Chicago, Illinois: Moody Press, ©1984).

[2] Quintilian, and Harold Edgeworth Butler. *The Instituto Oratoria of Quintilian: with an English translation by H.E. Butler*. (Cambridge, Massachusetts: Harvard University Press, 1920-1922). Also online: <https://catalog.hathitrust.org/Record/011719724/Home>.

[3] Ware, Henry. *Hints on Extemporaneous Preaching*. Boston: Cummings, Hilliard, 1824. Also online: <https://archive.org/details/hintsonextempor00waregoog/>.

[4] Also called the coronavirus disease 2019 pandemic.

[5] Whitaker, Albert Preston, Jr. with Stephen L. Robbins. *This Is Olio: From Where I Sit*. (Brewer, Maine: North Wind Publishing, ©2020). See pages 91-92, 199.

[6] The population of 54 in 1790 increased to 127 by 1800. Most were recruited by proprietor Robbins and initially worked for him.

[7] Settlers named place after the man from whom they'd bought land on easy terms – lawyer Edward H. Robbins of Milton, Massachusetts. Robbins bought the entire township (17,860 acres) in 1786 when the Massachusetts General Court needed money to pay for the Revolutionary War. Robbins had been a delegate to the Massachusetts Constitutional Convention in 1778; later he was a representative in the Massachusetts House, Speaker of the House (1793-1802), and Lieutenant Governor (1803-1806).

[8] Vose, Thomas, *[Personal papers] [manuscript]*. As quoted in: Johnson, Dorothy, "A Story and a Recipe," *Calais Advertiser* (Calais, Maine), 26 May 2016, (volume 181, number 21), page 23 ; online: http://www.thecalaisadvertiser.com/digital_ca/2016/May_26.pdf ; accessed 20 July 2020.

Chapter 5

Reverend ROLLA LEE UTLEY *Junior*

The year was 1926, in the *Roaring Twenties*, and our president was Herbert Hoover. Over the next few years, the notorious gangster Al Capone emerged, and Wall Street's 1929 crash heralded in the *Great Depression*. Male life expectancy was then at 55.8 years.

In Missouri, by the Mississippi River, arose the city of Hannibal. A famous American writer was born nearby in 1835, Samuel Langhorne Clemens (later known as Mark Twain). Clemens spent his early life in Hannibal and the area inspired his writing of *The Adventures of Tom Sawyer* (1876) and *The Adventures of Huckleberry Finn* (1884).

But this area also produced ROLLA LEE UTLEY JR. on June 1st, 1926.[1] He was born about 3 miles northeast of Hannibal in Oakwood, a sparsely-inhabited crossroads with few buildings. Tradition says he was named Rolla after a location in Missouri called "Rolla," which was named for the North Carolina place where an early settler was born – "Raleigh," but spelled as pronounced in a Missouri accent.

Sadly, Rolla's mother died in 1939[2] when he was only 13 years old. Rolla's father,[3] unable to handle reduced finances and caring for 4 boys[4] (the youngest only a toddler), sent them to a nearby orphanage called *The Home*. Rolla recalls their only transportation was walking. They had no car, nor

(above, right:) **Rolla Lee Utley, Jr.'s mother, Gladys Leotha (Young) Utley, holding one of her babies [unidentified].** *(ancestry.com)*

(below, left:) **Rolla Lee Utley Jr.'s father, Rolla Lee Utley, Sr. [the woman and baby are unidentified].** *(ancestry.com)*

was one affordable. After only a month at *The Home*, Rolla walked away and rejoined his father.

But Hannibal had produced and inspired another native son than Mark Twain. Rolla soon went to live with a married sister in St. Louis for a time. Then in April 1944, at 17 years of age, he traveled to Oakland, California to enlist in the U.S. Navy. Rolla served during 7 major Pacific battles.

Rolla's son, Joseph King, tells this story:

> When I was a young teenage boy, Dad [Rolla Utley] would always tell us stories of the action he experienced in World War II. Dad served on the aircraft carrier CVL-30, USS San Jacinto. One story in particular was a favorite of mine. He told me when he was the helmsman (driver) in the tower (the place above the flight deck) during a battle in the Marianas, South Pacific [on 5 April 1945]. He recalls a kamikaze coming toward his ship intending to crash upon it to inflict as much damage and death as possible. The airplane got closer and closer, yet after going through covering fire from the USS Alabama and other ships, and the carrier firing fiercely at the plane, when it looked like it was going to hit the carrier, at the last moment a round from one of the battery guns hit it and it crashed right in front of the bow of the ship – spraying water and debris all over the tower's window and the surrounding areas.
>
> Captain Harold M. Martin ordered dad to go on top of the tower, which is approximately 90 feet above the deck, and wash off the window – by hand. As ordered,

REGISTRATION CARD — Gray Card 58

SERIAL NUMBER: U	ORDER NUMBER:
1. NAME (Print): Rolla Lee Utley Jr.	

2. PLACE OF RESIDENCE (Print): 5303 East 12th St., Oakland 1, Alamda Co., California
   [THE PLACE OF RESIDENCE GIVEN ON THE LINE ABOVE WILL DETERMINE LOCAL BOARD JURISDICTION; LINE 2 OF REGISTRATION CERTIFICATE WILL BE IDENTICAL]

3. MAILING ADDRESS: same

4. TELEPHONE: —
5. AGE IN YEARS: 19 — DATE OF BIRTH: June 1, 1926
6. PLACE OF BIRTH: Hannibal, Mo.

7. NAME AND ADDRESS OF PERSON WHO WILL ALWAYS KNOW YOUR ADDRESS: Mr. Joseph Atkins, bro-in-law, 1501 Turn St., Hannibal, Mo.

8. EMPLOYER'S NAME AND ADDRESS: None

9. PLACE OF EMPLOYMENT OR BUSINESS: Veteran — Disc 5/20/46

D.S.S. Form 1 (Revised 4-1-42)   16—21650-2

Signature: Rolla Lee Utley Jr.

MUSTER ROLL OF THE CREW

Page 32 of the U.S.S. SAN JACINTO for the quarter ending 31 March 1945

NAMES (Alphabetically arranged without regard to ratings, with surname to the left and the first name written in full)	SERVICE NUMBER (The service number must under no condition be omitted)	Present Rating	DATE OF ENLISTMENT — Day	Month	Year	Date first received on board
UTLEY, Rolla L., Jr.	338 71 48	S2c V6				11/2/44

Dad did exactly that. He said he was scared to death because there was nothing to hang onto, and he had to wipe off more than just airplane parts, grease, and gasoline. One of the engine cylinders ended up on the flight deck.

Years later (when he was 90 years old), I was visiting him for the Christmas holidays and I remembered the story he had told me. And I wondered if I could find it on *YouTube*. So, I looked and there it was!![5] – just as he had said. [As I watched the *YouTube* video,] the kamikaze plane flew past *USS Alabama* toward the *USS San Jacinto* with guns blazing, fire coming from the plane. And just as it seems it's going to hit the ship, one more round hit the plane. And [the plane] plummets widely in front of the bow, barely hitting the ship and spraying all the debris toward the tower.

So [then], I took the computer to Dad's room. And I said, "Dad, I want you to look at something." As he watched the video, his eyes got big – as if he were reliving that moment. He looked up at me and said, "I was there! I was right there when it happened! I was there when the plane hit us in front of the deck! Do you remember the story I used to tell you, Son?" And I replied, "Yes, Dad, you got it right in every detail."[6]

Rolla was discharged on 20 May 1946.[7]

With an improving post-war economy, the ambitious Navy veteran returned to Missouri. Rolla joined Hill-Behan Lumber Company, a prominent retailer of lumber and building materials in 4 states, and a pioneer in prefabricating windows and doors. Rolla remained

REVIVAL

JULY 30 - AUG. 4

SERVICES DAILY
7 A.M. & 7:45 P.M.

Dinner on the ground after Sunday morning services.

Nursery provided for all services.

ROLLA UTLEY

Rolla Utley will be visiting evangelist.

Richard Jenkins, minister of music at the First Baptist Church in Sumner, will lead the music.

Pastor Laddie Pierce invites public to attend.

COWART BAPTIST CHURCH

Cowart Ill.

UTLEY, Rolla & Polly

with this firm for several years as a most trusted and capable employee.

During these years Rolla began to sense the calling of the Lord on his life. In 1962 he became the bi-vocational pastor of Brighton Church in Brighton, Arkansas and changed its name to Brighton Baptist Church, believing "Baptist" was both an unashamed designation and one that identified their beliefs.

Then when South Side Baptist Church in Kennett, Missouri sought a pastor, Rolla accepted their call. This *fragmented* congregation presented a challenge to Mr. Utley. They had no youth ministry. The pianist had recently left because a parishioner accused her of playing a wrong note. Rolla went to visit her and convinced her to return. His methods and concern for all began to bring people back and they started *loving one-another* again. Church attendance grew from a low of 20 to over 100. This ministry lasted about two years, until Rolla's company transferred him again, this time a hundred miles away to Memphis to assume responsibility of their sales office.

Rolla did *supply preaching* where needed, at various churches over the next 5 years, while devoting most of his time to the building materials business. Here his wife Marjorie died on 22 November 1966.[8] Despite his young age, he expressed his desire to remain unmarried and continue his bi-vocational endeavors. That is, until 3 years later when he was introduced to Polly, a young, exciting, beautiful red-head, also recently widowed. Polly was a native of Maine, having come to Memphis as a military wife, but now alone with her 3 children.[9] Rolla's stated intention to remain a widower quickly changed! Rolla and Polly married in 1969 in Memphis at East Park Baptist Church. In that time, the "gentleman" Rolla, always would open the car door for Polly. Not only to enter, but encouraged her to remain seated until he accessed the door and assisted her in exiting. This was his routine until recent years when they ceased driving. In 2019, this couple celebrated 50 years together.

In Pleasant Hill, southeast of Memphis, Pleasant Hill Baptist Church organized in 1940. In 1947 they built and occupied their first building, dedicating it debt-free in 1950. Rolla was called to this church as an interim pastor in October 1969, was ordained here in April 1970, then becoming their full-time pastor and served until September 1979. Rolla was not only bi-vocational, but managed to retain 2 full-time positions and be home with his melded family almost every night. A busy man.

Busy? In addition, and despite his motto that "I learn by doing," Rolla enrolled at Mid-America Baptist Theological Seminary at its nearby South Germantown campus, graduating in 1978.

A daughter later noted, "Sure, you were home every night, but there was little interaction; you were always in your office-study." Not many could handle being a father while employed full-time in 2 organizations. Rolla was the exception, faithfully and productively doing it all well. A high point in Rolla's mind is Pleasant Hill Baptist

Church's building program, buying land in 1972 to build a parsonage, then dedicating it in 1974. Rolla served 10 years there.

Rolla was next called to the Cornerstone Baptist Church. However, their small closely-knit group had no desire to grow, engage in any new programs or visitation. Rolla soon felt the need to move on, but left them with no debt, money in the bank, and the parsonage paid for. This "sweet little country church" wanted to stay that way.

In 1979 Rolla and a small group of people formed the Bridgetown Baptist Church at Nesbit, Mississippi, south of Memphis but across the state line, about 45 minutes from his home. They first met under a carport at a recently-built home in a development. As attendance grew the singing got louder. Soon, as winter drew near, they needed a better meeting place. Through one parishioner's contacts, they got permission to use the local fire station each Sunday morning and evening. With their own folding chairs and a donated piano, fire trucks were moved out and a church environment set up. Rolla preached his first Sunday morning "firehouse sermon" and the little congregation was "praising the Lord."

But that evening, Rolla arrived at the fire station to discover a fire had consumed everything – fire trucks, building, their chairs and piano; only a foundation slab remained. Had Rev. Utley's morning sermon been so real that Hell's fire and brimstone visited this place? Back to the carport! But not for long. Rolla, already a member of the clergy group, immediately contacted a Seventh-day Adventist pastor to express the possibility of using the Adventist building on Sundays (Adventists worshipped on Saturdays). This arrangement was quickly contracted and successfully continued. Rolla notes that the 2 congregations celebrated a combined Thanksgiving service.

This new Baptist congregation bought an old 3-acre pasture with $13,000 borrowed dollars (paid back as $20,000). They cleared the site, dug a well, and bought a relocatable 30 x 30 structure. But 3 years later a larger building was needed. So, Rolla drew plans and an expanded facility was made, with seating for over 200 persons; when Rolla left there in 1994 it was overfull.

Polly, otherwise known as Mrs. Rolla Utley, often wrote poetry. In January of 1993, Pastor Utley preached a series of sermons on the family, home and marriage. He also taught a Sunday School class. On the morning of January 24, 1993, Polly boldly entered Rolla's classroom to bravely read her poem, *How To Be King Of Your Castle* (see Appendix A).

In 1999 Polly penned a poem on their experiences at Bridgetown Baptist Church, *Memories Of My Church* (see Appendix B). When the Utleys returned to visit in 2019, they were thrilled to know many folks who were still there.

After serving Bridgetown Baptist Church for fifteen years, the Utleys retired in 1994,[10] moving to Ellsworth, Maine (Polly's home state). They also bought a cabin back in fishing territory, where Rolla could enjoy fishing with his brother-in-law, a retired Maine State Police officer. Rolla quickly adapted to Maine with its unique accents, unpredictable cold and winter snow.

The Utleys accepted a call to pastor two small churches on the rugged Maine coast, at Corea and Birch Harbor. The Corea Baptist Church, constructed on a ledge outcropping at water's edge, was one in which Polly's family had worshipped. Polly's mother Stella (née Young) played the piano here for years. Polly's father Herbert was of the large Bunker family in that area.

But Maine winters were increasingly a strain on the Utleys and it became apparent that retirement should be their lifestyle. So, when a daughter and her husband returned from military assignment in Germany, deciding to settle in mid-state Florida at Dover, Rolla and Polly joined them in building a home there with an "in-law" section. Around the corner was the First Baptist Church which they could attend and join. And guess what? You know! The Reverend Rolla became an associate pastor. His duties included a very active visitation ministry to senior adults, posting a daily prayer line, and weekly staff meetings. On his 90th birthday, Rolla preached the Sunday evening sermon and quoted, from memory, the entire 39 verses of Romans chapter 8.

Rolla's son-in-law, Larry Streur (married to daughter Cindy), tells the story of his father-in-law and Rolla's selection to take an *Honor Flight* to Washington, D.C. in the Spring of 2014:[11]

> Rolla was not a man to outwardly show his military service but loved to show his

support for others that served. We got him a WWII veteran hat that he wore proudly during that trip and every time that we went on vacation. He was proud he had served and of what he did during his service. He was excited that he was selected for this trip to Washington with other Veterans of World War II and the Korean Conflict. It was fun to sit and hear him and the other veterans speak about their time in the war. Obviously, he enjoyed this trip to the fullest.

On the way back from Washington the activities included a mail call for each one. People from all over sent letters to each veteran present on the flight. I remember him being so surprised that he had mail from friends, family and some people that didn't know him...not just a couple of letters, but a large stack of them. He began reading the letters on the flight and became very emotional of the many who were thanking him for his sacrifices and service, to the point he could not read anymore until he arrived home.

When we arrived back in St. Petersburg, we were greeted by hundreds of people in the terminal welcoming them back home and showing their respect. You could see his face light up with joy when he saw this crowd and especially those of his family there to greet him. I will tell you he did not like the fact that he had to be seated in a wheelchair to be escorted through the terminal. But it was a great pleasure for me to wheel this World War II veteran through Washington and the terminal, and that he allowed me to do this.

I have always been so proud to be known as Rolla's son in law, although he would always say to people that I was his son, and made me feel very humble and honored to be that to him. He was a great man in all aspects of his life and always willing to talk about anything and to assure me of his support whenever I needed it. I considered him a true saint and one who lived his life for God and the church.[12]

Rolla Utley remained an active associate pastor at First Baptist Church of Dover, Florida until he was 94 (in 2020), when he reluctantly passed on most of his responsibilities to others. Oh, and do you recall that when he was born the expected life span was 55.8 years!

On November 28th, 2020, Rolla Utley passed from this active life into the presence of his Lord Jesus. Most of Rolla's family participated in the service celebrating his life, held December 4th, 2020 at the First Baptist Church of Dover, Florida. Widow Polly Utley read an original poem she had composed about his life. Son Joe King and son-in-law Larry Streur each shared their remembrances. The author also spoke a tribute (see Appendix H).

Rolla's interment was at the Memorial Gardens in Memphis, Tennessee, with Pastor Larry Dean speaking at the committal service. Rolla's replacement, Clayton Yates, and Deacon John Minton of the Dover Church attended.

Not just any preacher —
Rolla Utley was
a real PASTOR

Rolla's son Joe King, in his message at the funeral, challenged: "Do you share your faith regularly?" *Rolla did!*

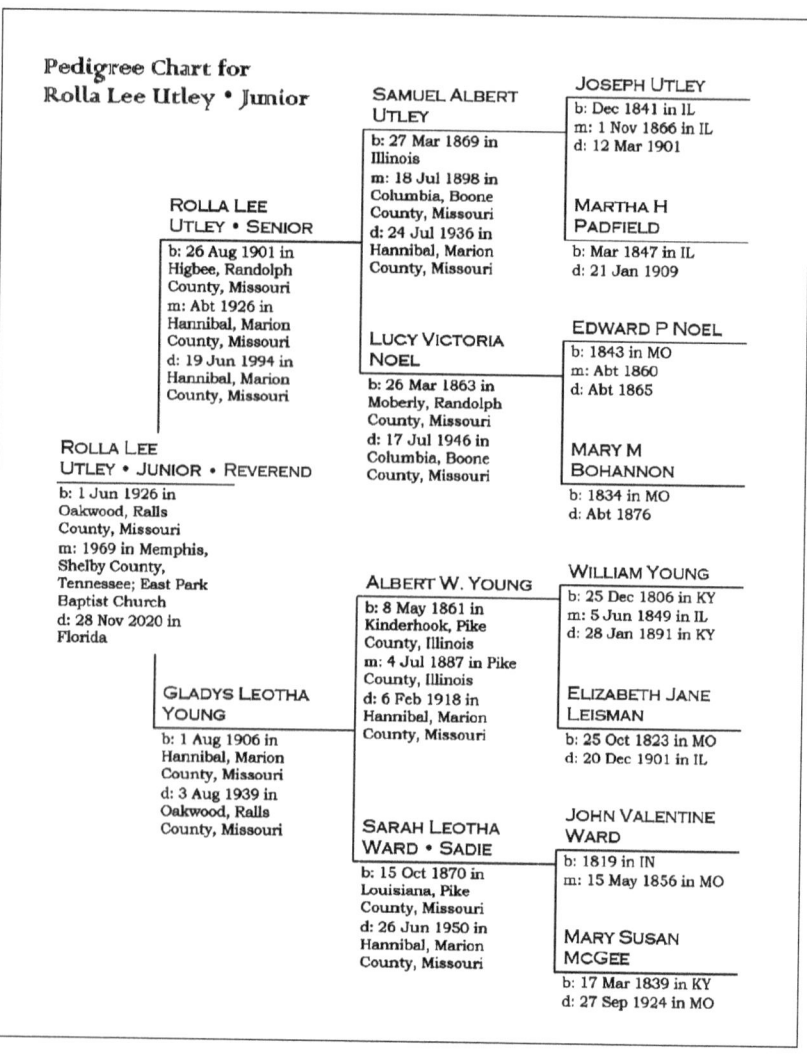

ENDNOTES

[1] U.S., WWII Draft Cards Young Men, 1940-1947 [image, ancestry.com].

[2] Missouri, Death Certificates, 1910-1962 [image, ancestry.com]; also, an undated newspaper obituary. Gladys Leotha (Young) Utley d. 3 Aug. 1939, 10 am at Levering Hospital, Hannibal, Marion County, Mo.

[3] Rolla Lee Utley, Senior, b. 26 Aug. 1901, Higbee, Randolph County, Mo.; d. 19 Jun. 1994, Hannibal, Marion County, Mo.

[4] Rolla Lee (b. 1 Jun. 1926); Albert Eugene (b. 16 Apr. 1930); Orville Clinton (b. 11 May 1934); Donald Lee (b. 8 Mar. 1937).

[5] "Kamikaze dives on USS San Jacinto (CVL-30) - 5 April 1945" [online video recording]. *YouTube*, posted 14 Oct. 2013 by "Colonel Tannenbusch": <https://www.youtube.com/watch?v=jyn5pNi9nEs>; accessed 4 Mar. 2021.

[6] King, Joseph. "Dad's Story." [Remembrances of Rolla Utley, read at his celebration of life service], 2020. Joseph King to Polly Utley, e-mail, 23 Dec. 2020.

[7] WWII Draft Cards Young Men, 1940-1947 [image, ancestry.com].

[8] "Marjorie Sue Miller Utley," *Find A Grave*, findagrave.com, memorial 63471690. Web: <https://www.findagrave.com/memorial/63471690/marjorie-sue-utley>. Marjorie b. 28 Sep. 1924, dau. of Edgar Hassel Miller and Ora Lee (Chipman) Miller; bur. in Oak Ridge Cemetery, Kennett, Dunklin County, Mo. (plot: sect. 6, row 51).

[9] Pauline "Polly" Janet Bunker, b. 11 Dec. 1932 in Me.; m. (1st) Foree Erasmus King, 7 Sep. 1951 in Me. They had 3 children: Cynthia Foraye (b. 1953); John Tarleton (b. 7 Mar. 1958); and Joe. Foree E. King d. 17 Nov. 1966, Memphis, Shelby County, Tenn.

[10] Pastor Larry Dean succeeded Rolla Utley at Bridgetown Baptist Church. Pastor Dean was still leading that church in 2021.

[11] Rolla Utley's *Honor Flight* took him to Washington, D.C. on 27 May 2014.

[12] Streur, Larry D. [Remembrances of Rolla Utley, read at his celebration of life service], 2020. Larry Streur to Albert P. Whitaker, e-mail, 31 Dec. 2020. This quote from Mr. Streur has been edited by the author, who has made only minor changes.

Eugene S. Philbrook
(photo is dated 1920; courtesy of JoAnn Randall; edited)

Chapter 6

Reverend Doctor EUGENE S. PHILBROOK

5 . . . endure hardship, do the work of an evangelist, discharge all the duties of your ministry.
–II Timothy 4:5 (New International Version)

North Bradford, Maine is a small, almost obscure hamlet tucked into mid-state Maine's Penobscot County, northwest of Bangor.

1871

Eugene Sumner Philbrook took his first breath on the 19th of February in 1871[1] at North Bradford. His parents, Francis Jerome Philbrook and Pauline (Moulton) had been married for just over five years.[2] North Bradford's

Several Maine towns where young "Gene" Philbrook lived (highlighted in dark blue, with white lettering).
(Detail from: "Penobscot County," In: George N. Colby, Atlas of the State of Maine, Houlton, Me.: G.N. Colby, 1885, p. 74. David Rumsey Map Collection, David Rumsey Map Center, Stanford Libraries. davidrumsey.com; edited)

population then was less than fifteen hundred people; today it is even lower than that.³

A view in Bradford, Maine, circa 1910s.

(ebay.com)

1880

By 1880, when "Gene" was nine years of age, the census shows him living in nearby Atkinson, Me. with his widowed grandmother, Rebecca (Cummings) Philbrook, at Frank McGregory's home.⁴ At that time, Eugene's mother was a "boarder" with her sister Abbie (Moulton) Page's family in Lawrence, Mass.;⁵ and Gene's father had moved to Bangor⁶ to manufacture and promote his new fishing reels sensations.

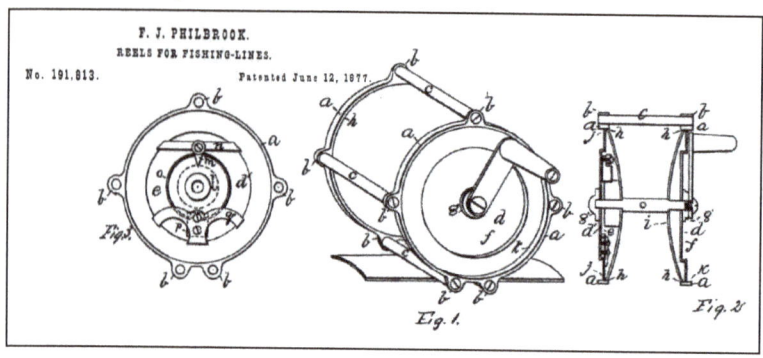

After a first glance at the 1880 census, one might suspect family trouble. Why was Gene with his grandmother in Atkinson, Me., his father living in a hotel in Bangor, Me., and his mother living in Lawrence, Mass. with her sister? A closer look at the details, however, reveals that all was well between Gene's parents. It was about 1880,

> at the age of nine years [when Gene] went with his parents to Bangor, his father, Francis J. Philbrook, being a machinist and engineer.[7]

Gene's mother had temporarily gone to Massachusetts to care for her dying mother, Susan (Howard) Moulton, who was suffering with "consumption" (tuberculosis). This gave some relief to Gene's aunt – at whose home this grandmother lived. During his mother's temporary absence, he stayed with his paternal grandmother in Atkinson, because his father was too busy working in Bangor to properly care for him. Gene and his parents were subsequently able to reunite.

Father Frank Philbrook was an inventive machinist. The 1880 census lists his occupation as "Fish Rod Man."[8] Born in Hermon, just west of Bangor, he was an exceptional, almost genius mechanical engineer, gunsmith and sportsman,

---

<--- (Opposite:) **Patent drawings for Francis J. Philbrook's fishing reels. Patent number 191,813 dated 12 June 1877.**
(United States Patent and Trademark Office. Web: https://pdfpiw.uspto.gov/.piw?Docid=00191813 . Edited)

who patented raised pillar fishing reel improvements.⁹ Later, in 1916, he applied for a patent on an air outlet valve for the internal combustion engine; he got patent 1,246,458 in 1917.¹⁰

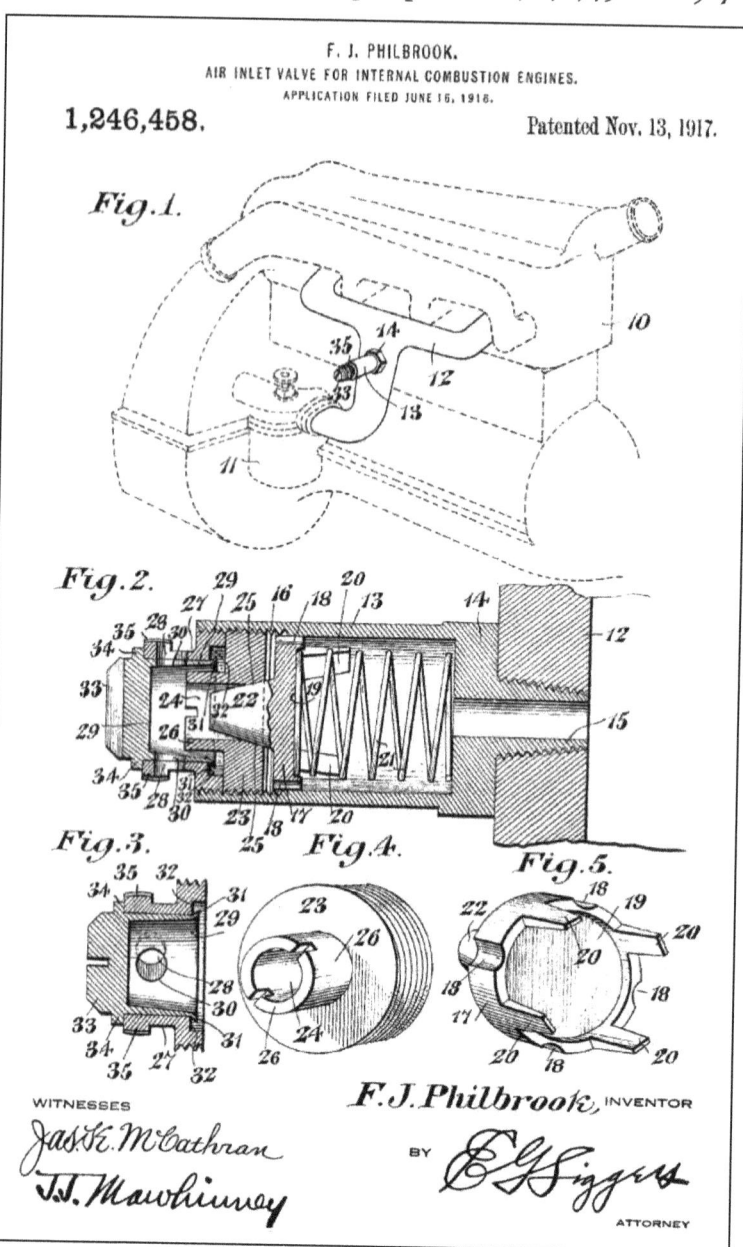

1888-1899

Knowing of his father's abilities, Gene Philbrook's early plan was to enter the engineering field as well.

But Gene Philbrook became a "born again" Christian at 17 years of age[11] (about 1888), under the preaching of Rev. George B. Ilsley at the Second Baptist Church of Bangor.[12] Gene was also

Second Baptist Church *(with towers),* on Columbia Street in Bangor, Me. (now called Columbia Street Baptist Church).
(postmarked 1912; ebay.com)

baptized by Rev. Ilsley and soon decided to prepare for the ministry.[13]

<--- *(Opposite:)* **Francis J. Philbrook's drawings for an air inlet valve. He was granted patent number 1,246,458 on 13 November 1917.**
(United States Patent and Trademark Office. Web: https://pdfpiw.uspto.gov/.piw?Docid=01246458)

Gene Philbrook graduated from Bangor High School in 1891. Thirty years later, he was identified as the only one from that class who had entered the ministry.[14]

Bangor High School, Bangor, Me. *(circa 1907-15; ebay.com)*

After graduating from the Bangor High School he was engaged in business for awhile and then entered Colby College in 1894.[15]

Chapel & Library, Colby College, built 1869 *(mailed 1914; ebay.com)*

Gene graduated from Colby, at Waterville, Me., in 1898.[16] Meanwhile, he apparently maintained a dual-enrollment; he simultaneously attended Coburn Classical Institute in Waterville, graduating in its class of 1896.[17]

Coburn Classical Institute, Waterville, Maine.
(circa 1905; ebay.com; edited)

While still a Colby student, Gene preached at a Baptist Church in Norway, Me. on Sunday, 30 May 1897.[18] Colby may have been asked to "send us a minister; any minister will do." But Gene Philbrook was not just "any minister."

1900

The 1900 census lists Eugene S. Philbrook twice. According to instructions printed on each census sheet, the census-taker was to record, in column 3, the "Name of each person whose place of abode on June 1, 1900, was in this family." Gene was counted as a "Student of Theology" on the campus of Newton Theological Institution in

Newton Theological Institution, Newton Centre, Mass.
(©1905; ebay.com)

Newton, Mass. (enumerated on June 1st).[19] Then, under a June 19th enumeration date, he was also listed as "Student, Theology" at his parents' home on Main Street in Brewer, Me.[20]

Main Street, Brewer Maine.   *(postmarked 1912; ebay.com)*

While still a student at Newton, Gene Philbrook did "student preaching" where he could.

He gave a Sunday evening sermon in Boston, 18 March 1900, at the First Baptist Church on Commonwealth Ave.[21] He also had a series of engagements with a Baptist church at South Willington, Conn.:

First Baptist Church, Commonwealth Avenue, Boston, Mass.
(circa 1905; ebay.com)

> **1900 Feb. 24 pm**
>
> A royal good time was had by those who attended the social at the hall Saturday evening [Feb. 24]. The social, which was arranged by . . . the Y.P.S.C.E., was for the purpose of giving Eugene Philbrook an opportunity to meet with the people in an informal way. . . . E. Philbrook closed the exercises by a talk on the Bible.[22]
>
> **1900 Apr. 1**
>
> Eugene Philbrook will preach at the hall next Sunday [i.e. Apr. 1st].[23]

South Willington, Conn. "village and thread works."
(Cole, J R. History of Tolland County, Connecticut [. . .]. New York: W.W. Preston, 1888, facing page 622. Image: FamilySearch.org)

When Eugene graduated from Newton in 1900,[24] he occupied an honored place at the ceremonies. He had earned the degree of B.D. (Bachelor of Divinity).[25] Not surprisingly, he delivered an essay titled "The Value of Nature Study to the Preacher."[26]

After graduating at Newton, Philbrook "supplied a church in N.H.,"[27] "preaching one year" there [i.e. 1900-1901] before "he accepted a call to the First Baptist church in Belfast," Me. in Aug. 1901.[28]

Nevertheless, he sensed the need for, and desired, further ministry preparation, so he "arranged for special advanced courses at Andover Newton Theological Seminary,"[29] in a two-year postgraduate program.[30] At its completion, he was awarded an S.T.M.[31] degree (Master of Sacred Theology) in 1926.[32]

1901

While continuing postgraduate studies at Newton, from January through May 1901 Gene Philbrook got in more preaching and lecturing, at a Baptist church in South Willington, Conn.:

1901 Jan. 5 pm
> a special religious meeting in the Baptist conference room . . . Messrs. Philbrook and Harding will be present.[33]

1901 Jan. 6
> Mr. E. S. Philbrook, who occupied the Baptist pulpit, assisting Pastor Snow, preached from Deut. 1:19—*And they came to Kadish-barnea*. It was a forceful and logical exhortation against lingering on the borders of the promised land – the kingdom of God.[34]

Pastorate at Belfast, Maine
30 Aug. 1901 - 30 Nov. 1906

About seven months later, on August 1st 1901, the Belfast, Me. *Republican Journal* reported that the First Baptist Church there had

> extended a call to Mr. Eugene S. Philbrook of Brewer to become its pastor. . . . [He] has given the best of satisfaction during a short stay in this city, both in the pulpit and among the people. . . . It is expected that he will be ordained here August 25th.[35]

Their previous pastor, Reverend R. T. Capen, had

Belfast First Baptist pastors preceding Eugene Philbrook.
(ebay.com; edited).

resigned

> in December 1900, and the pulpit was supplied by different preachers until Aug. 30th, when Eugene S. Philbrook was ordained and installed as pastor.[36]

First Baptist Church, Belfast, Maine.
(Williamson, Joseph, Alfred Johnson, and William C. Williamson. <u>History of the City of Belfast in the State of Maine</u>*. Portland [Maine]: Loring, Short and Harmon, 1877-1913, volume [1], pages 297 [left], 300 [right]. Images: hathitrust.org)*

Pastor Philbrook, 30 years old, was just beginning his fruitful ministry years with a dedicated resolve and purpose. Ordained at the end of August, the

Main Street, Belfast, Maine. *(mailed 1909; ebay.com; edited)*

local newspaper began reporting his upcoming sermon topics for the Sept. 15th am[37] and pm[38] services. Very soon, however, *the enemy* attempted to hamper Gene's ministry. Belfast's newspaper reported that, even as Reverend Philbrook

> [w]ith his mother and sister Beulah . . . will soon begin housekeeping in the Rogers house on Northport avenue[,] [he has also] been critically ill with typhoid fever . . .[39]

At the beginning of 1902, the newspaper summarized the previous year's important local events, which included this update:

> Mr. Philbrook had a severe illness soon after his ordination, and was unable to preach until December.[40]

Reverend Philbrook was always accomplishing new things and was very visible in the local community. His stereopticon lectures became increasingly popular, even in secular circles. At the Belfast church, he organized and led the Brotherhood of Andrew and Philip and their gospel meetings,[41] and promoted the Christian Endeavor organization, in addition to many

A stereopticon projector used by Rev. Eugene Philbrook to show images on glass slides, as a way to illustrate his lectures.

(courtesy of JoAnn Randall)

other activities. Marriages and funerals were a constant responsibility, but also an opportunity to present the gospel in a dignified and appreciated manner.

1904

Rev. Philbrook went to Nova Scotia, Aug. 1904,[42] resulting in a 50-slide stereopticon show at Belfast, Oct. 21;[43] then to Presque Isle, Nov. 1904,

> assisting Rev. A. W. Lorimer in evangelistic work, holding general meetings every evening and young people's meetings afternoons.[44]

1905

Rev. Philbrook apparently gave a series of stereopticon lectures in Conn. early in 1905. On Wed. 18 Jan. 1905 in Norwich, Conn.,

> the Third Baptist church was filled to overflowing—both the audience room and gallery—to listen to a most scholarly lecture by the Rev. Eugene S. Philbrook of Belfast, Me., on "The Life of the Master," which was clearly illustrated with beautiful stereopicon [sic] views. The lecturer held the audience, even the little children, in rapt attention.... The lecture was in all respects most successful, an assurance to all those who have season tickets for the course that their time and money are well spent.—Norwich, Conn., Bulletin Jan. 19th.[45]

On Fri. 20 Jan. 1905 at South Willington, Conn.:

> Rev. Eugene Philbrook and Rev. C. L. Snow gave their stereopticon views in the hall Friday evening to a well pleased and

Image from one of Rev. Philbrook's glass stereopticon slides. This one, showing Jesus carrying the Cross to Calvary, may have been shown with Philbrook's "The Life of the Master" lecture, delivered in Norwich, Conn. on 18 January 1905.

(courtesy of Howard Randall)

appreciative audience. One-third of the proceeds go to the Endeavor society. It is expected that they will give views on Scotland a month or six weeks later.[46]

Ten days later Gene Philbrook was back in Me., giving a visual lecture on Mon. Jan. 30th at the Morrill church:

> Rev. C. N. [sic] Snow of Norwich, Conn., assisted by Rev. Eugene S. Philbrook of Belfast, gave a stereopticon lecture . . . .

Morrill Union Church, Morrill, Maine, circa 1910s.
Erected in 1847, this house of worship was shared by four denominations simultaneously, each using the building for one Sunday every month. Destroyed by fire in 1972, the replacement structure was home to Morrill Baptist Church (which changed its name in 2020 to Veracity Chapel). *(ebay.com)*

The views were taken from historic scenes in Scotland.[47]

Rev. Philbrook was not afraid to speak his mind on social and political issues, especially about Prohibition and the liquor trade. He spoke on those subjects 09 May 1905 at the annual meeting of the Christian Civic League of Maine held in Waterville. He mentions "the Sturgis bill" which the Maine Legislature had passed in 1904 "for the purpose of enforcing the prohibitory laws."[48] The Belfast paper reported on May 11th:

> At the annual meeting of the Christian Civic League of Maine in Waterville Tuesday E.S. Philbrook of Belfast reported for York County. He said "things are not as

favorable as the friends of temperance wish. Rum is being sold in Belfast still. The Sturgis bill has had little or no effect there." While there is almost daily evidence that the sale of liquor in Belfast has not been entirely stopped, the Sturgis bill has certainly had its effect—as witness the [dark ?] saloons and absence of open bars.[49]

But Gene Philbrook felt his remarks were reported out-of-context and could possibly be misinterpreted, so wrote this letter to the editor:

The Liquor Situation in Waldo County.

TO THE EDITOR OF THE JOURNAL: The few sentences quoted in last week's Journal from remarks made by me at the recent meeting of the Civic League in Waterville are apt, as they stand alone, to give an erroneous impression. It is

Maine prohibition characterized: farmer & "cold tea," 1907.
(Detail from: Glackens, L. M. "Said prohibition Maine to prohibition Georgia: 'Here's looking at you'." Puck, 28 Aug. 1907, v.62, no.1591, [cover p.1]. Web: Library of Congress; <https://www.loc.gov/item/2011647232/>); edited.

true that in Belfast things are not "as favorable as friends of temperance wish," and expect soon to see.

. . . . In my report the statement was made that in Sheriff Carleton we have an efficient and trustworthy officer, who has already done much to suppress the rum traffic in our city and elsewhere in he county. . . . It is hardly to be expected that those who have defied that law and violated the moral sense of the community for years will quit their iniquitous practice until actually compelled to do so. . . . Give to our Governor and his associates the loyal and active support which his fearless and dignified attitude demands and do everything possible to assist county officials in their performance of their duty.

EUGENE S. PHILBROOK.[50]

Gene Philbrook loved outdoor life: setting up a camp, canoeing, fishing and hunting. At the same time, he enjoyed capturing

In The Maine Woods: 1905 edition.

Bangor and Aroostook Railroad put out this annual guide for sportsmen, describing the best Maine wild areas, accessible by their trains, to hunt and fish.

(Bangor Public Library. <https://digicom.bpl.lib.me.us/railroad_pubs/32>.)

photographs of nature, then hand-tinting those glass slides to show in his stereopticon lectures. In 1905 he "got his deer" on Saturday, October 14th, it being one of

> 52 deer being received in the various trains into Bangor during the day. It was the high line day of the present season[51]

in which game receipts at Bangor, so far, totaled 401 deer and 6 bears.[52]

1906

"New" train station, Bangor, Maine.
Note the hunting-themed border decorations on this postcard.
(postmarked 1907; ebay.com; edited)

After five-and-one-half years at Belfast, Reverend Eugene S. Philbrook resigned, "and went to Sanford, Maine, December 1st" 1906. He had accepted a call to Sanford's First Baptist Church.[53] Before his departure, the Belfast congregation honored Rev. Philbrook with a reception on Nov. 23rd, a gold watch and chain from the deacons, and a tribute from Woman's Christian Temperance Union for his "conscientious" and "fearless" advocacy of their cause.[54]

Pastorate at Sanford, Maine
1 Dec. 1906 – 31 Oct. 1915

Gene Philbrook's marriage to Bessie B. Smalley took place back at Belfast, on Thursday, 7 February 1907. He was 35 years old and his bride was 19. The goings-on were described by *Sanford*

Marriage Record for Eugene S. Philbrook & Bessie B. Smalley
(FamilySearch.org)

Rev. & Mrs. Philbrook.

(left:) **Gene Philbrook**. *[grainy photo in:* Belfast Republican *(Belfast. Maine), 04 July 1907, page 6; web: Library of Congress].*

(right:) **Bessie (Smalley) Philbrook**. *(detail from a glass slide, hand-colored by Rev. Philbrook; courtesy of Howard Randall; edited).*

Tribune on February 15th[55] and also reprinted in Belfast's *Republican Journal* on February 21st:

WELCOMED TO SANFORD.

Reception to Rev. E.S. and Mrs. Philbrook.

Rev. Eugene S. Philbrook, who was recently installed as pastor of the Baptist church, was wedded to Miss Bessie Smalley of Belfast Thursday, February 7th. The happy couple arrived in Sanford on the morning train last Monday and were given a glad surprise when they were greeted by about fifty of their friends who had chartered a special car to meet them at Springvale depot. As soon as Mrs. Philbrook entered the

Sanford and Springvale Station, Maine, circa 1908-1909.
(ebay.com; edited)

car she was presented with a beautiful bouquet of pinks.

On Wednesday evening a formal reception was given the pastor and his wife in the Baptist church vestry and proved to be one of the most happy events of its kind ever held in town. . . .

After the reception Mr. Hersey . . . presented the couple with a beautiful silver set . . , stating as he did so, that the people wanted to present them with something lasting and would be useful in the new parsonage, that will soon be built. Mr. Philbrook made a splendid response which endeared him to all present.[56]

Sanford's First Baptist Church is the oldest

First Baptist Church, Sanford, Maine.
(postmarked 1915; ebay.com)

continuously operating Baptist church in Maine, having been founded in September 1772.⁵⁷

Enter Rev. Eugene Philbrook, a thirty-five-year-old pastor, full of wisdom and vitality! The Baptist Church at Sanford and the community were about to experience the impact of this dedicated, ambitious leader.

Views of Downtown Sanford, Maine.
(above:) "The Square, looking from Main Street" *(mailed 1911; ebay; edited).*
(below:) "Main Street" *(circa 1907-1915; ebay).*

Both of the local newspapers, the <u>Sanford Tribune</u> and the <u>Springvale Advocate</u>, contain numerous, almost daily, accounts of this busy pastor's activities. Pastor Philbrook officiated at

<u>Sanford Tribune</u> published weekly local church times. (Friday, 19 Jan. 1912, p. 6; image online: springvale.advantage-preservation.com)

funerals and weddings. He gave high school baccalaureate addresses, spoke to, prayed for, or served in civic events, special services, and local organizations such as the *Odd Fellows*, *YMCA*, *Knights of Pythias*, and *Library Association*. And on it goes. His involvement in the community became well-established.

In what may seem unusual for a Baptist preacher, Reverend Philbrook was a life member of the Masons[58] (i.e. for 55 years at his death in 1956).[59] He was a Mason through each of his pastorates "in Belfast, Sanford, and Augusta, Maine and in Randolph," Mass., where he became "a life member at Norfolk Union Lodge."[60] On

> **Record of Eugene Philbrook's Masonic membership.**
> (*Massachusetts, Mason Membership Cards, 1733-1990* [database], Record for Philbrook, Eugene Sumner.; image: ancestry.com.)

Sunday 23 June 1907,[61]

> 85 members of local Masonic lodges celebrated St. John's Day . . . by attending divine service at the Baptist Church and listening to an excellent sermon by Pastor Philbrook.[62]

The *Sanford Tribune* even reprinted the text of that sermon.[63] St. John's Day was identically celebrated four years later (1911).[64]

Gene Philbrook kept membership in Sons of Union Veterans of the Civil War[65] since 1902, based on the service of his father and three uncles.[66] Gene was also a member of the Randolph, Mass. Grange[67] which he had joined in 1920.[68] He also had "the distinction of being an honorary member of the Girl Scouts of America."[69]

Reading the local newspapers in areas where Reverend Philbrook served reveal a very busy pastor who was well-known, recognized and respected in the community. He was involved, had influence, earned respect, and was appreciated. People looked up to him as a leader in the town and often sought his guidance, advice, wisdom and

Looking up School Street, Sanford, Maine.
(circa 1910; ebay.com)

leadership. With his unusual nature-themed lectures, his ability to relate with the youth, the elderly, and even politicians, Philbrook became a vital and integral part of the community. And he served the community with full and uncompromising faith.

Today's preachers should take note of Reverend Philbrook's example – a very active pastor and minister who was also involved in the local community. A true Christian witness is *not* having the church, or its pastor-shepherd, separated from the local community, which it should be serving. Engagement in and with the community is necessary.

At one point, Gene Philbrook was encouraged to seek a seat on the school committee; this he discouraged, but expressed appreciation for the consideration.

The record shows he took a large group of boys on a camping trip, where they engaged in fishing, playing ball, shooting, boating and bathing.

1908

Camping Trip.
(detail, Philbrook lecture poster; courtesy of Howard Randall; edited)

In 1908 God gifted Gene and Bessie Philbrook with their first child, a son born on August 24th in Sanford, whom they named Frank Randolf Philbrook.[70]

1909

Two years after Rev. Eugene Philbrook had moved away from Belfast, its newspaper, the <u>Republican Journal</u>, kept reporting on their former pastor's recent activities, now in Sanford. The Belfast paper's issue of 18 Feb. 1909 printed this item:

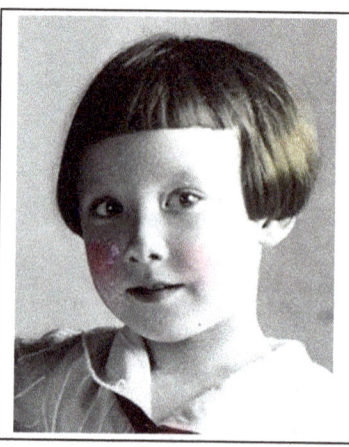

Frank Randolf Philbrook
(circa 1912; detail from a glass slide, hand-colored by Rev. Philbrook; courtesy of Howard Randall; edited)

> Rev. Eugene S. Philbrook, formerly of Belfast, was a member of the orchestra formed for the "Concert of Nations," which was given in Sanford last week under the direction of N. W. Littlefield.[71]

In Sanford, the local newspaper published his upcoming sermon titles each week. On several occasions, the <u>Sanford Tribune</u> even printed the full text of Philbrook's sermons. The issue of 15 Jan. 1909 reprinted "The Sunday Stone,"[72] which we include in Appendix C. And the paper's Nov. 26th issue reprinted another Philbrook sermon text, "Our Gibraltar."[73]

Curiosity leads us to speculate on the sermon titled "Burmah," which the <u>Sanford Tribune</u> reported in its issue of Fri., 26 Nov. 1909:

> The illustrated lecture which was given by Rev. E. S. Philbrook at the Baptist church Sunday evening [i.e. 21 Nov. 1909] was greatly enjoyed. The subject was "Burmah."[74]

There was a passenger ship named *Burmah* which disappeared in 1859 while *en route* from England to New Zealand. "Burmah" was also a variant spelling for the country of Burma.[75] Reverend Philbrook may have read the 26-page article, "Notes on Burma," in the October 1909 issue of *The National Geographic Magazine*,[76] to which he subscribed. Note that this article included 34 illustrations.

It may also be noted that three years previous (in 1906) at Belfast, and while Pastor Philbrook was there, "Fred M. Armstrong of Rangoon, Burmah, addressed a missionary meeting July 16th."[77] But we cannot know for sure exactly what Pastor Philbrook's *Burmah* lecture emphasized.

What was happening outside of Sanford Baptist Church during Eugene Philbrook's nine-year pastorate there, from 1907 through 1915? William Howard Taft was our 27th President from 1909 to 1913. And the first Lincoln pennies were minted and introduced in 1909.

Also in 1909, the "Blue Laws" became a political issue. The April 23rd edition of *Sanford Tribune* printed Pastor Philbrook's entire "Letter to the Editor"[78] (dated April 21) which, from a Christian understanding, condemns the conducting of business on the Lord's Day. Rev. Philbrook was certainly familiar with the enacted laws regarding this subject, and he presented a commendable position. As might be expected, the editor's response, in the next issue, ignored the basis and presented the progressive arguments. Although Reverend Philbrook likely did not win this argument, he did advance the Christian position in a scholarly manner.

Gene's "time off" in 1909 included a "three weeks fishing trip in Caratunk"[79] in August, and

Pleasant Pond, Caratunk, Maine
(circa 1905; ebay.com)

"a hunting trip in northern Maine"[80] in October:

> A post card received from Rev. Eugene S. Philbrook was dated Oakfield, October 22nd, saying he arrived there October 21st and with a friend had succeeded in bringing down a fine buck. They had a grand time in climbing Mount Katahdin, but found no

game there. He left for his home in Sanford Friday.[81]

(top:) **"A Shipment of Game at Masardis."** (In The Maine Woods: 1909 edition. *Bangor & Aroostook Railroad, p. 74; archive.org).*

(center:) **Mt. Katahdin** *(green),* **Oakfield** *(yellow)* **on** *BAR* **map** *(ibid.).*

(bottom:) **Mt. Katahdin photo by Eugene Philbrook on glass slide and hand-colored by him.** *(courtesy of Howard Randall; edited).*

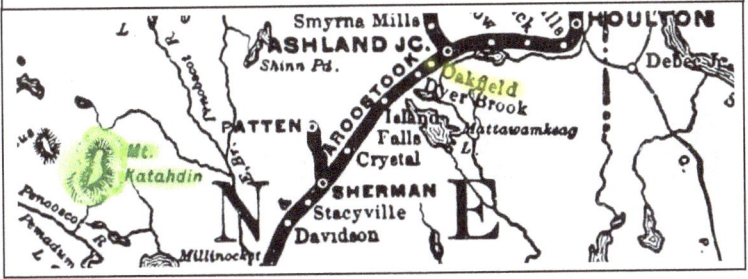

1910

At a Prohibition Convention held in August 1910, Reverend Philbrook made a strong speech in favor of a particular Sheriff's nomination.[82] The nomination thereafter drew a strong second from Reverend Philbrook. When the ballots were tallied, Philbrook's candidate won with unanimous vote (except for one blank ballot)![83]

It is interesting that Pastor Philbrook also served as chaplain to the York County Supreme

York County Court House, Alfred, Maine.
(mailed 1908; ebay.com)

Court, meeting at Alfred, Maine, for the September 1910 term.[84]

Probably the biggest highlight of 1910, for Gene and Bessie Philbrook, occurred on Tuesday, November 29th with the birth of an eight-pound daughter, whom they named Isabel Allegra Philbrook.[85]

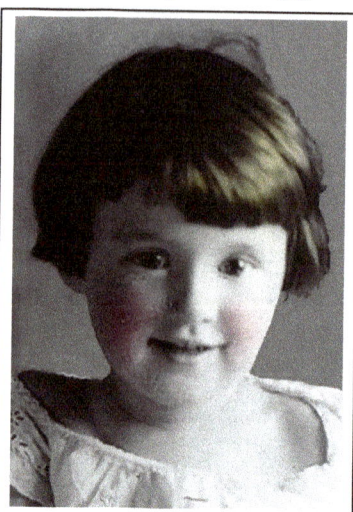

Isabel Allegra Philbrook
(circa 1912; detail from a glass slide, hand-colored by Rev. Philbrook; courtesy of Howard Randall; edited)

1911

On Memorial Day, 30 May 1911, Rev. Philbrook was "orator of the day" to Willard Post, No. 70, Dept. of Maine, Grand Army of the Republic (G.A.R.), which met at the Free Baptist Church.[86] At that celebration service, noting that it was the 50th anniversary since the start of the Civil War, the Rev. Philbrook's address was about "the great cyclorama of the Battle of Gettysburg." The local newspaper, <u>Springvale Advocate</u>, noted how Philbrook carried his hearers along with him, in a review of the great events which had transpired and closed with a fervid appeal to all his hearers to take the right side in the great conflict now on for the honor of Maine in the Constitutional amendment campaign.[87]

Free Baptist Church, Springvale, Me. *J. B. Ranger, Pastor.* (circa 1906; ebay.com)

Here Pastor Philbrook refers to Maine's 26th Constitutional Amendment, in effect since 1884, which made Maine the first Prohibition state. But on the ballot in the upcoming September 11th election was an attempt to repeal this Prohibition amendment.[88] Indeed, the name "Rev. E. Philbrook" was on a list of men styled "Prohibition Citizens Committee," who from July

LIST IS STILL INCREASING

Many Prominent Men Of Sanford Declare Themselves In Favor Of The Present Maine Law, And Will Vote For Prohibition Next September

(above:) **"List is still increasing"** [Sanford Tribune (Sanford, Me.), Fri., 28 Jul. 1911, p. 4; image: springvale.advantage-preservation.com; edited]. (below:) **"The Saloon"** (ibid., Fri., 04 Aug. 1911, p. 4).

THE SALOON

Geo. B Hugo of Boston, for many years engaged in the bottling and wholesaling of malt liquors, and President of the Massachusetts Organization of Beer Bottlers, says

"By Saloon I mean the place that has no other reason for existing than to supply drink, the congregating spot for all that is vile and vicious in a neighborhood, and the poorer the neighborhood the more prosperous is the saloon, as a rule. It has no defenders outside of its direct or indirect beneficiaries. No consistent or logical argument can be advanced for its continuance, unless it be the hackneyed one that it is the poor man's club

If it is the poor man's club, then I contend that the dues are too high, it costs too much to keep the club steward in a prosperous condition, and therefore should be disbanded for the benefit of the club members their families and the community at large."

The following men will vote for Prohibition—in other words they vote NO September 11 These names will be added to from week to week We trust that our opponents may publish a similar list.

E. M Goodall, Louis B. Goodall, Geo. B. Goodall, E E Hussey, Geo. Emery, Samuel Littlefield, Wm Batchelder, Wm Nutter, Herbert Hope, Geo. Nowell, E. M Hewett, F J Allen, Esq, N H Fogg, John V Tucker, Esq, Geo Hanson, Esq, Geo. Allen, O W. Brown, S. B. Emery Orville Libby, Edgar Bacon, M A Hewett, Geo. P Chase, E. L. Gowen, Dr D. W Wentworth, S J Nowell A C Hanscom, D. D. S, Moses Wentworth, Geo. Batchelder, N T Fogg, Dr C W Blagden, Dr R S. Gove, O D Clark, Rev E J Prescott, Rev. J A. Davis, Rev D Faulkner, Rev E Philbrook, Dr E L. Burnham, Moses S. Moulton, L. A.

28th to August 18th bravely published their names in large newspaper ads, under this statement:

> The following men will vote for Prohibition—in other words they [will] vote NO September 11. These names will be added to from week to week. We trust our opponents may publish a similar list.[89]

Philbrook's cause was barely successful:

> By a cliff-hanging 60,853 to 60,095 margin the adult men who did participate voted to retain Prohibition.[90]

Note that at this time women did not have the right to vote; if they had, the margin might have been wider.

Note also that after Maine's Prohibition began in 1884, Sanford's mills were hiring more and more immigrants[91] whose cultures accepted alcohol consumption. Sanford could almost be described as *a small mill town with a drinking problem*.[92]

**Goodall Mill workers, Sanford, Maine, April 1909.
Photographer Hine noted that he couldn't get the girls to pose.**
(Hine, Lewis W., photographer. "Noon hour. . . ." [photograph]. Library of Congress, <www.loc.gov/item/2018675108/>; detail.)

Goodall's Plush Mills, Sanford, Maine.
(circa 1915; greenerpasture.com; edited)

Years into the future, Prohibition would be repealed (Dec. 1933).[93] And even later, most New England textile mills closed[94] as the industry moved to southern states.[95] Sanford's Goodall Mills closed in 1954; shoe factories would follow. Sanford could now be described as *a small drinking town with a mill problem.*

Bessie Philbrook's mother, Eliza (Stearns) Smalley, passed away on Fri., 28 July 1911 in Belfast "after a long and brave struggle with a complication of diseases."[96]

1912

Prayer was offered by Reverend Philbrook at a joint installation service for Riverside Lodge, No. 12, Knights of Pythias and Arbutus Temple, No. 27, Pythian Sisters, held at the Sanford Town Hall on Saturday, 20 Jan. 1912.[97]

(above:) **Letterhead for Sanford's Knights of Pythias Lodge.** *(on letters dated between 1907 and 1911; ebay.com).*

(below:) **Town Hall Sanford, Me.** *(postmark 1913; ebay.com).*

In July, Gene Philbrook got away to fish:

> Rev. E. S. Philbrook and John Johnson enjoyed another of those quiet and successful expeditions after trout this week.[98]

"Brook Trout" by S.F. Denton, 1896. *(In: N.Y. 1st Annual Report of the Commissioners of Fisheries ...; ebay.com)*

1913

Gene Philbrook's now-annual Memorial Day sermon, titled "Christianity and Patriotism," was preached Sunday morning, 25 May 1913 at his church, to visiting "members of William Reed Post, No. 164, and Lieut. W. H. Miller Camp No. 44, Sons of Veterans."[99]

Veterans march in Springvale's Memorial Day Parade, 30 May 1904. *(ebay.com)*

Pastor Philbrook liked camping. For two weeks in July 1913, he went with a large group of boys to "the fifth annual encampment of the Sanford Chapter of the Brotherhood of Andrew and Philip, held at Kennebunk Beach this year."[100]

Kennebunk Beach, Maine. *(circa 1909; ebay.com)*

1914

It was probably at the suggestion of Dr. Philbrook that the two local newspapers helped promote a "Go-to-Church Sunday" movement.

Springvale Advocate ran three large advertisements from 26 Dec. 1913 to 9 Jan. 1914.[101] On 9 Jan., *Sanford Tribune* responded in its own editorial: "A great deal has been said about going to church, in connection with the 'Go-to-Church Sunday

3 REASONS 3

Why People Should Go To Church

1. The demand of to-day is all-around men. No man can be such who neglects his religious nature.

2. Every man has influence. The influence that touches life most profoundly is religious.

3. The Church is the only institution that affords training for the religious life.

Think This Matter Over

Begin 1914 Right by Attending the Church of Your Choice

JANUARY 4th, '14

AND KEEP IT UP

"3 Reasons Why People Should Go To Church"
[*Springvale Advocate* (Springvale, Me.) Fri., 26 Dec. 1913, p. 4]

Movement'" that was advertised in the local papers "gratuitously." They continue, "Rev. Eugene S. Philbrook came to us and expressed his thanks for the Tribune's cooperation" in the

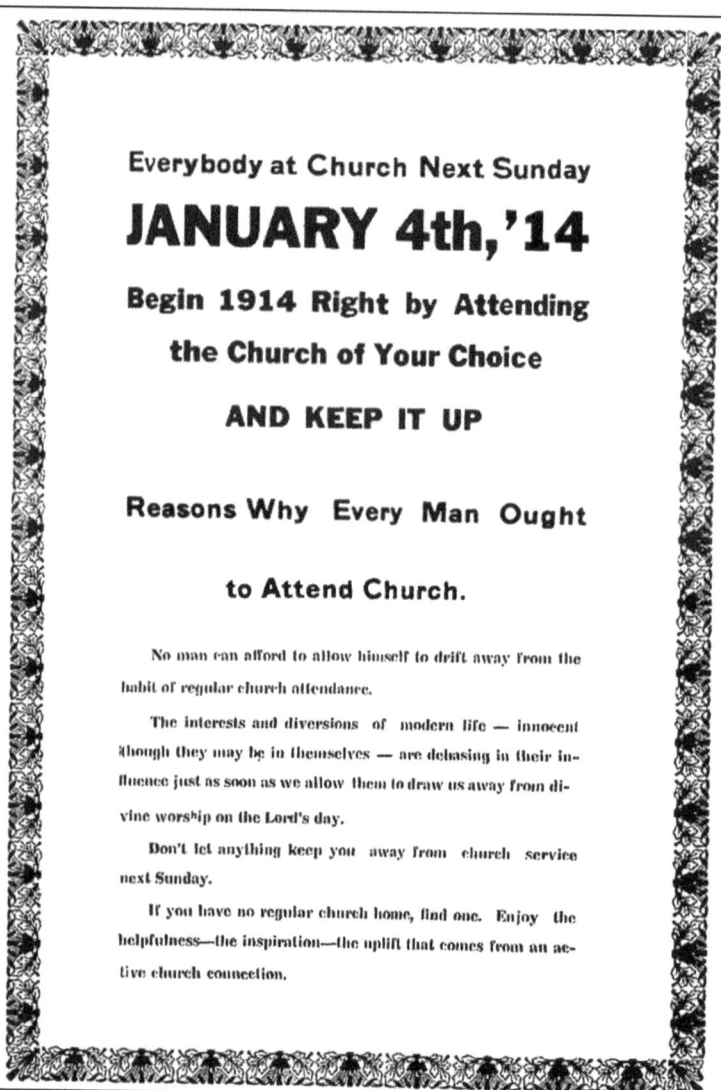

"Everybody At Church Next Sunday, January 4th, '14"
[Springvale Advocate (Springvale, Me.) Fri., 2 Jan. 1914, p. 4]

> **Everybody at Church Next Sunday**
>
> # JANUARY 11, '14
>
> In Spite of the unpleasant weather, last Sunday's Go-To-Church program was a Great Success.
>
> Try it again next Sunday. The Services are Adjourned to January 11th, 1914.
>
> **Reasons Why Every Man Ought to Attend Church.**
>
> No man can afford to allow himself to drift away from the habit of regular church attendance.
>
> The interests and diversions of modern life — innocent though they may be in themselves — are debasing in their influence just as soon as we allow them to draw us away from divine worship on the Lord's day.
>
> Don't let anything keep you away from church service next Sunday.
>
> If you have no regular church home, find one. Enjoy the helpfulness—the inspiration—the uplift that comes from an active church connection.

"Everybody At Church Next Sunday, January 11, '14"
[Springvale Advocate *(Springvale, Me.) Fri., 9 Jan. 1914, p. 4]*

campaign. But the news editor appeared sad that no other area pastors had expressed any "thank you" to the newspaper.[102] Today most of our churches are quick to criticize the press and almost never compliment.

It was reported during the first week of February 1914 that "Rev. E. S. Philbrook returned . . . from a successful lecture tour in the eastern part of the State."[103]

The *Springvale Advocate* noted in Feb. 1914 when "a delegation of five young men led by Rev. E. S. Philbrook went from Sanford to attend the sixth annual Y.M.C.A. Students Conference held in Waterville," Feb. 20-22.[104]

Y.M.C.A., Waterville, Me. *(mailed 1912; digitalcommonwealth.org)*

On Sun. 03 May 1914, Rev. Philbrook preached to several Odd Fellows and Rebekah lodges:

> In observance of the 95th anniversary of the International Order of Odd Fellows, Canton J. H. Dearborn of Biddeford, Moreh Encampment of Sanford, Friendship Lodge and Ruhamah Rebekah Lodge of Springvale united in attending services at the Sanford Baptist Church. . . .
>
> A parade . . . marched to the church. . . . one of the longest parades ever turned out by any fraternal body in Sanford."[105]

The *Sanford Tribune* reported,

> The pastor, Rev. Eugene S. Philbrook, took for his subject, "The Question of the Ages." His text [was] from the scene in the judgment hall of Pilate at the trial of Christ, when Pilate said to the Saviour, "What is Truth?" Mr. Philbrook said that just seven years ago he preached to these same bodies,

and his subject was from the emblem of Odd Fellowship, "Love, the Binding Link." This time his theme was "The Link of Truth."

Mr. Philbrook, in welcoming the orders, said "One of the oldest churches in Maine welcomes one of the oldest orders in the country...."[106]

On Sunday 14 June 1914, the Sanford High School baccalaureate service was held at the Baptist Church for 19 graduating seniors. "The church was filled . . . to its full capacity" and "Mr. Philbrook's sermon was one of the best ever given before a graduating class in Sanford." This was also the first time in the school's history that caps and gowns were worn.[107]

The next day, Monday, June 19th, "Rev. E. S. Philbrook" and four others were appointed to the book committee of the Sanford Library Association, at a meeting of its trustees.[108]

The papers reported in July 1914 when "Rev. Eugene S. Philbrook has started on a tour of the White Mountains."[109]

"Heart of the Notch," White Mts., NH *(circa 1914; ebay.com)*

Readers of the <u>Springvale Advocate</u> learned on Friday 30 October 1914 that "Rev. Eugene S. Philbrook will make a trip through the northern part of the State next week" [i.e. the first week in September 1914].[110]

1915

The East Lebanon, Maine correspondent for the <u>Springvale Advocate</u> wrote in the issue of 14 May 1915 that

> Memorial exercises will be held on Sunday afternoon, May 23, at Grange Hall at East Lebanon. Everyone is invited to attend. Rev. E. S. Philbrook, of Sanford, will give the address, and anyone who has heard him speak will know it will be worth going to hear.[111]

On Monday 26 July 1915 "Rev. Eugene S. Philbrook and family left town for their annual vacation" which included "an extended trip up the west branch of the Penobscot River" with "a camping outfit and canoe."[112] Belfast's paper gave specifics on Aug. 5th:

(<u>In The Maine Woods: 1915 edition</u>. Bangor & Aroostook Railroad, p. 75; image: babel.hathitrust.org)

> Rev. and Mrs. Eugene S. Philbrook of Sanford, who arrived last week with their two children for a visit with Mrs. Philbrook's sister, Miss Isabel Smalley, will spend the first two weeks in August with Mr. Philbrook's people in Brewer, after

which Mr. Philbrook with his sister, Miss Beulah F. Philbrook, and Mr. and Mrs. George Robertson of this city will spend two weeks on a canoe and hiking trip to Mt. Katahdin, taking a different route than that of last season's trip. During his absence Mr. Philbrook's family will visit in Belfast."[113]

Katahdin on 13 May 2005. *[image by "TJ aka Teej"; (https://commons.wikimedia.org/wiki/File:TjWikiKatahdin.jpg).]*

After a whole month away "in the eastern part of the state,"[114] the Philbrook family returned to Sanford about first of September.[115]

In November of 1915, after ministering in Sanford for nine years, Reverend Philbrook moved on to the Winthrop Street Baptist Church of Augusta, Maine. The Sanford community gave a "farewell reception" to Pastor and Mrs. Philbrook. The <u>Springvale Advocate</u> reported, "Mr. Philbrook carries with him the esteem and best wishes of his church and parish and of the whole town as well."[116] Likewise, the Sanford Tribune recognized the good Gene Philbrook had done during his Sanford pastorate:

February 4, 1916
In Rev. E. S. Philbrook . . . Sanford loses an able and faithful preacher of the gospel and worker for the upbuilding of the church.

> In Mr. Philbrook's pastorate here he proved himself to be a man of wonderful ability and untiring devotion to his calling. His many friends, while sorry to see him go, congratulate him on his new position.[117]

Gene Philbrook's *alma mater*, Colby College, proudly summarized his successful ministry at Sanford:

> Since going to Sanford, Mr. Philbrook has been instrumental in greatly increasing the membership of the church and several thousand dollars have been expended for the betterment of the church and parsonage. The present year [i.e. 1915] has been one of great success in the Sunday school work, the church having one of the largest Baptist Sunday schools in Maine.
>
> A special feature has been work among boys and the annual encampment at Kennebunk Beach every Summer. He also brought about the organization of the Brotherhood Orchestra, which has furnished music for so many concerts held in the church during the past few years. Among the new organizations he has formed in connection with the church are the Young Men's Class, the Brotherhood of Andrew and Philip, the Pathfinder Girls, the Junior Congregation and the Older Men's Club.[118]

A pastor's wife also makes a huge contribution to her husband's ministry. Bessie Philbrook's efforts at Sanford were not overlooked by <u>Colby Alumnus</u>:

Mrs. Philbrook is also an earnest worker in the church and has put in considerable time in Sunday school and children's work. She is the leader of the large organization of girls.[119]

From 1906, when he first went to Sanford, until he left there in 1915, the Sanford Tribune and the Springvale Advocate published much of the whereabouts, activities, sermons, weddings and funerals of Reverend Philbrook. It is interesting

Mastheads for *Sanford Tribune* (top) and *The Springvale Advocate* (bottom), **both dated January 1, 1915.**
(springvale.advantage-preservation.com)

that, for many years after he'd left the Sanford area, these newspapers continued to cover Philbrook's exploits. Through these newspapers, the community remembered and honored his ministry with them.

From time-to-time, Reverend Philbrook would be invited back to Sanford to preach, such as when a pastor there took vacation. In August 1920, the Springvale Advocate reported: "Rev. E. S. Philbrook will supply the pulpit at the Baptist church Sunday" [i.e. at the Sanford First Baptist Church].[120] Similarly the next year, Sanford Tribune noted on July 31st: "This is the pastor's last message before vacation," so Rev. Philbrook and three other pastors would fill the Baptist pulpit on August Sundays.[121] Philbrook spoke again at Sanford Baptist church on 31 July 1930,[122] and the next year (23 August 1931) at the Emery Mills Baptist Church;[123] and again at Sanford Baptist in 1935 (August 4),[124] 1938 (July 31),[125] 1940 (August 11),[126] and 1944 (August 27).[127] It's obvious that Gene Philbrook had earned a special place in the hearts of Sanford's people.

Pastorate at Augusta, Maine
1 Nov. 1915 - 30 Apr. 1920

Reverend Philbrook "began his duties as pastor of the First Baptist Church in Augusta on November first"[128] in 1915. He remained at Augusta, residing at 21 Weston Street,[129] until early in 1920 when he accepted a call to the First Baptist Church in Randolph, Massachusetts.[130]

The first Baptists in Augusta "occupied the Old Court House, after 1831 until 1835, when their meeting-house was erected on Winthrop Street."[131]

> **Kennebec.**
> The Journal says a census of church-goers in Augusta, Sunday, showed that about one-half of the population are attendants.

Half of Augusta's population were church-goers in 1882.
[Lewiston Evening Journal (Lewiston, Me.), Tue., 25 Apr. 1882 (2 p.m. edition), p. [2]. Image: MyHeritage.com]

This was the church to which Gene Philbrook came in 1915; by then, several other Baptist churches had also appeared in Augusta.

Winthrop Street Baptist Church in Augusta, Maine was formerly named First Baptist Church. *(circa 1907; ebay.com)*

During Philbrook's five years at the Augusta church he was

> president of the Maine Education Society, secretary of the Maine Cumberland Association, and moderator of the South Kennebec United Baptist Association and the South Kennebec Association. While at Augusta the church was reorganized and the repaired and renovated. A men's Bible class and a girls' society was [sic] organized, and a troop of Boy Scouts registered and 75 persons were added to the membership of the church.[132]

Despite the gains made at Winthrop Street Baptist Church during Rev. Philbrook's pastorate there, within three years of his leaving this organization seems to have disintegrated. A startling July 1923 advertisement in *The Congregationalist* reveals the aftermath, although it doesn't explain exactly what happened:

EXCEPTIONAL OPPORTUNITY

To Secure First Class Church Furniture and Fittings at Record Low Prices

> The Penney Memorial United Baptist Church, Augusta, Maine, offers for quick sale in part or whole the entire fittings of the former Winthrop Street Baptist Church, Augusta.
> First class twenty-one stop, two manual pipe organ with electric blower; complete pulpit set; pews; settees; pulpit painting (work of Harry Coch-

rane); carpet; bell; decorated stained glass windows.

Extremely low prices as sale of building makes early removal of contents necessary. Wire, write or call on E. W. CHURCH, 217 Water St., Augusta, Me.[133]

(left:) **Winthrop Street Baptist Church** [Burrage, Henry S., History of the Baptists in Maine (Portland, Me: Marks Printing House, 1904), facing p. 314; archive.org].

(above:) **Penney Memorial United Baptist Church** (formerly Free Baptist Church; ebay.com).

1917

Gene Philbrook took some "time off" in early July 1917 for "a short vacation in Northern Maine." He then joined his wife Bessie and their two kids who were "visiting relatives in Belfast."[134] While at Belfast, he "preached a very

(In The Maine Woods: 1917 edition. Bangor & Aroostook Railroad, p. 7; Bangor Public Library. <https://digicom.bpl.lib.me.us/railroad_pubs/24/>)

able sermon on Colossians 3-17" at the Baptist church on July 15th.[135]

1918

While still pastoring the Augusta church during the first World War, Rev. Philbrook also

PERSONNEL OF STATE HEADQUARTERS SELECTIVE SERVICE

THE GOVERNOR
HON. CARL E. MILLIKEN

THE PROVOST MARSHAL
BRIGADIER GENERAL GEORGE McL. PRESSON

DISBURSING OFFICER AND AGENT OF UNITED STATES IN MAINE
HON. TIMOTHY F. CALLAHAN (Resigned)
CAPTAIN WILLIAM E. LAWRY, U. S. A. (Died September 23, 1918)
CAPTAIN GEORGE McL. PRESSON, Inf., U. S. A.

ASSISTANT EXECUTIVE OFFICER
REV. EUGENE S. PHILBROOK

(Report of the Adjutant General of the State of Maine for the Period of the World War, 1917-1919. (Augusta, Me.: Adjutant General, 1929), v. 2, p. [5]; image: archive.org)

Maine State House, where Rev. Philbrook worked for Adjutant General of Maine.
(photo by Jack E. Boucher, Aug. 1965; wikimedia.org)

Military Preparedness Parade, 8 May 1917, Augusta, Maine.
(from glass negative; ebay.com)

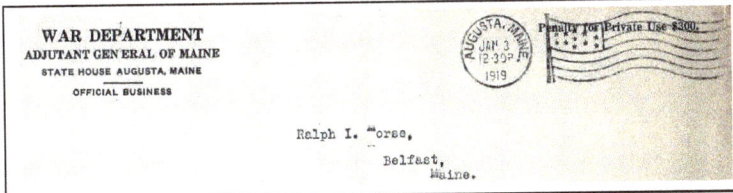

Envelope from the office of Adjutant General of Maine.
(postmarked 3 Jan. 1919; ebay.com)

served two years[136] as *assistant executive officer* for the Maine Selective Service. He signed this notice, placed in newspapers in August 1918:

> ### Registration of September, 1918.
> Under the supervision of the Draft Executives at Augusta, the 24 Local Boards in the State of Maine are rapidly completing their arrangements for the registration of between seventy and eighty thousand men in the State of Maine. This registration will take place early in September, possibly on or about the fifth day of the month.
> .... Companies needing deputized registrars should report at once to E. S. Philbrook, Assistant Executive Officer, at Augusta.
> .... It is confidently expected that when the President's Proclamation shall be issued the State of Maine will be found worthy of her motto,[137] a leader among the commonwealth of the union.
> GEORGE McL. PRESSON,
The Adjutant General.
By E. S. PHILBROOK,
Assistant Executive Officer.[138]

Subsequent to the president's proclamation on August 31, a similar directive signed by Philbrook appeared in newspapers on September 10. It specified a registration deadline of September 12 for males "between the ages of 18 and 45 inclusive" except those already registered or in the military.[139]

But the men who signed up in this "Third Registration" never had to serve. Their processing abruptly ended on 11 November 1918, when the Armistice was signed.[140] The "Great War" was over. Now Gene Philbrook could devote his full attention again to the Lord's work.

Bessie Philbrook's father, Alexander D. Smalley, passed away in Belfast on 08 Oct. 1918.[141]

1919

Tragedy came suddenly to Gene and Bessie Philbrook's family at Augusta early in February 1919. The Belfast newspaper explains the details:

> Miss Isabel M. Smalley of this city [Belfast] died Sunday, Feb. 2nd, at 6 p. m., at the home of her sister, Mrs. Eugene S. Philbrook of Augusta. She had been in failing health since last summer and had grown gradually worse since the death of her father in October. Her nervousness took the form of melancholy and fearing she would never be well again, she took her own life by shooting at about 4 p. m. Sunday and lingered until six. . . . She had practically given her young life for her father and mother's comfort and the greatest incentive to get well was to live at home with her only brother. . . . The day of her death she had attended church and took part in the services and seemed stronger than for some time, gladly accepting an invitation from some girl friends to spend Thursday evening with them. When taken with the desire to end her

mental suffering she was writing a letter to her brother and seemed unable to concentrate her thoughts as she wished. ....¹⁴²

Understandably, Gene Philbrook did not officiate

"When taken with the desire to end her mental suffering she was writing a letter to her brother and seemed unable to concentrate her thoughts as she wished."
(Detail from "The Letter" by Albert Lynch [wikimedia.org]; gun and bullet inserts from "gun-with-bullets" [jooinn.com].)

at Isabel's funeral; that responsibility was given to "Rev. Charles W. Martin of the Methodist church." Gene did attend the funeral, held at the

Smalley home in Belfast, but "Mrs. Philbrook was ill and unable to make the trip."[143]

Rev. Philbrook's moral and legal crusade against addictive substances moved beyond just alcohol to also include tobacco. In many ways his moral and social activism mirrored the interests

> **3—HOME INTERESTS.**
>
> Resolved, That we will also do all in our power towards the enforcement of these other laws of our State which have direct reference to home interests, including laws against cigarettes, gambling, Sabbath desecration, impure literature and immoral exhibitions, and for the protection of women and children.

A resolution from Maine Woman's Christian Temperance Union supporting "laws against cigarettes" and other vices.
[Thirty-first Annual Report of the Woman's Christian Temperance Union of Maine . . . Year Ending September, 1905 (Rockland, Me.: Press of the Courier-Gazette, 1905), p. 32; image: <https://digitalcommons.library.umaine.edu/maine_women_pubs_all/657>]

and activity of the Maine Woman's Christian Temperance Union. Indeed, the Maine W.C.T.U. had paid him a tribute on 23 Nov 1906 at Belfast, for his "conscientious" and "fearless" advocacy of their cause.[144]

In 1919, "Eugene S. Philbrook and 18 others of Augusta" petitioned for a bill in the Maine legislature "favoring an act prohibiting the manufacture and sale of cigarettes within the State of Maine." After state senator Gannett of Kennebec County presented the petition, it was "Placed on File" on 14 March 1919.[145] Now, 101 years later, that petition and its cause remain ignored.

When corporate boards elect a president, often he or she is expected or required to mix with the community. This may include being active in the chamber of commerce, professional clubs and civic organizations. These interactions have always proven very valuable and rewarding, not only for the individual but also for their organization. Rev. Philbrook obviously understood and practiced this art during each of his pastorates, but especially at his next (and final) assignment: Randolph, Massachusetts.

Pastorate at Randolph, Massachusetts
1 May 1920 – 1952

NEW PASTOR FOR RANDOLPH CHURCH

In 1920, Gene Philbrook "accepted a unanimous call to become pastor of the First Baptist Church

> **Rev. Philbrook, May 1920**
> ["New pastor for Randolph church," Boston Herald (Boston, Mass.), Sun., 16 May 1920, p. 31; image: genealogybank.com]

THE REV. E. S. PHILBROOK

in Randolph."[146] Son Randolf was eleven years old, and daughter Isabel was nine.

Randolph,[147] just south of Boston, had a "flourishing Baptist Church" according to one newspaper.[148] Rev. Philbrook began his work there on the First of May in 1920, successor to Rev.

"Main Street, Randolph, Mass."
(postmark 1907; ebay.com)

Herbert L. Howard who had moved on to the First Baptist Church of Peabody, Mass.[149]

As Eugene Philbrook began his long pastorate First Baptist Church in Randolph, Mass., big social changes were taking place across the country. These times would be called *The Roaring Twenties* and *The Decade of Change*. Prohibition had just gone into effect via the 18th Amendment to the Constitution (1919; until rescinded in 1933). Women were about to gain the right to vote by the 19th Amendment (1920). Families bought their first radios. In the national arena of religion, citizens debated Charles Darwin's controversial evolution theory. America was on its way to becoming a world power in industry and creativity.

Reverend Philbrook could be described as a

North Main Street (from West Street), Randolph, Mass.
(postmark 1917; ebay.com)

"lifelong learner." His son Randolf recalled:

> Still not satisfied in his quest for knowledge and the ability to interpret the Holy Scriptures, he soon enrolled at Gordon College of Theology & Missions and also at Harvard Divinity School to work for a Doctorate in Sacred Theology on the same part-time basis as used in acquiring his Master's Degree. His studies never interfered with his pastoral duties but instead enhanced them.[150]

This "2 years of special study,"[151] in Boston at Gordon College of Theology and Missions, earned Rev. Philbrook a Doctor of Sacred Theology degree (STD)[152] in 1935.[153] His dissertation is titled *The Concept of Progressive Creation in Ascending*

Levels as the Determinative Factor in the Rise and Destiny of Man.[154]

By 1898, about 12 years prior to Pastor Philbrook's advent in Randolph, the church building had been replaced after an 1873 fire destroyed an earlier building. The architect for the new construction was W. J. Paine of Boston. "The entire cost, including clock, bell, organ and pews," was $18,000.[155]

The history explains the name change from

First Baptist Church, Randolph, Massachusetts
(postmark 1909; ebay.com)

"North Baptist Church of Christ in Randolph" to "The First Baptist Church." Much more had changed over the one-hundred-and-fifty years of its existence. Founded in 1819, it was "Calvinistic in sentiment" and of a membership where only the males could vote (this changed in 1905).

This church also stressed the importance of correct deportment, including a ban on movies, playing cards, dancing, and much more.

The Baptist church in Randolph did experience a period in which those excommunicated were restored from their verdict of dismissal. At that time, members supported the budget by paying for the pews they occupied, by taxation, and by special assessments.

Churches at the end of the nineteenth century were undergoing changes, as they still do today, whether for good or bad. Positive approaches were certainly destined under Rev. Philbrook's leadership.

Newspapers spanning the ministry years of Dr. Philbrook record the expansion and growth of ministries and membership. He continually formed new organizations for every age and interest within the church. A photographer and nature enthusiast, he presented illustrated lectures which were enthusiastically received throughout the Northeast.

In contrast to the slower pace of many current pastors, newspaper articles during Dr. Philbrook's era confirm his constant involvement in community activities, lectures, weddings, funerals, political advocacy, mountain climbing, camping, fraternal lodges, and even a community orchestra. He accomplished all of this, in addition to preaching and leading an active, prospering church.

Note also that in Rev. Philbrook's era there were no assistant pastors, associate pastors or administrators. His constant visiting of parishioners was recognized and greatly appreciated. He was always *on the move*. A vibrant church was testimony of his successful ministry.

Dr. Philbrook was generally a very quiet, humble gentleman. His frame was not large, but appeared somewhat frail. His sermons were delivered forcibly when required, but without shouting; never ear-piercing; convincing, but not clamorous; always reverent.

Rev. Dr. Eugene Philbrook was pastor of the First Baptist Church in Randolph for thirty-three years until retiring in 1952.[156] At that time, his lengthy tenure was considered unusual.

First Baptist Church, Randolph, Massachusetts
(courtesy of JoAnn Randall)

Rev. Philbrook was my pastor during my growing up years and through my time in college. In 1947, our family moved from 68 Center Street to 536 North Main Street, next door to the parsonage. If the Whitaker kids had ever misbehaved, our best behavior would be required now!

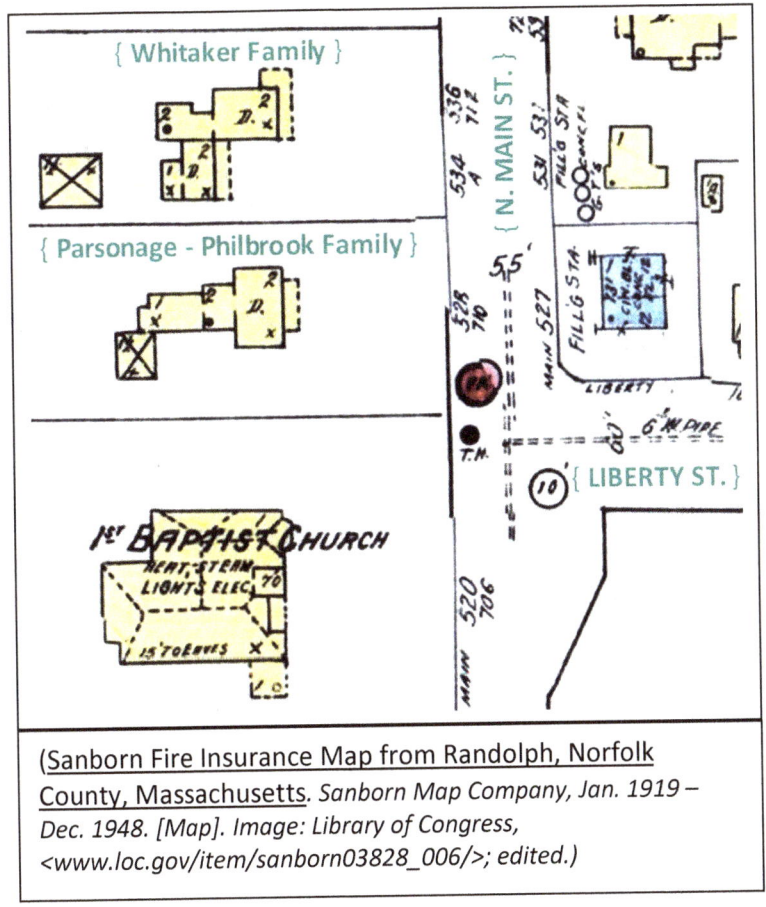

(Sanborn Fire Insurance Map from Randolph, Norfolk County, Massachusetts. *Sanborn Map Company, Jan. 1919 – Dec. 1948. [Map]. Image: Library of Congress, <www.loc.gov/item/sanborn03828_006/>; edited.)

The stately parsonage still had an attached carriage shed, though it no longer housed a horse or carriage. Sometime later, during Pastor Knox's

Parsonage for First Baptist Church, Randolph, Mass.
(courtesy of JoAnn Randall)

tenure, he excavated the dirt floor and large embedded rocks, then installed a concrete floor and overhead garage doors.

This parsonage was originally purchased in 1824 from a church deacon, Daniel Alden. Despite several subsequent upgrades, at over 200 years old it remains an architectural specimen of the historic North Main Street neighborhood, once lined with stately elms.

1920

Seven months after Gene Philbrook's arrival at Randolph, he had a mishap on Dec. 9th, 1920.

Newspaper reports varied, even conflicted, on some details. *Boston Herald* had the longest report:

RANDOLPH MINISTER RUN DOWN BY MOTOR
Rev. E. S. Philbrook Has Slight Concussion of Skull

The Rev. Eugene S. Philbrook, pastor of the First Baptist Church in Randolph, was struck by an automobile on North Main street yesterday [i.e. Dec. 9] while riding a bicycle with his nine-year-old son. He was thrown to the street and struck his head on the edge of the sidewalk, becoming unconscious. The driver of a second automobile picked him up and took him to the office of Dr. Alfred W. Mirick, who

"Main Street, North from Randolph Square, Randolph, Mass."
(postmark 1915; amazon.com)

gave first aid treatment for a slight concusion [sic] of the brain, a scalp wound three inches long and multiple bruises. He was then taken to his home on North Main street. The man who picked him up said that the driver of the machine which struck him stopped long enough to give his name and to say he lived in Brockton and then drove away. Chief of Police Hadley is trying to locate him.[157]

(above:) **Central Square (looking North), Randolph, Mass.**
(photo by W.M. Shipman; postmark 1906; ebay.com)

(below: postcard, circa 1920; ebay.com)

Boston Globe printed its report on Dec. 10th, although the dateline is "Dec. 9":

MINISTER KNOCKED FROM BICYCLE AND HURT BY AUTO

RANDOLPH, Dec 9—Rev Eugene T. Philbrook, pastor of the First Baptist Church, was severely injured this evening when hit by an unidentified automobile, while riding a bicycle on North Main st.

He was thrown from his wheel, and his head struck on the cement pavement. His son, who was riding ahead, heard the crash and, assisted by an automobile operator, who came along, took his father to the office of Dr Alfred W. Myrick, North Main st.

The doctor said the minister had a three-inch scalp wound, concussion of the brain and body bruises.

Mr Philbrook was later taken to his home on North Main st by Dr Myrick.[158]

The *Boston Post* report confused the story even more by indicating that father and son were on the same bicycle:[159]

RANDOLPH PASTOR INJURED BY AUTO

The Rev. Eugene S. Philbrook, pastor of the First Baptist Church of Randolph, was seriously injured yesterday, when an automobile collided with a bicycle on which he and his nine-year-old son were riding in North Main street. After assisting the Rev. Mr. Philbrook to the office of Dr. Alfred W. Myrick, the driver of the machine is said to have left without making his identity known to the police.

It was one week later, Dec. 16th, when Gene's former parishoners in Belfast, Maine read an account in the *Republican Journal*:[160]

> Belfast relatives of Rev. Eugene S Philbrook of Randolph, Mass., formerly pastor of the Belfast Baptist Church, have received news of his recent accident which caused a slight concussion of the brain. While riding a bicycle with his son they were in collision with an auto when Mr. Philbrook was thrown against a building and received a cut on his head. His son was not injured. Later advices said the injury was not so serious as first feared.

So which paper's report is the most correct?

Boston Herald: "...thrown to the street and struck his head on the edge of the sidewalk."

Boston Globe: "...thrown from his wheel, and his head struck on the cement pavement."

Republican Journal: "...thrown against a building and received a cut on his head."

Other than walking, the bicycle no doubt provided some of Gene's mobility. In 1920, motor vehicles were not the heavy machines they are today, which was fortunate for the bicycle. No account was given of damages, if any, to Gene's "wheel," or to the "machine" which hit him.

(above:) **"What Happened?"**
(by A.B. Frost; Harper's Weekly, Nov. 1897; ebay.com; edited)
(below:) **"Fact and fiction about a great annoyance"**
(Puck, July 1886; ebay.com; edited)

The First Baptist Church's steeple housed a large bell that sometime later was electrified to peal hourly – and it did! – all night long! This *took some getting-used-to*. Guests at our house often asked, in frustration, how we could sleep with "that thing" reporting every hour of the night! In our vain attempt at a humorous reply, we sometimes proffered that it was to prompt the parson and parishoners to prayer.

I was baptized by Rev. Philbrook in 1945 on June 17th (his 611th baptism). He also baptized my brother Wayne and my father in 1952 on June 15th

> 703 Wayne Calvin Whitaker
>
> 710 Albert Preston Whitaker, Sr.

Baptism entries from Rev. Philbrook's record book
(courtesy of Howard Randall; edited)

(numbers 703 and 710, respectively). Dad served many years on this church's Board of Trustees.

Dr. Philbrook trained me, and others in the youth group, to read Scripture from the pulpit.[161] In his advanced years by then, Pastor Philbrook

Stained glass window at First Baptist Church, Randolph, Mass.

(image courtesy of the Church)

A door without a handle
  Is like the human heart
As Jesus, waiting, knocks;
  A person must decide
To open latch and lock
  And let HIM come inside.

(©2021 Stephen L. Robbins)

Behold, I stand at the door and knock. If anyone hears my voice and opens the door, I will come in to him and eat with him, and he with me.

—Revelation 3:20
(English Standard Version)

sat in the rear pew to observe and coach us. There was no electro-mechanical sound system in that day, so we were taught how to 'THROW' out, or project, our voices so that all could hear. Next, we learned to incorporate into that projection the proper annunciation, pronunciation and inflection – so that this senior clergyman could not only hear, but also *understand* our reading, even from the back pew. Many times, Dr. Philbrook interrupted us with "slow down," "breathe," "pause," or other corrections, including "repeat" – until it's almost perfect!

Only after we had mastered Scripture reading and received Pastor Philbrook's approval did he use us in the very formal Sunday morning service. – But – As I recall, only one or two of us qualified in that "art" to his standards. I was proudly and boldly one of those.

Gene and Bessie Philbrook's daughter Isabel married Donald Randall, a high school teacher and collector of antique and classic automobiles.

Gene and Bessie's son, Frank Randolf Philbrook, became a medical doctor (M.D.), serving many years in the U.S. Navy and reaching the rank of Commander. He held medical degrees from

**Isabel (Philbrook) Randall
May 1998**
(courtesy of JoAnn Randall)

Boston University and a Master of Public Health degree from Harvard University. In the Navy, he was senior medical officer responsible for the public health of the entire Pacific Fleet. Later he was appointed to the staff of the Secretary of Defense at the Pentagon.

After Dr. Randolf Philbrook retired from the Navy, he served on the staff of the Commonwealth of Massachusetts, Department of Public Health. He was recognized by Dr. Jonas Salk for his assistance in the effective development of polio immunization.

Randolf was also an accomplished musician, playing both organ and flute.

(above:) **Dr. Frank Randolf Philbrook, circa 1947.**

(below:) **Madeline (Hartford) Philbrook** *(left)* **and Dr. Frank Randolph Philbrook** *(right).*

(images courtesy of JoAnn Randall)

His original compositions of carillon music have been played in churches throughout the world. He had his own organ aboard ship, evidenced by grey deck paint that could be seen around its base of after he returned home with it.

It was on this organ that Randolf gave me several lessons, in both theory and practice. But I never mastered the art of playing organ, not even well enough to attempt "Happy Birthday." It is a very good thing that my reading of the King James Bible was more accomplished!

Bessie Philbrook often related how her son Randolf had a great interest in medicine, even from his early years. Her favorite, oft-repeated, story noted how little Randolf attempted to insert an isinglass (mica) window onto the side of their house cat, hoping to see how it worked. She never mentioned what was the cat's ultimate fate. Her

reading glasses, normally on a chain around her neck, must have been raised, the glass rubbed clean with her fingers, then pinched to her nose for a closer look at his work!

My interest in old vehicles was probably engendered by Isabel (Philbrook) Randall's husband, Donald H. Randall. At one time Don let us put an old 1910 REO truck in our barn and encouraged us to do some "elbow grease" work on it toward full restoration.

In those days, the Brockton Fair was a big doing in our area and one of the attractions was a classic automobile parade and race. The REO was entered, and Harvey Cossaboom[162] and I commissioned to drive it.

At the appointed time we joined other cars at the track and grandstand to participate. When the starting gun was fired, we set out – literally like "a herd of turtles." With a manufacturer's posted top

A Good Finish at the Brockton Fair *(postcard, circa 1909, ebay.com.; photo inserts from author's and editor's collections; edited).*

speed of ten miles per hour, we were obviously destined to be last. But the crowd loved it, and cheered anyway. Realizing the race was lost for us, we reversed our part, made a U-turn and went to the finish line – even before the others – to WIN in reverse! The crowd roared!

The next day, the local newspaper featured our picture in the REO – and a nice article, believe it or not! I think we took the fans' attention away from some fine restored classic and antique vehicles that were more deserving of it than our 1910 REO. But this birthed within me an enthusiasm for antique and classic vehicles which occupied much of my time during the years ahead.

While in my senior year at Boston University, I bought my cousin John Ivester's 1939 Buick Roadmaster, a black four-door sedan. It was parked in his yard in Arlington, Mass. and I was allowed to drive it on some occasions.

When John enlisted in the Coast Guard, he decided to dispose of the car. After some negotiations, he agreed to sell it to me for $150.00. In those days, that price was just below the fifteen-year-old machine's fair market value. But its registration had lapsed, and I had to get it home to Randolph.

My hope was that Mr. Donald Randall, Dr. Philbrook's son-in-law, would know how to accomplish this. Perhaps he might even find a temporary license plate to affix on the car. However, the Buick refused to run, most likely due to its lack of use. Motor work was obviously necessary.

Don Randall suggested he would tow it to Randolph with his vehicle. What else could I do? So, on the appointed day, we drove to Arlington, affixed a heavy rope between his car's rear bumper and the Buick's front end. Off we went – me behind the wheel of the Buick, steering and biting my lip!

In those days, the noted "Circumferential Highway" (Route 128) was a winding and scenic

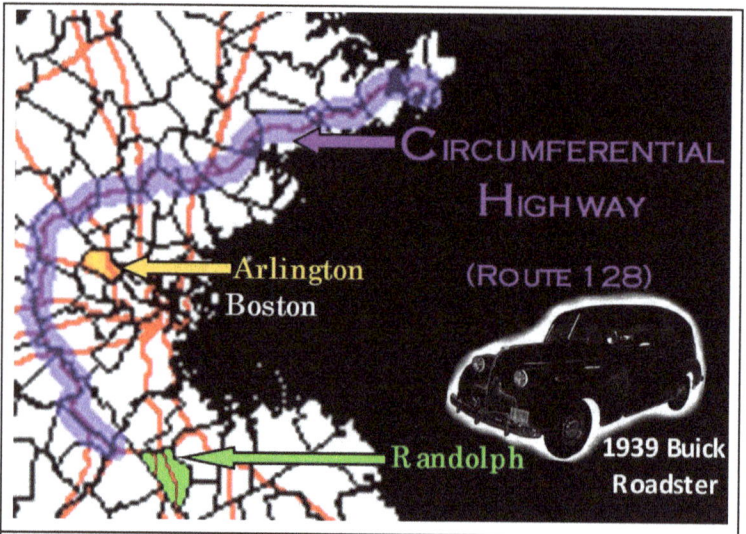

(Map: wikimedia.org; edited). (1939 Buick Roadster: German Medeot, CC BY 2.0 <https://creativecommons.org/licenses/by/2.0>, via Wikimedia Commons; edited by Stephen Robbins).

road around Boston. This road's southern end meandered through the Blue Hills. It was a well-maintained two-lane road. But, for those days, it was heavily-traveled and traffic moved at a fairly fast pace. It always carried a good amount of automobile traffic, but no trucks!

Frankly, this about scared me to death, and I am sure I applied the brakes more than once. It was no wonder that I needed to install new brake linings afterwards! But we made it! Tethered only by a rope, we somehow survived this hazardous journey – all the way from Arlington to Randolph.

Randolph Road, showing Blue Hills, Randolph, Mass.
Al Whitaker's 1939 Buick Roadster, towed with a rope.
(<u>Postcard</u>: postmark 1920; amazon.com; edited). (<u>1939 Buick Roadster</u>: German Medeot, CC BY 2.0 <https://creativecommons.org/licenses/by/2.0>, via Wikimedia Commons; edited by Stephen Robbins). (<u>Portrait photo</u>: author's collection). (<u>Rope 1</u>: Andre Furtado, pexels.com; edited). (<u>Rope 2</u>: Engin Akyurt, pexels.com; edited).

I expressed my genuine appreciation to Mr. Randall, despite his giving me the thrill of a lifetime at full speed ahead! As I remember, Dr. Philbrook, with some alarm, exclaimed, "You did WHAT!?"

Oh yeah – in addition to the brakes, I did a full motor job on the Buick, after it was pushed into our barn.

By this time, Rev. Frederick Knox had succeeded Dr. Philbrook in the Randolph pastorate. His son, Kenny Knox (later became the Rev. Kenneth Knox), and my brother Wayne were close friends. At one point, they decided to use my Buick to "run the bases" on a backyard baseball field, and nearly tipped it over. This happened while I was at work in Boston; by the time I arrived home, the Buick was safely stored back in the barn. No one, ever, should have even suspected it had been the object of two playful high school boys. But "Father Knox", as the boys knew him, had noticed these antics; he quietly, gracefully, but forcibly, lectured Kenny and Wayne that this sneaky and risky activity was, really, *not* what they should be doing.

Incidentally, this Buick was later traded for a Henry J automobile which, in turn, was traded for the first A. P. Whitaker & Sons vehicle: a new 1955 Studebaker truck. The used Buick car was bought and traded for $150. With trade, the Henry J automobile was $900. The trade value of the Henry J on the Studebaker pickup truck was the $900. The total new cost of the 1955 pickup was $1800. So, less the $900. trade-in, the net cost of this deal was $900. High finance!

Had it not been for Dr. Philbrook, retaining my faith during my college years might have been much more difficult, especially with the rapid dissemination of liberal thought throughout academia. Almost every night, I found myself next door in Dr. Philbrook's study, seeking answers to questions, obtaining his advice and counsel, and preparing my papers.

Dr. Philbrook was especially helpful with my two dissertations: *Scientific Theories and the Doctrine of Creation*, and *Greek Mythology and Christian Theology*. Despite one professor stating his disagreement with my theses, both papers had been effectively done and were convincing enough to merit my degree. Thanks, Dr. Philbrook!

In the pulpit, Dr. Philbrook always wore his neatly-pressed black robe, with three bands on the sleeves signifying the doctorate degree. Often during his preaching, Dr. Philbrook lifted his arms outward, making them appear as angel wings – but black and not white! On special occasions such as Communion Sunday he wore an academic collar having a striking burgundy lining, which signified his degree and the seminary granting it. Somehow this seemed to add some dignity and reverence into the worship experience.

Rev. Dr. Philbrook in his black robe
(courtesy of First Baptist Church, Randolph, Mass.)

Dr. Philbrook's sermons were well-prepared. He wrote out most of them with his ink-dipped pen, then converted them into notes on 8 ½-inch-by-11-inch sheets of paper. After neatly folding these sheets of notes, he wrote a sermon title on the outside (like on a book) – sometimes in red ink.

Cover sheet for the "Seven by the Sea" sermon notes of Rev. Philbrook.
(author's collection)

Also written on the outside, the sermon's Scripture verses were identified, as well as the date(s) of its delivery (which sometimes included other speaking locations).

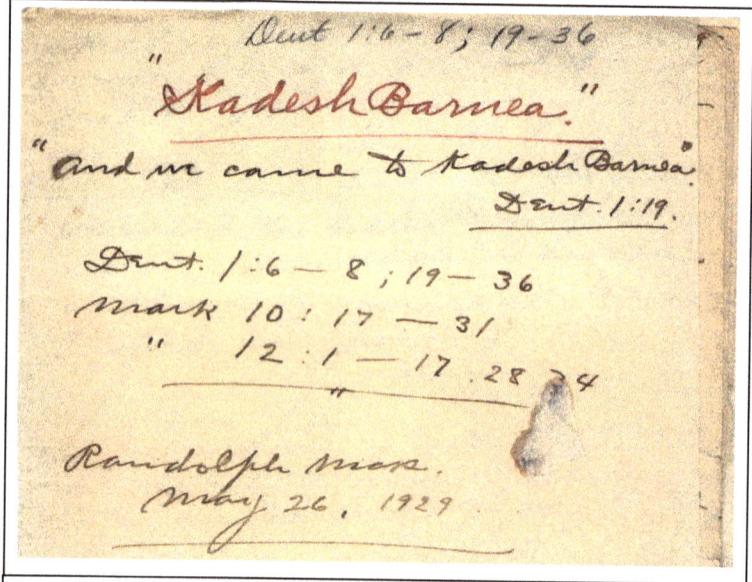

Cover sheet for the "Kadesh Barnea" sermon notes of Rev. Philbrook. (author's collection)

After Rev. Philbrook's death, his wife emptied the barrel and gave boxes of these sermon outlines to Harvey Cossaboom and me. Harvey and I divided the sermons between us, according to our interests. Many of these, or at least parts of them, were used by both of us during the ensuing years.

My favorite, of all Dr. Philbrook's sermons, is "Plus Ultra" – its title and message were captivating. According to the Morning Call, a Patterson, N.J. newspaper, Dr. Philbrook was

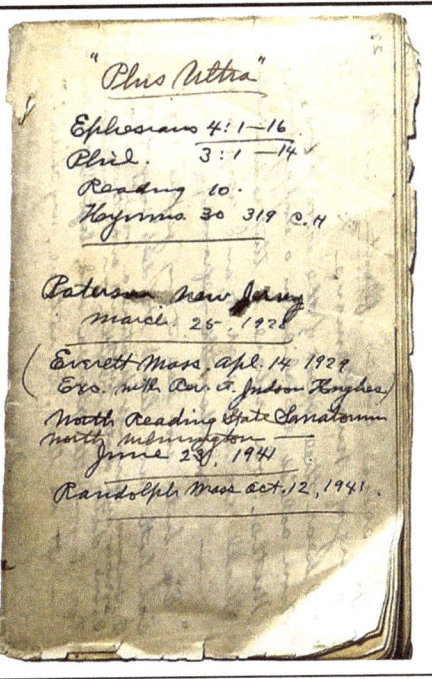

(above:) **Newspaper ad for Rev. Philbrook's speaking at First Baptist Church in Patterson, New Jersey on 25 March 1928.**

["Sermon Topics, Times and Places of Services," Morning Call (Patterson, N.J.), Sat., 24 Mar. 1928, p. 10. Image: newspapers.com.]

(below:) **Cover sheet for the "Plus Ultra" sermon notes of Rev. Philbrook.**

(author's collection)

coming on Sunday, 25 Mar. 1928 to preach his sermon "Plus Ultra" for the evening service at

First page of Rev. Philbrook's "Plus Ultra" sermon notes.

(author's collection)

First Baptist Church in Patterson.[163] I am excited to have this original valued manuscript in my possession! I wrote about "Plus Ultra" in chapter 55 of our earlier book, *This Is My Story*. A copy of this chapter is attached as APPENDIX E at the back of this book.

Gene Philbrook's son, Randolf,[164] told me the story of his father's handwritten notes which were stored in a barrel in the parsonage attic. At times, Rev. Philbrook would pull out an old sermon – perhaps to repeat after several years, or to use in another church. Sometimes these sermons seemed to get shorter – maybe instead of 35 or 40 minutes, now 20-to-25 minutes. Somehow mice had nested in that barrel and had shredded the paper on which the sermons were written. When he complained to Mrs. Philbrook, she had no sympathy. Her comment: "I hope they have chewed 10 minutes off of every one of them."

Randolf noted it was "a pleasant joke between us– that he [Rev. Philbrook] became a doctor before I did." (Three days before!).

The emphasis of the Christian message, although delivered more formally in those days, was never compromised by Dr. Philbrook. He was a constant encourager of all, including the youth. In my case, no one could have done it better or accomplished more during my years in academia and in later life.

After assuming the pastorate at Randolph, Pastor Philbrook taught the Men's Bible Class in the church sanctuary every Sunday, where the attendance quickly increased to over 150 men each week. His sermons and teaching included current scientific information, presented in an understandable and interesting way, and illustrating a Biblical truth or concept. He obviously spent many hours in Bible study and in other research, to prepare for his sermons and lectures. Some current "preachers" would do well to emulate him.

A *calling* to a church involved not just preaching, but someone who could also direct, manage, and administer everything. Most assemblies didn't have a secretary; and some not even a janitor! Computers were not even thought about.

The papers retained by Dr. Philbrook's family include a hardbound book[165] in which he recorded child dedications, conversions, marriages, baptisms and funerals. These events and their

> 137
>
> 694 Virginia D. Randall Jn.15,'52
> 695 Bette Ellen Johnson
> 696 Anne Elizabeth Johnson
> 697 Nancy Linda Feed
> 698 Emile Carol Condon
> 699 Florence Elaine Charron
> 700 Neal De Boer
> 701 Bette" West
> 702 Neil West
> 703 Wayne Calvin Whitaker
> 704 John Robert Pepper
> 705 George Melvin Berry
> 706 Robert Bruce Fraser
> 707 Donald Allen Pilgrim
> 708 Alfred Holbrook, Jr.
> 709 Alfred Holbrook, Sr.
> 710 Albert Preston Whitaker, Sr.
>
> 711 Elizabeth Jean Randall Apl. 5,'53
> 712 Roger Sumner Randall
> 713 Donald Howard Randall Jr.

dates were neatly-entered, using a steel pen dipped into ink. Each entry was also numbered serially.

Gene Philbrook's daughter, Isabel (Philbrook) Randall, played the violin. He had purchased a "Bachelder" violin for her on 30 Aug. 1922, from its father-and-son makers, Edwin R. and Alvah M. Bachelder[166] of Frankfort, Maine. This violin cost $50.[167]

When Harvey Cossaboom and I occasionally had our *Gospel Crusaders* group conducting an evening service,[168] Isabel often played for us.

Isabel also coordinated other music. One such production, *The Life of Christ* in vocal and instrumental selections, proved to be a highlight of our involvement. Musicians included my brother Malcolm with his trumpet.

Dr. Philbrook was a nature lover,

(above:)
"The Christmas Hymn"
drawn by Marcella Walker
(<u>Illustrated London News</u>, *Dec. 1890; ebay.com; edited*)

(opposite:) **Some baptisms in Rev. Philbrook's record book**
(courtesy of Howard Randall)

appreciative of God's creations.

> As a camera fan, he made hundreds of negatives from which slides were made for lectures which were given in various places in New England and in New York State.[169]

Gene had a black "slide box" in which he carried his homemade slides. The slides were approximately 3-inches-by-3-inches window glass sections, held together with black tape along their

Glass slide of a Showy Lady's Slipper orchid
(Cypripedium reginae)
photographed and hand-colored by Eugene Philbrook
(courtesy of Howard Randall)

edges. Inside were drawings, diagrams and samples of flowers, bugs and such, many of which he'd hand-painted. Many slides contained Gene's photographs of natural life.

Dr. Philbrook often traveled to lecture with these handmade visual aids and a rather large and cumbersome homemade stereopticon projector. At one point, Harvey Cossaboom and I were entrusted with this "kit" and presented *The Twenty-third Psalm* using these materials.

I had often wondered what ever disposition may have been made of Gene Philbrook's handmade slides and the homemade projector. I was pleased to learn recently that they have been carefully preserved by his grandchildren.

There are several other collections of Gene Philbrook's slides, which he prepared for two institutions:

> Lecture sets were also prepared for the Good Will Home for needy boys and girls in Hinckley, Maine and also the Andover Newton Theological School. At Good Will there is a large display of flower transparencies in natural size and color known as the Philbrook collection.[170]

<u>The Boston Globe</u>, a widely-read newspaper in the early nineteen-hundreds, often reported on Dr. Philbrook's "illustrated lectures" at various meetings around New England.

Regardless of his interest in lecturing about nature, he always gave direct reference to God's hand in all of it. His sermons were always Bible-based and Scripture-referenced, and called sinners to faith in Jesus. Obviously, he was somewhat in-demand for his exciting, informative lectures, and for sermon delivery at special occasions.

Gene Philbrook was not a "shouting" or even a loud speaker. It was exciting to listen to him speak with full articulation and in learned moderation and inflection. He spoke clearly, was heard and understood. Some of today's expounders who use a fast pitch and rapid delivery could learn much from Dr. Philbrook and his expert delivery.

1921

Gene Philbrook joined the Norfolk Union Lodge of Masons, Randolph, Mass., 11 June 1921.[171]

"Masonic Building and Post Office, Randolph, Mass."
(postmark 1912; ebay.com)

1922

Gene Philbrook gave his "Sportsman's Paradise" talk in several states during 1922 and 1923:

> # THE SPORTSMAN'S PARADISE
> ### STEREOPTICON LECTURE
> ## By Rev. Eugene S. Philbrook
> Original colored views of hunting, fishing, canoeing and mountain climbing in
> ## New Hampshire and Maine
> ### VACATION MEMORIES
> ## WEDNESDAY, JAN. 18, 7.45 P. M.
> ### Middle Street Baptist Church
> Admission Free. Silver Offering.

"The Sportsman's Paradise" [advertisement]
[Portsmouth Herald *(Portsmouth, N.H.), Wed., 18 Jan. 1922, p. 5. Image: newspapers.com]*

1922 Jan. 18 pm at Middle Street Baptist Church, Portsmouth, N.H.;[172]

1923 Dec. 17 pm for the Men's Club of the South Congregational Church, Braintree, Mass.;[173]

and at unspecified dates in "Boston and Syracuse" (according to poster on next page).

"The Sportsman's Paradise" [poster]
(circa 1922-1923; courtesy of Howard Randall)

1923

Gene Philbrook's mother, Pauline (Moulton) Philbrook, died "in her 79th year" on 2 Feb. 1923 at her Rockland, Mass. home, from bronchial pneumonia. The funeral service at her home (122 Union St.), at 2 p.m. Monday [the 5th] was conducted by Rev. Willard Pratt, Stoughton Street Baptist church, Boston. The obituary mentions Beulah Philbrook (Gene's sister), a teacher at Rockland Junior High School.[174]

1926

Rev. Philbrook gave an address, "The Aristocracy of Character," at the 26th annual reunion of the

NEARLY 300 OF ALDEN KINDRED AT REUNION

Rev Eugene S. Philbrook of Randolph Speaks on "The Aristocracy of Character"

Rev. Philbrook's speech headlined
[above: Boston Globe (Boston, Mass.), Thur., 29 July 1926, p. 1; newspapers.com]

Unitarian Church, Duxbury, Mass.
(above: postmark 1910; cardcow.com)

Alden Kindred of America, meeting on 28 July 1926 at the Unitarian Church, Duxbury, Mass. The Boston Globe printed Dr. Philbrook's speech text the next day.

1928

Readers of The Morning Call (Patterson, N.J.) were invited by a nice display ad to hear Rev. Eugene Philbrook give three sermons on Sunday,

March 25th, 1928 at their city's First Baptist Church. Good publicity!

Back at home in Randolph, Mass., Gene Philbrook was installed as chaplain for Norfolk Lodge, A.F.& A.M. (Ancient Free & Accepted Masons), on 14 Dec. 1928 at Masonic Hall.[175]

"Post Office, Randolph, Mass."
Masonic Lodge rooms are on upper levels.
Post Office is on the ground floor.

(postmark 1912; ebay.com)

1930

On 9 May 1930, Gene Philbrook's father passed away. The newspaper death notice recalls Francis J. Philbrook's military service in the Civil War: Company A, 2nd Regiment, of the Maine Infantry. It also mentions that Beulah F. Philbrook (Gene's sister) was then living in Rockland, Mass. North Bradford, Maine's inhabitants may not have been aware of all the important people who had roots there.

1934

Beulah Philbrook of Rockland and her brother, Rev. Eugene Philbrook of Randolph, each received a bequest $300 in the will of Helen M. Pike, late of Brookline. Her late husband was a jeweler and optician in Boston. The will, dated 28 June 1919, was finally "allowed" by a probate judge on Mar. 1st, 1934. It's interesting that the judge also

> disallowed a will, alleged to have been made by Mrs. Pike in 1932, in which she left her entire estate to Mme. Effie Walton, Boston numerologist, on the grounds of undue influence of Mme. Walton.[176]

At Randolph's Memorial Day activities on 30 May 1934, a parade marched, pausing for ceremonies at each cemetery. "Prayers were given by Rev. Eugene S. Philbrook" at both Central and at Oakland cemeteries. Curiously, although Philbrook was designated "chaplain of the day," "Prayers were read at the cross at St Mary's Cemetery by Rev Dominic Rock."[177]

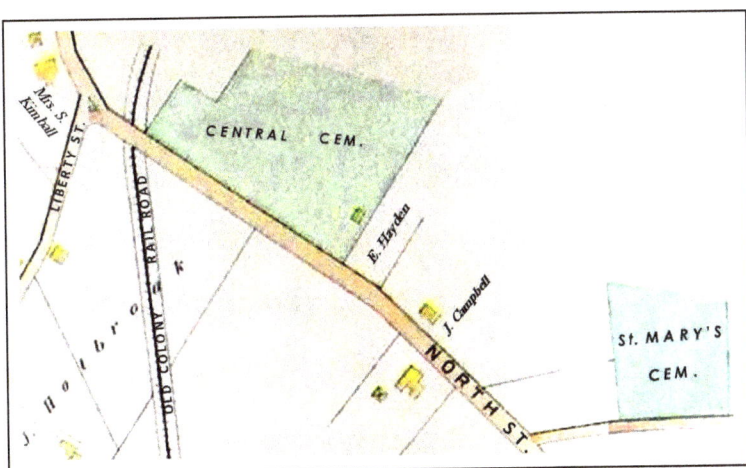

Sites of the two largest cemeteries in Randolph, Mass. in 1888.
(Detail from: "Randolph; Holbrook" [map]. In: Robinson, E., A.H. Mueller, and F. Bourquin. Robinson's Atlas of Norfolk County, Massachusetts. [New York]: E. Robinson, publisher; Phila[delphia]: Engraved by A.H. Mueller; Printed by F. Bourquin, 1888. Image: ebay.com; edited.)

1937

A clipping from an unidentified, undated (but 1937) newspaper reported:

> Frank Perry, a Gloucester fisherman, gave a stirring talk last evening at the service in the First Baptist church. . . . After the service the members remained for an informal reception to Dr. and Mrs. Philbrook in recognition of the 30th anniversary of their marriage. The affair was a complete surprise and was arranged by Mrs. McNeill and Mrs. Cossaboom. Edwin Stetson, superintendent of the Bible school, presented them, in behalf of the members, a six-branched candlabra [sic], a purse of money, and a large bouquet of flowers."[178]

1939

A *Boston Globe* story on 18 Oct. 1939 listed Rev. Eugene S. Philbrook as one of six speakers at a "conservation conference," held at First Congregational Church in Braintree, Mass. About 200 women attended this event, which was put on by the 2d District of the Massachusetts State Federation of Women's Clubs. The only other male speaker was Egbert Hans of the Mass. Dept. of Conservation.[179] Rev. Philbrook's topic was not stated.

1940

Gene Philbrook's parishoners at First Baptist Church of Randolph certainly appreciated their faithful pastor, hosting a surprise celebration for the 20th anniversary of his pastorate there, on 16

May 1940. "Rev. Mr. Philbrook knew nothing of the affair and was taken completely by surprise."[180]

In July 1940, Gene Philbrook "went to lead 160 boys at Royal Ambassador Baptist camp in Ocean Park, Maine."[181] More details:

When the Royal Ambassador Camp for boys was started at Ocean Park, Maine, he was chosen to have charge of the nature department. He served sixteen years as counsellor, teacher, photographer and lecturer.[182]

(above:) **Rev. Philbrook's handbook for nature study at Ocean Park, Maine.**
(courtesy of Howard Randall)

(below:) **"[Y]oung boys and perhaps a camp counselor at a Baptist camp in Ocean Park, Maine"; a glass slide photo, taken and hand-colored by Rev. Eugene Philbrook.**
(courtesy of Howard Randall)

1942

In November 1942 the U.S. State Department confirmed that Germany was actively pursuing the extermination of all European Jews.[183] And on November 10th, German troops took control of France's Vichy region, effectively occupying all of France.[184] Expressing moral outrage, Rev. Philbrook and 946 other North American clergy signed a petition urging military action against the fascists, instead of failed diplomacy and appeasement. The petition and the names of its signers were printed in a Canadian newspaper on Nov. 13th., under this headline:[185]

> # 947 Ministers Call For Break With All Fascist Nations
>
> (Ottawa Citizen *(Ottawa, Ontario, Canada), Fri., 13 Nov. 1942, p. 11; newspapers.com)*

1945

As the 25th anniversary of Gene Philbrook's Randolph pastorate arrived, the congregation duly celebrated it on 6 June 1945 at the church.[186]

1951

Among Gene Philbrook's writings were daily devotionals published in *The Secret Place*,[187] both before and after retirement. Two of special note were "The Thrill of My Life" (Friday, 12 January 1951), and "Our Trustworthy Guide" (Wednesday, 10 March 1954).

Rev. Philbrook was honored by First Baptist Church for his fifty years in the gospel ministry, with a special afternoon service held at the church on 21 Oct. 1951. The details appeared the next day in a local newspaper, which stated the "church was filled to capacity."[188] Another article reported, "The occasion was attended by hundreds of his parishoners and friends. A fine testimonial was given."[189]

```
* * * * * * * * *
  PROGRAM OF SERVICE HONORING
  REV. EUGENE S. PHILBROOK, S.T.D.
         ON THE OCCASION OF
  HIS FIFTIETH YEAR IN THE MINISTRY
       * * * * * * * * *
Prelude          "Thine Own" - Lange - Reuben Willis
Processional     Hymn No. 56
Opening Greeting Albin W. Johnson, Moderator
Welcome          Rev. E. Stacy Harrison
Invocation       Rev. Eugene Dolloff, S.T.D.
Anthem           "March On" - Holton - Choir
Scripture        Rev. Frank T. Valdina
Greetings from Fellow Clergy
                 Rev. Isaac Higginbotham, D.D.
                 Rev. E. Carl Herrick, D.D.
                 Rev. Albert W. Lorimer
Presentation     Orrin B. White
Poem             Mrs. Marguerite Monahan
Recognition of visiting clergy and others
Negro Spiritual  "Steal Away to Jesus" - Choir
Reading of letters and greetings
Presentation     Albin W. Johnson
Benediction      Rev. Albert W. Lorimer

       * * * * * * * * *
       RECEPTION IN CHURCH PARLOR
       * * * * * * * * *
       COLLATION IN VESTRY
       * * * * * * * * *
"OUR PASTOR" - By Mrs. Edwin Stetson
```

(courtesy of Howard Randall)

Mrs. Edwin Stetson read a poem she wrote, *Our Pastor: A Tribute to Dr. Eugene S. Philbrook* (reproduced in Appendix D).

1952

After serving for 32 years as pastor at the First Baptist Church in Randolph, Mass.,[190] Rev. Philbrook retired in June 1952. He was also "elected pastor emeritus."[191] He moved from the parsonage (next door to us), to his son's (Dr. Frank Philbrook's) home at 22 Roel Street,[192] about a quarter mile down the street, and where I often visited with him.

A typical bulletin cover (undated) during Rev. Philbrook's ministry years at First Baptist Church, Randolph, Mass.
(courtesy of Howard Randall)

1953

The *Brockton Enterprise* of 5 Aug. 1953 named Rev. Philbrook an "Outstanding Person," describing him as

cultured, educated . . . . a lover of nature . . . an ardent student of the stars and flowers, and with a knowledge far beyond the ordinary person. . . . The spiritual outlook of this man is the highest . . . [He is an] unusual leader . . .[193]

An oil painting by Gene Philbrook — one of his many hobbies and interests. *(courtesy of Howard Randall)*

Eugene Philbrook designed his own bookplate. The various design elements represent significant parts of his life story and reflect his many interests.

(courtesy of Howard Randall)

1956

At the age of eighty-three years, Rev. Dr. Eugene S. Philbrook passed from this life to his eternal home, on October 24th, 1956. No other pastor could have hoped to accomplished more than he did during his lifetime on this earth. And so, my beloved former pastor, mentor and friend was no longer available as my close and dear counselor.

[Boston Globe (Boston, Mass.), Fri., 26 Oct. 1956, p. 43; newspapers.com]

Printed in the church bulletin for Rev. Philbrook's funeral service was a poem by a church member, Mrs. Edwin Stetson: *Our Pastor: A Tribute to Dr. Eugene S. Philbrook* (reproduced in Appendix D).

1969

Many people in Randolph and others now scattered continue to remember Dr. Philbrook. He was loved by not only his church members, but was also respected by those of other faiths in the town. In 1969, the First Baptist Church of Randolph celebrated the 150th anniversary of its founding. Included in the printed program was a fitting tribute to the legacy of Dr. Philbrook. It reads, in part:

Rev. Eugene S. Philbrook was a devoted Christian leader, dearly loved by all, a true friend, and a faithful servant of the living God he loved, admired and respected throughout the community, for he lived the Christian life he preached. He was an ardent scholar.... He loved all nature... an expert at photography.... interested in astronomy ... preaching... teaching... revival services .... He Walks With God.

1984

Gene Philbrook's widow, Bessie, died on 21 Mar. 1984 in Halifax, Mass., 27 ½ years after him. Her funeral was held on Sunday afternoon, Mar. 25th, at First Baptist Church, Randolph. She was buried beside Gene at Knollwood Memorial Park in Canton, Mass.[194]

2021

Today, almost seventy years after Gene Philbrook's passing, most of his descendants, surnamed Philbrook and Randall, live in the "South Shore" area of Massachusetts. Grandson Carl Philbrook still resides in Randolph. Five Randall grandchildren still reside in southeastern Massachusetts, and one lives in California.

~ ~ ~ ~ ~ ~ ~ ~ ~ ~ ~ ~ ~ ~ ~ ~ ~ ~ ~

In Pastor Eugene Philbrook, the world had been the benefactor of a truly great and *real PASTOR* ~ a *PREACHER* most extraordinary!

~ ~ ~ ~ ~ ~ ~ ~ ~ ~ ~ ~ ~ ~ ~ ~ ~ ~ ~

Eugene Philbrook's Children and Grandchildren

Son: **F. Randolf Philbrook**
(1908-1998)
m. Madeline D. Hartford
(1910-1968)
Grandchild: **Carl E. Philbrook**, (1952-)

(right:) **Madeline (Hartford) Philbrook, F. Randolf Philbrook.**
(circa 1947; courtesy of JoAnn Randall)

(below:) **JoAnn Randall, Isabel (Philbrook) Randall, Carl Philbrook, Virginia (Randall) Lee.**
(dated May 1998; courtesy of JoAnn Randall)

Daughter: **Isabel A. Philbrook** (1910-2002)
m. Donald H. Randall (1908-1987)
Grandchildren: **Virginia D. Randall**, (1940-)
Elizabeth J. Randall, (1941-)
Donald "Howard" Randall, Jr., (1942-)
Roger S. Randall, (1943-)
JoAnn N. Randall, (1945-)
Robert E. B. Randall, (1946-)

Pedigree Chart for Eugene Sumner Philbrook • Rev. • Dr. • Gene

EUGENE SUMNER PHILBROOK • REV. • DR. • GENE
b: 18 Feb 1871 in North Bradford, Maine
m: 7 Feb 1907 in Belfast, Maine
d: 24 Oct 1956 in Randolph, Mass.

- **FRANCIS J PHILBROOK**
  b: Feb 1837 in Hermon, Maine
  m: 30 Dec 1865 in Weymouth, Mass.
  d: 9 May 1930 in Rockland, Mass.
  - **FRANCIS D. PHILBROOK**
    b: Abt 1815 in Maine
    m: Abt 1838 in Maine
    d: Oct 1852 in California
    - **JEPSON WILLIAM PHILBROOK**
      b: 6 Feb 1789 in ME
      m: 10 Apr 1814 in ME
    - **MARIA A DREW**
      b: 4 Jun 1794 in ME
      d: 7 Jan 1879 in ME
  - **REBECCA R CUMMINGS**
    b: 20 Oct 1813 in Freedom, Maine
    d: 25 Aug 1904 in Lewiston, Maine
    - **JASON CUMMINGS**
      b: 23 Oct 1787 in ME
      m: 19 Dec 1810
      d: 2 Mar 1861 in ME
    - **ANNA REED MILLER**
      b: 9 Jul 1786 in ME
      d: 18 May 1872

- **PAULINE MOULTON**
  b: Aug 1843 in Sedgwick, Maine
  d: 2 Feb 1923 in Rockland, Mass.
  - **RUFUS H. MOULTON**
    b: 14 Feb 1811 in Bucksport, Maine
    m:
    d: 22 Apr 1877 in Cambridge, Mass.
    - **RUFUS MOULTON**
      b: 15 Oct 1775 in ME
      m: 18 Jun 1806 in ME
      d: 23 Sep 1833 in ME
    - **REBEKAH PAGE**
      b: 9 Feb 1778 in ME
  - **SUSAN HOWARD**
    b: 28 May 1812 in Deer Isle, Maine
    d: 8 Jun 1880 in Lawrence, Mass.
    - **JOHN HOWARD**
      b: 20 Jun 1784 in ME
      m: Abt 1802
      d: 1832 in ME
    - **SUSAN FOSTER • SUKEY**
      b: 1787 in ME
      d: 22 Mar 1847 in ME

Known Lecture and Sermon Topics of Rev. Dr. Eugene S. Philbrook
(as reported by newspapers)

1901 Jan. 06	And They Came to Kadish-Barnea[195]
1901 Sep. 15 am	Christian Strength, or, Christ our Pattern and Power[196]
1901 Sep. 15 pm	The Architecture of Character[197]
1903 Apr. 09 pm	Christ our Passover[198]
1903 Apr. 12 am	The Resurrection, a Challenge to Unbelief[199]
1903 Apr. 12 pm	Intimations and Confirmations of Immortality[200]
1904 May 01 am	Paul's Word to a Young Man[201]
1904 Oct. 21 pm	The Land of Evangeline[202]
1905 May 21 pm	Looking for the [illegible][203]
1905 Nov. 26 am	Our Great Reasons for Thanksgiving[204]
1905 Nov. 26 pm	The Turning of the Soul[205]
1906 Jun. 17 pm	Africa[206]
1906 Sep 13 pm	Prayer for the Holy Spirit[207]
1906 Sep 16 am	The Testimony of Jesus as the Spirit of Prophesy[208]
1907 May 09 pm	The Land of Evangeline[209]
1908 Dec 22	The Place & Power of Personal Work[210]
1909 Jan 10	The Sunday Stone[211]
1909 Jan 24 am	Seeing Rome[212]
1909 Jan 24 pm	Life and Death in Haran[213]
1909 Jan 31 am	Apprehended and Apprehending[214]
1909 Jan 31 pm	The Triumph of Wireless Telegraphy[215]
1909 Feb 28 am	"The Kings Business" As I Saw It Transacted in Boston[216]
1909 Feb 28 pm	The Greatest Power in the World[217]
1909 Mar 14-Apr	Powerful Incentives to Godliness [sermon series]: The Holiness of God The Eye of God Influence The Coming of Christ

	The Judgment
	Heaven[218]
1909 Apr 25 am	*Elijah's Mantle and Ours*[219]
1909 July 18 am	*Heaven – Its Inhabitants: Who Are They?*[220]
1909 Nov 14	*Our Gibraltar*[221]
1909 Nov 21 pm	*BURMAH*[222]
1910 Jan 02 am	*Christ Préeminent*[223]
1912 Mar. 7 pm	*South America*[224]
1912 Mar. 11	*The Spiritual Life of the Minister*[225]
1914 Feb. 3 pm	*Majestic Katahdin, Monarch of Maine*[226]
1914 "Winter"	*Mt. Katahdin*[227]
1914 May 03	*The Question of the Ages*[228]
1921 Jan. 17 pm	*The Pine Tree State.*[229]
1922 Jan. 18 pm	*The Sportsman's Paradise.*[230]
1923 Mar. 07 pm	*The Glories of the White Mountains.*[231]
1923 Dec. 17 pm	*A Sportsman's Paradise.*[232]
1926 July 28 pm	*The Aristocracy of Character.*[233]
1927 Jan. 08 pm	*[an illustrated lecture]*[234]
1928 Mar. 25 am	*The Blue Hills.*[235]
1928 Mar. 25 am	*The Honest Woodman.*[236]
1928 Mar. 25 pm	*Plus Ultra.*[237]
1929 May 15 pm	*The Land of Evangeline.*[238]
1929 Dec. 08 am	*Christ Préeminent.*[239]
1930 Jan. 06 pm	*Out-of-Doors With a Camera in New England.*[240]
1930 Oct. 20 pm	*God's Out-Of-Doors.*[241]
1931 Jun. 15 pm	*The Great Out[-Of-]Doors.*[242]
1932 Jan. 25 pm	*A Sportsman's Paradise.*[243]
1933 Nov. 9 pm	*Views of the Pine Tree State.*[244]
1934 Feb. 12 pm	*Sweet Land of Liberty.*[245]
1935 Jan. 27 pm	*Life of Christ.*[246]
1935 Mar. 31 pm	*Life of Christ.*[247]
1936 Jan. 15 pm	*The Land of Evangeline.*[248]
1937 Apr. 8 pm	*[Birds]*[249]
1937 Oct. 8 pm	*God's Out-of-Doors.*[250]
1938 Mar. 22 pm	*[a stereopticon lecture].*[251]
1940 May 18 am	*God or Gold.*[252]

1940 May 18 pm	*Lessons from Niagara.*[253]
1940 May 22 pm	*The Marvels of Vegetable Growth.*[254]
1941 Feb. 20 pm	*Sportsman's Paradise.*[255]
1941 Jun. 09 pm	*National Anthem.*[256]
1942 Feb. 10 pm	*Arcadia*[257] [i.e. Acadia]
1942 Nov. 15 pm	*Readings of Great Gospel Prayer Hymns*[258]
1942 Nov. 22 pm	*The Lilies of the Field; The Hand of God in Nature*[259]
1943 May 11 pm	*God's Great Outdoors*[260]
1943 Dec. 12 am	*Our Bible Goes to War*[261]
1943 Dec. 12 pm	*Quo Vadis?*[262]
1944 May 28 am	*My Country's Call*[263]
1944 Nov. 15 pm	*History of the Christian Attitude Toward Other Races*[264]
1947 Feb. 26 pm	*Flowers, Fruits and Their Growth*[265]

==

Open Air Preaching at the Seaside
(Harper's Bazaar, *1885; ebay.com*)

ENDNOTES

[1] The complete birth date "February 19, 1871" was found in only one source: the handwritten notes of Ms. JoAnn Randall of Plymouth, Massachusetts, a granddaughter of Eugene S. Philbrook. Ms. Randall graciously lent family archives and photos to the authors in June 2020.

[2] Massachusetts Marriages, 1695-1910 [database, familysearch.org]. The marriage was on 31 December 1865 at Weymouth, Mass.

[3] "Bradford, Maine", *Wikipedia, the free encyclopedia*, online: <https://en.wikipedia.org/wiki/Bradford,_Maine>. Population was 1,487 in 1870, and 1,290 in 2010.

[4] Eugene S. Philbrook and Rebea [sic] R. Philbrook in Frank McGregory household, 1880 U.S. Census, Atkinson, Piscataquis County, Me., p. 10. Grandma, age 67, "Keeps house"; McGregory, age 38 and married (but no wife present), "Runs saw mill."

[5] Pauline Philbrick [sic] in Calvin S. Page household, 1880 U.S. Census, Lawrence, Essex County, Mass., p. 26. Pauline's and Abbe's widowed mother, Susan (Howard) Moulton, age 67, was also in that household with "consumption" [tuberculosis]. That census, enumerated June 5th, listed those living in the household on June 1st; Grandma Moulton died June 8th—[*Boston Press and Post*, (Boston, Mass.), Mon., 14 Jun. 1880, p. 1; *New England Farmer*, (Boston, Mass.), Sat., 19 Jun. 1880, p. 3].

[6] Living at Horace W. Chase's hotel on Harlow Street. Frank J. Philbrook in Horace W. Chase "household," 1880 U.S. Census, Bangor, Penobscot County, Me., p. 35.

[7] "1898 [class notes]," Colby College, Colby Alumnus, v. 5, no. 1 (Nov. 1915), p. 19 [image, digitalcommons.colby.edu/alumnus/31].

[8] Frank J. Philbrook in Horace W. Chase "household," 1880 U.S. Census, Bangor, Penobscot County, Me., p. 35.

[9] United States Patent 191,813 dated 12 June 1877.

[10] United States Patent 1,246,458 dated 16 June 1916.

[11] "1898 [class notes]," op cit.

[12] Now known as Columbia Street Baptist Church.

[13] "1898 [class notes]," op. cit.

[14] *Republican Journal* (Belfast, Me.), 14 Jul. 1921, p. 5, citing: *Bangor Commercial* (Bangor, Me., 07 July 1921.

[15] "1898 [class notes]," op cit.

[16] Delta Upsilon Fraternity, Lynne John Bevan, and William Henry Dannat Pell. *Catalogue of Delta Upsilon, 1917*. (New York: Delta Upsilon Fraternity, Inc., ©1917), p. 350. [books.google.com/books?id=4_tMAAAAMAAJ].

[17] "Coburn Classical Institute Graduates." *Republican Journal* (Belfast, Me.), 21 Feb. 1907, p. 2.

[18] *Oxford Democrat* (Paris, Me.), 01 Jun. 1897, p. 3.
[19] Nathan E. Wood "household" [i.e., president], 1900 U.S. Census, Newton, Middlesex Co., Mass., p. 2.
[20] Francis J. Philbrook household, 1900 U.S. Census, Brewer, Penobscot Co., Me., p. 22.
[21] *Boston Herald* (Boston, Mass.), Sat., 17 March 1900, p. 10.
[22] "South Willington" [local news column], *Press* (Stafford Springs, Conn.), Thur., 01 Mar. 1900, p. 4.
[23] *Press* (Stafford Springs, Conn.), Thur., 29 Mar. 1900, p. 4.
[24] "1898 [class notes]," op. cit.
[25] Philbrook family papers.
[26] "Willington" [local news column], *Press*, (Stafford Springs, Conn.), Thur., 28 June 1900, p. 4.
[27] *Republican Journal* (Belfast, Me.), Thur., 01 Aug. 1901, p. 5.
[28] *Sanford Tribune* (Sanford, Maine), Fri., 09 Nov. 1906, p. 1.
[29] Philbrook, F. Randall. "Recollections of Recent Pastorates" [unpublished typescript manuscript in Philbrook family papers].
[30] "1898 [class notes]," op. cit.; "New Pastor For Randolph Church," *Boston Herald* (Boston, Mass.), Sun., 16 May 1920, p. 31.
[31] STM stands for *Sacrae Theologiae Magister* in Latin.
[32] Philbrook family papers.
[33] "Willington" [local news column], *Press* (Stafford Springs, Conn.), Thur., 03 Jan. 1901, p. 4.
[34] "Willington" [local news column], *Press* (Stafford Springs, Conn.), Thur., 10 Jan. 1901, p. 4.
[35] *Republican Journal* (Belfast, Me.), Thur., 01 Aug. 1901, p. 5.
[36] *Republican Journal* (Belfast, Me.), Thur., 09 Jan. 1902, p. 6. The *Colby Alumnus* in 1915 reported a wrong ordination date: August 3, 1901—["1898 [class notes]," op. cit.].
[37] *Republican Journal* (Belfast, Me.), Thur., 12 Sep. 1901, p. 5.
[38] ibid.
[39] *Republican Journal* (Belfast, Me.), Thur., 17 Oct. 1901, p. 1.
[40] *Republican Journal* (Belfast, Me.), Thur., 09 Jan. 1902, p. 6.
[41] "Maine," *The Watchman: A Baptist Journal* (Boston, Mass.), 12 May 1904 (v. 86, no. 19), p. 24. Web: <https://books.google.com/books?id=hhZQAAAAYAAJ>. On Sun., 1 May 1904 were "anniversary exercises of . . . the Brotherhood of Andrew and Philip. . . . The morning audience completely filled the church; and in the evening many persons were obliged to go away, there not being even standing room."
[42] "Maine Letter," *The Watchman: A Baptist Journal* (Boston, Mass.), 18 Aug. 1904 (v. 86, no. 33), p. 28. Web: <https://books.google.com/books?id=hhZQAAAAYAAJ>.

[43] *Republican Journal* (Belfast, Me.), Thur., 20 Oct. 1904, p. [1]. Web: <https://core.ac.uk/download/pdf/230098385.pdf>.
[44] *Republican Journal* (Belfast, Me.), Thur., 03 Nov. 1904, p. 4.
[45] "Mr. Philbrook in Connecticut," *Republican Journal* (Belfast, Me.), Thur., 26 Jan. 1905, p. 1. Reprinted from *Norwich Bulletin* (Norwich, Conn.), Thur., 19 Jan. 1905.
[46] "Willington" [local news column], *Press* (Stafford Springs, Conn.), Wed., 25 Jan. 1905, p. 4.
[47] "Morrill" [local news column], *Republican Journal* (Belfast, Me.), Thur., 09 Feb. 1905, p. 8.
[48] "Republicans Again Carry the State of Maine," *Pullman Herald* (Pullman, Wash.), Sat., 15 Sep. 1906, p. 2.
[49] *Republican Journal* (Belfast, Me.), Thur., 11 May 1905, p. 5.
[50] *Republican Journal* (Belfast, Me.), Thur., 18 May 1905, p. 1.
[51] "Saturday High Line Day," *Boston Herald* (Boston, Mass.), Tue., 17 Oct. 1905, p. 14.
[52] ibid.
[53] *Republican Journal* (Belfast, Me.), Thur., 10 Jan. 1907, p. 2.
[54] "Reception for Eugene S. Philbrook," *Republican Journal* (Belfast, Me.), 29 Nov.1906, p. 1. The page image is poor and partly illegible.
[55] "Pastor Wedded. Rev. and Mrs. Philbrook Arrive Monday. Reception Wednesday."*Sanford Tribune* (Sanford, Me.), Fri., 15 Feb. 1907, p. 1.
[56] *Republican Journal* (Belfast, Me.), Thur., 21 Feb. 1907, p. 2.
[57] The Town of Sanford, on the Mousam River, was incorporated just four years earlier (1768). One well-known Sandfordite was Everett Joseph "Vik" Firth (1930-2015), a percussionist in the Boston Symphony; although born in Massachusetts, "Vic" grew up in Sanford.
[58] Preble Lodge No. 143, Ancient Free & Accepted Masons, Sanford, Me.; see <https://tms.edu/msj/msj5-2-2/>.
[59] "Rev. E.S. Philbrook Services Saturday," *Boston Traveler* (Boston, Mass.), Thur., 25 Oct. 1956, p. D-17.
[60] "Man Of The Week," [unidentified newspaper, between 1952 and 1956]. From a clipping, courtesy of Howard Randall.
[61] *Sanford Tribune* (Sanford, Me.), Fri., 21 Jun. 1907, p. 5; *Springvale Advocate* (Springvale, Me.), Fri., 28 Jun. 1907, p. 2.
[62] *Springvale Advocate* (Springvale, Me.), Fri., 28 Jun. 1907, p. 2.
[63] *Sanford Tribune* (Sanford, Me.), Wed., 03 Jul. 1907, p. 4.
[64] *Sanford Tribune* (Sanford, Me.), Fri., 16 Jun. 1911, p. 5.
[65] *Sanford Tribune* (Sanford, Me.), Fri., 04 Jun. 1909, p. 8.
[66] "Man Of The Week," op cit.
[67] "Rev. E.S. Philbrook Services Saturday," *Boston Traveler* (Boston, Mass.), Thur., 25 Oct., 1956, p. D-17.

[68] "Rev., Mrs. Philbrook Are Feted At Baptist Church," *Patriot Ledger* (Quincy, Mass.), Thur., 07 June 1945, p. 4.
[69] "Man Of The Week," op. cit.
[70] Maine Vital Records, 1670-1921 [database, familysearch.org].
[71] *Republican Journal* (Belfast, Me.), 18 Feb. 1909, p. 1.
[72] *Sanford Tribune* (Sanford, Me.), Fri., 15 Jan. 1909, p. 4.
[73] *Sanford Tribune* (Sanford, Me.), Fri., 26 Nov. 1909, p. 1, 4. "Our Gibraltar" was preached on Sun., 21 Nov. 1909.
[74] *Sanford Tribune* (Sanford, Me.), Fri., 26 Nov. 1909, p. 1.
[75] Now also called Myanmar.
[76] Barbour, Thomas. "Notes on Burma." *The National Geographic Magazine*, 20:10 (Oct. 1909), p. 841-866. With 34 illustrations.
[77] *Republican Journal* (Belfast, Me.), Thur., 10 Jan. 1907, p. 2.
[78] Philbrook, Eugene S. to F. B. Averill, editor, [Letter], 21 Apr. 1909. In: *Sanford Tribune* (Sanford, Me.), Fri., 23 Apr. 1909, p. 4.
[79] *Republican Journal* (Belfast, Me.), Thur., 05 Aug. 1909, p. 1.
[80] *Republican Journal* (Belfast, Me.), Thur., 14 Oct. 1909, p. 1.
[81] *Republican Journal* (Belfast, Me.), Thur., 28 Oct. 1909, p. 1
[82] The then-current York County Sheriff, Charles O. Emery.
[83] "The Prohibition Convention." *Springvale Advocate* (Springvale, Me.), Fri., 05 Aug. 1910, p. 2.
[84] "Will Be Short: September Term of the Supreme Court Opened Tuesday." *Sanford Tribune* (Sanford, Me.), Fri., 23 Sep. 1910, p. 1. This body is now known as York County Superior Court.
[85] *Sanford Tribune* (Sanford, Me.), Fri., 02 Dec. 1910, p. 6; *Republican Journal* (Belfast, Me.), Thur., 08 Dec. 1910, p. 1.
[86] *Springvale Advocate* (Springvale, Me.), Fri., 26 May 1911, p. 3.
[87] *Springvale Advocate* (Springvale, Me.), Fri., 02 Jun. 1911, p. 3.
[88] Mills, Paul, "The 9-11 election of 1911." *Sun Journal* (Lewiston, Me.), 11 Sep. 2011. Online: <https://www.sunjournal.com/2011/09/11/9-11-election-1911/>.
[89] "List is Still Increasing," *Sanford Tribune* (Sanford, Me.), Fri., 28 Jul. 1911, p. 4; "The Saloon," *Sanford Tribune* (Sanford, Me.), Fri., 04 Aug. 1911, p. 4; "The Saloon," *Sanford Tribune* (Sanford, Me.), Fri., 18 Aug. 1911, p. 4.
[90] Mills, op cit.
[91] Sanford's population in 1883 "was only 2,700. By 1910 it had grown to 9,000, thanks mostly to mohair plush. 3,000 of Sanford's citizens by then were employed in the Goodall Mills. . . . The growth of industry in Sanford brought workers from many countries and gave our city a rich blend of nationalities" --[City of Sanford, Maine, "History of Sanford & Springvale," *Sanford Maine*. Online: <https://www.sanfordmaine.org/townhistory>].

[92] In 2011 and 2013, 64% of adults in York County imbibed at least one alcoholic drink a month, 5% more than the average for all of Maine—[*Substance Abuse Trends in Maine: Epidemiological Profile 2015: York*. (South Portland, Me.: Hornby Zeller Associates, Oct. 2015), p. 6. Online: <https://www.maine.gov/dhhs/samhs/osa/data/cesn/Files/York_EPI_2015_FINAL.pdf>].

[93] Repealed on 5 Dec. 1933.

[94] "In 1954 the Goodall Mills closed and the shoe factories in both Sanford and Springvale were about to disappear"—[City of Sanford, Maine, "History of Sanford . . . ," op. cit.]

[95] Brooks, Rebecca Beatrice. "What Was the Lowell System Used in the Lowell Mills?" *History of Massachusetts Blog*. Online: <https://historyofmassachusetts.org/lowell-mills-factory-system/>.

[96] *Republican Journal* (Belfast, Me.), Thur., 03 Aug. 1911, p. 1.

[97] "Joint Installation: Knights of Pythias and Sisters Will Unite in Ceremonies Tomorrow Night," *Sanford Tribune* (Sanford, Me.), Fri., 19 Jan. 1912, p. 8.

[98] *Springvale Advocate* (Springvale, Me.), Fri., 19 Jul. 1912, p. 2.

[99] *Sanford Tribune* (Sanford, Me.), Fri., 23 May 1913, p. 5.

[100] *Republican Journal* (Belfast, Me.), Thur., 24 Jul. 1913, p. 5.

[101] "3 Reasons Why People Should Go To Church," *Springvale Advocate* (Springvale, Me.), Fri., 26 Dec. 1913, p. 4; "Everybody At Church Next Sunday, January 4th, '14," *Springvale Advocate* (Springvale, Me.), Fri., 02 Jan. 1914, p. 4; "Everybody At Church Next Sunday, January 11, '14," *Springvale Advocate* (Springvale, Me.), Fri., 09 Jan. 1914, p. 4.

[102] *Sanford Tribune* (Sanford, Me.), Fri., 09 Jan. 1914, p. 4.

[103] *Springvale Advocate* (Springvale, Me.), Fri., 13 Feb. 1914, p. 4.

[104] *Springvale Advocate* (Springvale, Me.), Fri., 27 Feb. 1914, p. 4.

[105] *Sanford Tribune* (Sanford, Me.), Fri., 08 May 1914, p. 1.

[106] Ibid.

[107] "Nineteen Seniors Receive Diplomas of S.H.S.," *Sanford Tribune* (Sanford, Me.), Fri., 19 Jun. 1914, p. 1.

[108] "Library Ass'n Appointments," *Sanford Tribune* (Sanford, Me.), Fri., 19 Jun. 1914, p. 1.

[109] *Springvale Advocate* (Springvale, Me.), Fri., 31 Jul. 1914, p. 4.

[110] *Springvale Advocate* (Springvale, Me), Fri., 30 Oct. 1914, p. 4.

[111] *Springvale Advocate* (Springvale, Me.), Fri., 14 May 1915, p. 8.

[112] *Springvale Advocate* (Springvale, Me.), Fri., 30 Jul. 1915, p. 4.

[113] *Republican Journal* (Belfast, Me.), Thur., Aug. 1915, p. 1.

[114] *Sanford Tribune* (Sanford, Me.), Fri., 06 Aug. 1915, p. 5.

[115] *Sanford Tribune* (Sanford, Me.), Fri., 03 Sep. 1915, p. 5.

[116] *Springvale Advocate* (Springvale, Me.), Fri., 05 Nov. 1915, p. 4.

[117] "50 Years Ago," *Sanford Tribune* (Sanford, Me.), Thur., 10 February 1966, p. 20
[118] "1898 [class notes]," op. cit.
[119] ibid., p. 20.
[120] "Sanford" [local news column], *Springvale Advocate* (Springvale, Me.), Fri., 27 Aug. 1920, p. 4.
[121] *Sanford Tribune* (Sanford, Me.), Fri., 29 Jul. 1921, p. 5.
[122] *Sanford Tribune and Advocate* (Sanford, Me.), Thur., 07 Aug., 1930, p. 4.
[123] *Sanford Tribune and Advocate* (Sanford, Me.), Thur., 27 Aug. 1931, p. 4.
[124] *Sanford Tribune and Advocate* (Sanford, Me.), Thur., 01 Aug. 1935, p. 4.
[125] *Sanford Tribune and Advocate* (Sanford, Me.), Thur., 07 Jul. 1938, p. 1.
[126] *Sanford Tribune and Advocate* (Sanford, Me.), Thur., 08 Aug. 1940, p. 4.
[127] *Sanford Tribune and Advocate* (Sanford, Me.), Thur., 24 Aug. 1944, p. 3.
[128] "1898 [class notes]," op cit.
[129] Delta Upsilon Fraternity, Lynne John Bevan, and William Henry Dannat Pell, op. cit., p. 53, 350.
[130] *Springvale Advocate* (Springvale, Me.), Fri., 07 May 1920, p. 6.
[131] *Maine Farmer* (Augusta, Me.), Thur., 12 May 1853, p. 3.
[132] *Springvale Advocate* (Springvale, Me.), Fri., 07 May 1920, p. 6.
[133] *The Congregationalist*, 12 July 1923 (v. 108, no. 28), p. 57. [image, <https://books.google.com/books?id=IXQ0AQAAMAAJ>].
[134] *Republican Journal* (Belfast, Me.), Thur., 05 Jul. 1917, p. 1.
[135] *Republican Journal* (Belfast, Me.), Thur., 19 Jul. 1917, p. 1.
[136] "Man Of The Week," [unidentified newspaper, between 1952 and 1956]. From a clipping, courtesy of Howard Randall.
[137] Maine's state motto is *Dirigo,* which is translated "I lead."
[138] "Registration of September 1918," *Oxford Democrat* (Paris, Me.), Tue., 27 Aug. 1918, p. 2.
[139] "Registration of September 12, 1918," *Oxford Democrat* (Paris, Me.), Tue., 10 Sep. 1918, p. 3.
[140] Geva, Dorit, "Different and Unequal? Breadwinning, Dependency Deferments, and the Gendered Origins of the U.S. Selective Service System." *Armed Forces & Society*, v. 37 (Oct. 2011), p. 609 [image, researchgate.net]. DOI:10.1177/0095327X09358654.
[141] *Republican Journal* (Belfast, Me.), 10 Oct. 1918, p. 5.
[142] *Republican Journal* (Belfast, Me.), 06 Feb. 1919, p. 1.
[143] ibid.

144 "Reception for Eugene S. Philbrook," *Republican Journal* (Belfast, Me.), 29 Nov.1906, p. 1. The page image is poor and partly illegible.
145 *Legislative Record of the Seventy-Ninth Legislature of the State of Maine, 1919*. (Augusta [Me.]: Kennebec Journal Print, 1919), p. 591 [image, https://books.google.com/books?id=ATQIAQAAIAAJ].
146 "Man Of The Week," [unidentified newspaper, between 1952 and 1956]. From a clipping, courtesy of Howard Randall.
147 Randolph's population of almost 4,800 persons was rapidly growing. Its major industry was footwear, primarily boots.
148 Republican Journal (Belfast, Me.), 14 July 1921, p. 5; quoting *Bangor Commercial*, 07 July 1921.
149 "New Pastor For Randolph Church," *Boston Herald* (Boston, Mass.), Sun., 16 May 1920, p. 31.
150 Philbrook, F. Randolf. "Recollections of Recent Pastorates" [unpublished typescript manuscript, in Philbrook family papers].
151 Philbrook family papers.
152 Now recognized as equivalent to a DD (Doctor of Divinity) degree, the STD stood for *Sacrae Theologiae Doctor* in Latin. (English: Doctor of Sacred Theology).
153 Philbrook family papers.
154 This dissertation was held in the Thesis Collection at Hamilton-Goddard Library, Gordon-Conwell Theological Seminary (call number BT701.P34). It has recently been released to granddaughter JoAnn Randall for family preservation. That collection also contains two more of Dr. Philbrook's degree dissertations.
155 "First Baptist Church, Randolph, Mass.," *American Architect and Building News*, 14 May 1898 (v. 60, no. 1168), p. 55. (image, <books.google.com/books?id=xYlMAAAAYAAJ>.
156 "Rev. E.S. Philbrook Services Saturday," *Boston Traveler* (Boston, Mass.) Thur., 25 Oct., 1956, page D-17.
157 *Boston Herald* (Boston, Mass.), Fri., 10 Dec. 1920, p. 7.
158 "Minister Knocked From Bicycle And Hurt By Auto," *Boston Globe* (Boston, Mass.), Fri., 10 Dec. 1920, p. 15.
159 "Randolph Pastor Injured By Auto," *Boston Post* (Boston, Mass.), Fri., 10 Dec. 1920, p. 22.
160 *Republican Journal* (Belfast, Me.), Thur., 16 Dec. 1920, p. 5.
161 Then, only the King James Version.
162 See *Chapter 7: Reverend Harvey Lee Cossaboom*.
163 "Sermon Topics, Times and Places of Services," *Morning Call* (Patterson, N.J.), Sat., 24 Mar. 1928, p. 10. Presented at First Baptist Church, Patterson, N.J., Sunday evening, 25 Mar. 1928.
164 Randolf Philbrook's mother was very formal, always addressing him as "Randolf" and never "Randy."

[165] This ledger-like book originally had blank (but numbered) pages.
[166] The Bachelders worked as blacksmiths at the Mt. Waldo Granite Quarries in Frankfort. They were members of the Frankfort Congregational Church and were well known for their music and dance fiddling. Records indicate that Alva was working on his 99th violin when he died. Dr. Philbrook's great-grandson Andrew, living in Idaho, now has this valuable instrument.
[167] This $50 in 1922 dollars equates to almost $800 in 2020 dollars!
[168] This was during my high school and college years.
[169] "Man Of The Week," [unidentified newspaper, between 1952 and 1956]. From a clipping, courtesy of Howard Randall.
[170] ibid.
[171] *Massachusetts, Mason Membership Cards, 1733-1990* [database], Record for Philbrook, Eugene Sumner.; image: ancestry.com.
[172] "The Sportsman's Paradise," *Portsmouth Herald* (Portsmouth, N.H.), Wed., 18 Jan. 1922, p. 5.
[173] "Braintree" [local news column], *Boston Globe* (Boston, Mass.), Tue., 18 Dec. 1923, p. 12.
[174] "Mrs. Francis J. Philbrook" [obituary], *Bangor Daily News* (Bangor, Me.), Mon., 05 Feb. 1923, p. 5.
[175] "Public Installation For Randolph Freemasons," *Boston Globe* (Boston, Mass.), Sat. 15 Dec. 1928, p. 7; <https://tms.edu/msj/msj5-2-2/>.
[176] "Court Allows Mrs Pike's Will," *Boston Globe* (Boston, Mass.), Fri. 02 Mar. 1934, p. 3. Mrs. Pike left $30,000 to her sister, $100 each to 5 persons, $200 each to 10 persons, and $300 each to 9 persons.
[177] "Randolph" [local news column], *Boston Globe* (Boston, Mass.), Thurs., 31 May 1934, p. 18.
[178] "Baptist Church," [unidentified newspaper, 1937]. From a clipping, courtesy of Howard Randall.
[179] "Federated Women's Clubs Conference Held in Braintree," *Boston Globe* (Boston, Mass.), Wed., 18 Oct. 1939, p. 15.
[180] "Rev. E.S. Philbrook Honored By Friends and Parishoners," *Patriot Ledger* (Quincy, Mass.), Fri., 17 May 1940, p. 18.
[181] *Patriot Ledger* (Quincy, Mass.), Tue., 17 Dec. 1940, p. 10.
[182] "Man Of The Week," [unidentified newspaper, between 1952 and 1956]. From a clipping, courtesy of Howard Randall.
[183] United States Holocaust Memorial Museum. *Holocaust encyclopedia*. 2000. <http://bibpurl.oclc.org/web/9469>, "Franklin Delano Roosevelt."
[184] History.com editors. "Germans Take Vichy, France." *History*. Accessed 02 Sep. 2020. <https://www.history.com/this-day-in-history/germans-take-vichy-france>.
[185] "947 Ministers Call For Break With All Fascist Nations," *Ottawa Citizen* (Ottawa, Ontario, Canada), Fri. 13 Nov. 1942, p. 11.

186 "Rev., Mrs. Philbrook Are Feted At Baptist Church," *Patriot Ledger* (Quincy, Mass.), Thur., 07 June 1945, p. 4.
187 *The Secret Place* (Philadelphia, Pa.: Northern Baptist Convention, 1939-). A devotional calendar, published quarterly.
188 "Large Crowd Honors Pastor on 50 Years in Ministry," [unidentified newspaper, 21 Oct. 1951]. From a clipping, courtesy of Howard Randall.
189 "Man Of The Week," [unidentified newspaper, between 1952 and 1956]. From a clipping, courtesy of Howard Randall.
190 "Rev. E.S. Philbrook Services Saturday," *Boston Traveler* (Boston, Mass.) Thur., 25 Oct., 1956, page D-17.
191 "Man Of The Week," [unidentified newspaper, between 1952 and 1956]. From a clipping, courtesy of Howard Randall.
192 ibid.
193 "Rev. Eugene Philbrook An 'Outstanding' Person," *Brockton Enterprise* (Brockton, Mass.), 05 Aug. 1953, p. [??]. From a clipping, courtesy of Howard Randall.
194 "Philbrook" [death notice], *Boston Globe* (Boston, Mass.), Fri. 23 Mar. 1984, p. 44.
195 "Willington" [local news column], *Press* (Stafford Springs, Conn.), Thur., 10 Jan. 1901, p. 4.
196 *Republican Journal* (Belfast, Me.), Thur., 12 Sep. 1901, p. 5.
197 ibid.
198 *Republican Journal* (Belfast, Me.), Thur., 09 Apr. 1903, p. 1.
199 ibid.
200 ibid.
201 *The Watchman: A Baptist Journal* (Boston, Mass.), 12 May 1904 (v. 86, no. 19), p. 24.
202 *Republican Journal* (Belfast, Me.), Thur., 20 Oct. 1904, p. [1]. Web: <https://core.ac.uk/download/pdf/230098385.pdf>: ". . . an outcome of Rev. E.S. Philbrook's trip to Nova Scotia . . . illustrated by 50 original stereopticon views.
203 *Republican Journal* (Belfast, Me.), Thur., 18 May 1905, p. 1: "one of the last addresses [in the] Powerful Incentives to Godliness [series]."
204 *Republican Journal* (Belfast, Me.), Thur., 23 Nov. 1905, p. 1.
205 ibid.
206 *Republican Journal* (Belfast, Me.), Thur., 14 Jun. 1906, p. 1: ". . . a stereopticon lecture on Africa."
207 *Republican Journal* (Belfast, Me.), Thur., 13 Sep. 1906, p. 1.
208 ibid.
209 *Republican Journal* (Belfast, Me.), Thur. 16 May 1907, p. 1. Reprinted from *Sanford Tribune* (Sanford, Me.), Fri., 10 May 1907, p. 5: ". . . it was illustrated by stereopticon views. It proved both interesting

and instructive and was heartily enjoyed by all. There were a number from Springvale present."
[210] *Springvale Advocate* (Springvale, Me.), Fri., 01 Jan. 1909, p. 2. Sermon was delivered on 22 Dec. 1908.
[211] *Sanford Tribune* (Sanford, Me.), Fri., 15 Jan. 1909, p. 4. Text reprinted in newspaper.
[212] *Sanford Tribune* (Sanford, Me.), Fri., 22 Jan. 1909, p. 8.
[213] ibid.
[214] *Sanford Tribune* (Sanford, Me.), Fri., 29 Jan. 1909, p. 4.
[215] ibid.
[216] *Sanford Tribune* (Sanford, Me.), Fri., 26 Feb. 1909, p. 4.
[217] ibid.
[218] *Sanford Tribune* (Sanford, Me.), Fri., 12 Mar. 1909, p. 7.
[219] *Sanford Tribune* (Sanford, Me.), Fri., 23 Apr. 1909, p. 1.
[220] *Sanford Tribune* (Sanford, Me.), Fri., 16 Jul. 1909, p. 4.
[221] *Sanford Tribune* (Sanford, Me.), Fri., 26 Nov. 1909, p. 1, 4. Text reprinted in newspaper.
[222] *Sanford Tribune* (Sanford, Me.), Fri., 26 Nov. 1909, p. 1.
[223] *Sanford Tribune* (Sanford, Me.), Fri., 31 Dec. 1909, p. 8.
[224] *Republican Journal* (Belfast, Me.), Thur., 14 Mar. 1912, p. 8. Reprinted from *Sanford Tribune* (Sanford, Me.), Fri. 08 Mar. 1912, p. 5: "a very interesting illustrated lecture on South America, showing a large number of views of Equador and the Andes."
[225] *Sanford Tribune*, ibid.
[226] *Republican Journal* (Belfast, Me.), Thur., 29 Jan. 1914, p. 1. Presented at Baptist Church in Belfast. "The illustrations will include 75 colored plates." The next week, this paper reported the lecture "was largely attended and very enjoyable. The pictures from photographs made by Mr. Philbrook were beautiful, and the accompanying lecture, in which he told of his camping experiences, was very interesting"— [*Republican Journal* (Belfast, Me.), Thur., 05 Feb. 1914, p. 5].
[227] Islesboro (Me.), *Annual Report of the Selectmen, Treasurer and Superintendent of Schools for the Town of Islesboro for the Year Ending March 2, 1914*, (1914), p. 32. Maine Town Documents; 5023. [image, digitalcommons.library.umaine.edu/towndocs/5023]: "[T]his winter an illustrated lecture by Rev. Eugene Philbrook has been given under the auspices netting $22.54. The lecture was much enjoyed by all present and the public in general appreciate the opportunity given them of taking a trip to Mt. Katahdin, climbing the rocky sides and enjoying the wonderful scenery without moving from their chairs. Fireside travel certainly has its conveniences." Presented at Islesboro, Maine.
[228] *Sanford Tribune* (Sanford, Me.), Fri., 08 May 1914, p. 1.
[229] "Roxbury District" [local news column], *Boston Globe* (Boston, Mass., Sat. 15 Jan. 1921, p. 6. A "lecture and entertainment."

230 "The Sportsman's Paradise," *Portsmouth Herald* (Portsmouth, N.H.), Wed., 18 Jan. 1922, p. 5. "Stereopticon Lecture" presented at Middle Street Baptist Church, Portsmouth, N.H. "Original colored views of hunting, fishing, canoeing and mountain climbing in New Hampshire and Maine; vacation memories."
231 "Braintree" [local news column], *Boston Globe* (Boston, Mass.), Mon., 05 Mar. 1923, p. 7. An "illustrated lecture" presented at South Congregational Church, Braintree, Mass.
232 "Braintree" [local news column], *Boston Globe* (Boston, Mass.), Tue., 18 Dec. 1923, p. 12. "An illustrated lecture" presented to Men's Club of the South Congregational Church, Braintree, Mass.
233 "Nearly 300 Alden Kindred At Reunion: Rev Eugene S. Philbrook of Randolph Speaks on 'The Aristocracy of Character'," *Boston Globe* (Boston, Mass.), Thur., 29 July 1926, p. 1. An address given to 26th annual reunion of the Alden Kindred of America, at Unitarian Church, Duxbury, Mass. This article reprints the text of Dr. Philbrook's address.
234 "Officers of Old Colony North Pomona Installed," *Boston Globe* (Boston, Mass.), Mon. 10 Jan. 1927, p. 19. Illustrated lecture for Old Colony North Pomona Grange with Randolph Grange at Odd Fellows' Hall, Randolph, Mass. The topic was not specified.
235 "Sermon Topics, Times and Places of Services," *Morning Call* (Patterson, N.J.), Sat., 24 Mar. 1928, p. 10. Presented at First Baptist Church, Patterson, N.J. This was the main Sunday morning sermon.
236 ibid. This was a "Message to Juniors," or the "Junior Sermon," as part of the morning service at First Baptist Church, Patterson, N.J.
237 ibid. This was the evening sermon at First Baptist Church, Patterson, N.J.
238 "Hyde Park District" [local news column], *Boston Globe* (Boston, Mass.), Thur., 16 May 1929, p. 6. "[I]llustrated talk" presented to Home Extension Dept. of Congregational Church School, in Hyde Park, Mass.
239 "Hingham" [local news column], *Boston Globe* (Boston, Mass.), Thur., 05 Dec. 1929, p. 27. Sermon at Methodist Episcopal Church, Hingham, Mass.
240 "Malden" [local news column], *Boston Globe* (Boston, Mass.), Tue., 07 Jan. 1930, p. 24. An "illustrated lecture" presented at Linden Baptist Church, Malden, Mass.
241 *Fitchburg Sentinel* (Fitchburg, Mass.), Wed., 22 Oct. 1930, p. 13. Presented "for the benefit of Townsend Grange," Townsend, Mass.
242 "Scituate" [local news column], *Boston Globe*, Tue., 16 Jun. 1931, p. 10. An "illustrated lecture" presented to Scituate Grange, Patrons of Husbandry at G.A.R. [Grand Army of the Republic] Hall, Scituate, Mass.

²⁴³ "Chelsea" [local news column], *Boston Globe* (Boston, Mass.), Sat. 23 Jan. 1932, p. 11. An "illustrated lecture" at Horace Memorial Church, Chelsea, Mass.

²⁴⁴ "Dorchester" [local news column], *Boston Globe* (Boston, Mass.), Mon. 06 Nov. 1933, p. 8. A public "entertainment" at Christ Church on Dix St., Dorchester (Boston), Mass.

²⁴⁵ "Quincy" [local news column], *Boston Globe*, Wed. 07 Feb. 1934, p. 28; ibid., Mon., 12 Feb. 1934, p. 9. An illustrated lecture, presented to Abigail Phillips Quincy Chapter of the Daughters of the American Revolution (D.A.R.), in Glenwood Hall, Wollaston (Quincy), Mass.

²⁴⁶ "Weymouth" [local news column], *Boston Globe* (Boston, Mass.), Mon. 28 Jan. 1935, p. 5: "an illustrated lecture." Presented at Weymouth Baptist Church, Weymouth, Mass.

²⁴⁷ *Boston Globe* (Boston, Mass.), Mon. 01 Apr. 1935, p. 5. An illustrated lecture at Brighton Avenue Baptist Church, Boston, Mass. "In addition . . . a musical program by Miss Isabel Philbrook, . . . assisted by Mr and Mrs Omar Cossaboom and Miss Ilsie Hylen."

²⁴⁸ "Braintree" [local news column], *Boston Globe* (Boston, Mass.), Tue. 14 Jan. 1936, p. 12; ibid, Thur. 16 Jan. 1936, p. 15. An "illustrated lecture" presented at Braintree Baptist Church, Braintree, Mass.

²⁴⁹ *Boston Globe* (Boston, Mass.), Fri., 09 Apr. 1937, p. 30. An illustrated lecture, Wollaston Garden Club at Wollaston Library, for "Bird Day."

²⁵⁰ "Ex-Regents' Club to Open Season Friday," *Boston Globe* (Boston, Mass.), Tue., 05 Oct. 1937, p. 6. An "illustrated lecture" presented to Massachusetts Ex-Regents' Club, D.A.R. [Daughters of the American Revolution] at Hotel Touraine, Boston, Mass.

²⁵¹ "Tomorrow's Events in Greater Boston . . . Dorchester," *Boston Globe* (Boston, Mass.), Mon. 21 Mar. 1938, p. 6. Presented to Live Wire Class at First Baptist Church, Dorchester, Mass.

²⁵² *Patriot Ledger* (Quincy, Mass.), Fri., 17 May 1940, p. 11.

²⁵³ ibid.

²⁵⁴ "Grange Will Hear Lecture Tomorrow," *Patriot Ledger* (Quincy, Mass.), Tue., 21 May 1940, p. 7.

²⁵⁵ *Patriot Ledger* (Quincy, Mass.), Wed., 19 Feb. 1941, p. 3: ". . . depicting the wilds of Maine. The Reverend gentleman does his hunting with a camera." Presented at Rabboni Lodge, A.F.&A.M. Uphams Corners and visiting Lafayette Lodge of Roxbury.

²⁵⁶ "Juvenile Grange Plans To Attend Field Day At Rehoboth Saturday," *Patriot Ledger* (Quincy, Mass.), Tue., 10 Jun. 1941, p. 13: ". . . in beautiful colors and taken by Rev. Mr. Philbrook, showed . . . historical . . . scenes of . . . states, the homes of . . . presidents and . . . of Maine to show many beautiful scenes of nature." Presented to Randolph Juvenile Grange, at Grange Hall.

[257] "Illustrated Talk on Arcadia [sic] Given for Junior Library Assn.," *Patriot Ledger*, (Quincy, Mass.), Wed., 11 Feb. 1942, p. 10: ". . . scenes from the Maine coastline up to Nova Scotia." Presented to Junior Ladies' Library Association, at Jonathan Belcher Hall.
[258] "Intermediate CE to See Moving Pictures," *Patriot Ledger* (Quincy, Mass.), Sat., 14 Nov. 1942, p. 8: ". . . Lieut. Comdr. F. Randolf Philbrook, M.D., on the Hammond electric Solovox to accompany the readings . . . by his father, Rev. Dr. Eugene S. Philbrook."
[259] "Illustrated Sermon Planned By Pastor," *Patriot Ledger* (Quincy, Mass.), Sat., 21 Nov. 1942, p. 13: "Beautiful pictures made by the speaker . . . also several flower pictures from Palestine."
[260] "Lecture Is Given On Wild Flowers," *Patriot Ledger* (Quincy, Mass.), Wed., 12 May 1943, p. 12: "Disclosing the zeal of a true enthusiast, the speaker told of making long trips and waiting for hours at a time for the right light in which to photograph his specimens." Presented to Troop 8 of the Milton Girl Scouts, at Cunningham Gymnasium, Milton.
[261] "Bible Sunday Planned At Baptist Church," *Patriot Ledger* (Quincy, Mass.), Sat., 11 Dec. 1943, p. 8.
[262] ibid.
[263] "Special Program At Baptist Church To Mark Memorial Day," *Patriot Ledger* (Quincy, Mass.), Sat., 27 May 1944, p. 8.
[264] "Benevolent Ass'n To Hear Talk On 'Race Relations'," *Patriot Ledger* (Quincy, Mass.), Mon., 13 Nov. 1944, p. 7. Presented to Ladies' Benevolent Association of the First Congregational Church.
[265] "Neighbors' Night Held By Grange," *Patriot Ledger* (Quincy, Mass.), Sat., 01 Mar. 1947, p. 5: ". . . colorful pictures, many of them being of local gardens." Presented at Randolph Grange.

Clifford E. Jones

(courtesy of Clifford Jones)

Chapter 7

Reverend Doctor CLIFFORD EARL JONES

"Call to me and I will answer you and tell you great and unsearchable things you do not know."
— *Jeremiah 33:3 (New International Version)*

Snow and cranberries are normally not part of a *preacher's* biography, and had nothing to do with Clifford Jones' *early* life. They became a necessary part of his story when, later, the Lord abruptly and unexpectedly transplanted him from Mississippi to a "northern opportunity" in Massachusetts. Snow and cranberries were part of the culture shock to which he had to adjust.

Clifford Earl Jones, thirteenth of sixteen siblings, was born in Laurel, Mississippi

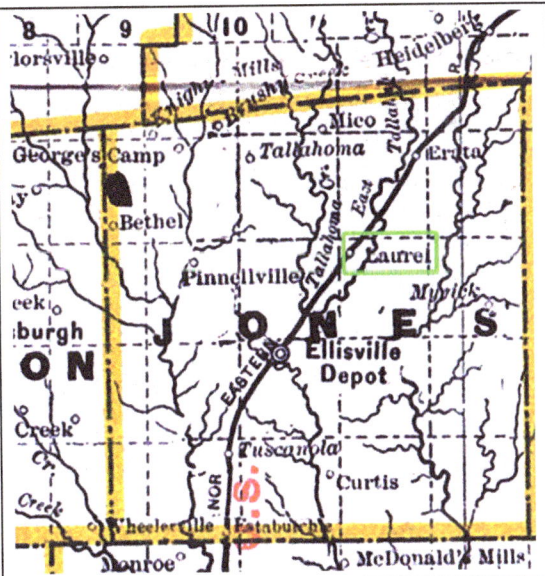

Cram, George Franklin. "Railroad and county map of Mississippi." Map. 1880. Norman B. Leventhal Map & Education Center, https://collections.leventhalmap.org/search/commonwealth:4m90f6675 (accessed 15 Dec. 2020). *(Map reproduction courtesy of Norman B. Leventhal Map and Education Center, Boston Public Library. Edited.)*

on February 14, 1946[1] to James 'Ira' Jones and Helen 'Geneva' (Ferguson) Jones.

Laurel was a farming community, about sixty percent African American[2] and deeply segregated; this was most evident in the schools, churches and

> **LIST OF EDUCABLE CHILDREN**
>
> County: Jones, Town: Laurel, Street or R.F.D. 4
> School Dist.: Mt. Olive, Race: Colored
>
> | Names of Parents or Guardians (Family Name) | Names of Children (Given Name) | Age | Month Born | Male | Fem. | School | Ward | Address |
> |---|---|---|---|---|---|---|---|---|
> | Jones, Ira | Wiley | 28 | 6 | m | | | | |
> | | Bernell | 29 | 9 | | f | | | |
> | | James | 30 | 11 Aug | m | | | | |
> | | Ray H. | 31 | 13 Sept | m | | | | |
> | | Ocei B. | 32 | 15 June | | f | | | |
> | | Willie L. | 33 | 18 | m | | | | |
> | | Otis | 34 | 20 | m | | | | |
>
> "Educable Children" in the Ira Jones family, 1945, in the "Colored" (segregated) Mt. Olive School District, R.F.D. 4 in Laurel, Mississippi. This was the year before Clifford Jones' birth. Another sibling, Earnest, appears on a 1943 list.
>
> ("Mississippi Enumeration of Educable Children, 1850-1892; 1908-1957," *database with images, FamilySearch* (https://familysearch.org/ark:/61903/3:1:939F-PJY1-L?cc=1856425&wc=M6NZ-NPL%3A167441501%2C167455301 : 18 September 2015), Jones > **1945** > image 511 of 552; Government Records, Jackson.")

other public places. In the early 1900s, Laurel produced lumber from its then-abundant yellow pine trees.[3] As the center of town grew, oaks were planted to line the village streets.[4] But most of Laurel was still rural, made up of family farms growing cotton, soybeans, corn, hogs and cattle.

(above:) **"Spring wagon and horse with farmers' staples of coal, oil and flour, Laurel, Mississippi." January 1939.**

(Lee, R., photographer. "Spring wagon and horse with farmers' staples of coal, oil and flour, Laurel, Mississippi." *January 1939. [photograph] Retrieved from the Library of Congress, https://www.loc.gov/item/2017738707/*).

==

(below:) **"Plowing up sweet potatoes near Laurel, Mississippi." November 1938.**

(Lee, R., photographer. "Plowing up sweet potatoes near Laurel, Mississippi." *November 1938. [Photograph] Retrieved from the Library of Congress, https://www.loc.gov/item/2017739091/.*

One forty-acre farm in the Laurel countryside was that of the Ira Jones family. Farming was not an easy existence, but provided a living for them. Ira Jones had fathered six boys and two girls with his first wife, Cammie (Gore), who died just five months after her youngest was born. Mr. Jones then married Helen 'Geneva' (Ferguson) on Dec.

Marriage license for Ira Jones and Geneva Ferguson, 1938.
("Mississippi, County Marriages, 1858-1979," database, FamilySearch (https://familysearch.org/ark:/61903/3:1:3Q9M-C91F-23R4-P?cc=3477669 : 25 July 2020), > image 1 of 1; citing multiple county clerks; Mississippi Department of Archives and History, Jackson. Cropped.)

16th, 1938[5] and had eight more children: seven boys and one girl. Clifford was the fifth child of Geneva's group of eight, and thirteenth of his father.

Clifford's father, Ira Jones, was a religious man and no doubt familiar with Psalm 127, an enlightening chapter about the family. Speaking of sons, this passage notes,

> 3 **Yes, sons are a gift from the Lord, the fruit of the womb is a reward.**

> 4 Sons born during one's youth are like arrows in a warrior's hand.
> 5 How blessed is the man who fills his quiver with them!
>
> --Psalm 127:3-5a (NET Bible)

As at most farms, there were always many things to be done, whether necessary or entertaining (sometimes mischievous). Above all, they were learning opportunities.

In his own words, Clifford recalls milking his first cow:

> I had seen it done but had not done it myself. I was pulling on the udder and pulled too

A boy milking the family cow, 1939.
Wolcott, Marion P., photographer. *"Pauline Clyburn, Manning, Clarendon County, South Carolina, rehabilitation client, has her children milking cows."* June 1939 [Photograph]. Retrieved from the Library of Congress, https://www.loc.gov/item/2017801137/. Cropped.

hard and the cow didn't like it so she kicked me and I tumbled over with the bucket of milk on top of me. I definitely learned a milking lesson the hard way.

Clifford Jones didn't become a champion cotton picker, either. He admits that he probably never picked a hundred pounds of cotton. While expending a minimal effort at his picking duty, Clifford's mind was engaged in daydreaming and

"Picking cotton"
([post card] "E. O. Kropp, Publ. Milwaukee, No. 1171" [circa 1905]. Retrieved from eBay)

thinking . . . . What would it be like not having to go into the cotton fields? Where could one be more productive than at the endless routine of picking cotton? What else was out there, beyond Laurel and Jones County?

Like many other encounters Clifford would "enjoy" in his lifetime, he met their challenges *head on*, thereby becoming a more rounded individual. Meeting challenges successfully is a part of this man's life.

Like so many southerners, church played an important role in the Jones family's lives. They were members of the Mt. Olive Baptist Church. All were *compelled* (as Clifford emphasizes!) to attend every Sunday and any scheduled events during the week. Clifford's father, Ira, was the superintendent of Sunday school and a deacon. Clifford's mother, Geneva, was secretary of the Sunday school and a member of the Missionary Society.

Clifford Jones recalls how, at the age of twelve, he "made a commitment to Jesus Christ" and was baptized in a pool behind the church. Even at this young age, he felt a strong desire to learn more about God. So, he decided to read through the Bible to learn all that his inquisitive mind could take in. He recalls,

> After I got through the first three chapters of Genesis, I lost interest because I couldn't pronounce the names and had no idea about what was being discussed.

With so many in the Jones household, there was always someone with whom to argue or to fight. Fighting was strictly *not* allowed, and any such activity engendered a good whipping. So, fighting had to be done far out in the fields, and with the hope that one of the others didn't divulge the incident. One can imagine how close the Jones family came to resembling the family of Joseph in the Bible. Though Clifford was not separated from his family, like Joseph he appears to have excelled and emerged as a leading personality, richly blessed by his God. Certainly, his vision of a life beyond the endless fields was a beginning.

Not the least in Clifford Jones' thinking was the tradition of separating people by their skin color. This concept was difficult for him to fully understand. He attended the segregated Roosevelt High School, eight miles away in the next town of Ellisville. But to get there, Clifford passed three all-white schools which, he mused, ought to be where he could get his education. He made the best of his situation and quickly became immersed in almost everything he could, academically and extra-curricular.

Clifford played just two football games. In the second game, his 140-pound frame was rammed mid-section by a 210-pound lineman. That left him counting stars for an hour. Quickly, he abandoned that sport and looked for something less hazardous to his health.

A much safer activity presented itself when Clifford learned that the school band needed a tuba player. Although he'd never played any instrument before, he suddenly volunteered as: "I'm that man," and learned to play tuba. Clifford would jump at any challenge, and now music took "center stage." He played tuba at Roosevelt High School for three years, and then at Alcorn State University for four more years. He was privileged to play in the university's *Sound of Dynamite* marching band and also in their concert band.

Alcorn State University, at Lorman, Mississippi, "is a public, historically black, land-grant university." Its many successful graduates include Medgar Evers, a well-known civil rights activist.[6]

At Alcorn, Clifford Jones was a busy member of the Baptist Student Union, YMCA, vesper services, and any other group he encountered. He became a member of the oldest Greek-lettered African American fraternity in the nation, Alpha Phi Alpha.

Oakland Chapel, Alcorn State University, Alcorn vicinity, MS
(Boucher, Jack, photographer. "Alcorn State University, Oakland Chapel." April 1972. [Photograph]. Library of Congress, Prints & Photographs Division, MISS,11-ALCO.V,2-4. Retrieved from Wikimedia.org.

The characteristics of an Alpha Phi Alpha Fraternity, Inc. man can be summed in sevens [sic] words: versatile, scholarly, ambitious, gentlemanly, tenacious, obedient and deferent.[7]

Alpha Phi Alpha Shield (original 1906 design, Morris Brown College monument)

[Clifflandis (https://commons.wikimedia.org/wiki/File:2019-05-15_Morris_Brown_College_Alpha_Phi_Alpha_Monument_2.jpg), „2019-05-15 Morris Brown College Alpha Phi Alpha Monument 2", cropped by Stephen Robbins, https://creativecommons.org/publicdomain/zero/1.0/legalcode]

This fraternity's "Missions Statement" reads:

> Alpha Phi Alpha Fraternity, Inc., develops leaders, promotes brotherhood and academic excellence, while providing service and advocacy for our communities.[8]

This fraternity give Clifford an opportunity to become heavily involved in community service and mentoring youth.

Clifford Jones graduated from Alcorn State University in 1969 with a Bachelor of Science degree in Agriculture Education. God was preparing him for an exceptional career!

College was over, including all that went with it. Now came the time for Clifford to find employment and see what was next in his life and dreams.

Clifford's studies had centered around agriculture – after growing up on a farm, what else? He accepted a position with the United

States Department of Agriculture, Soil Conservation Service (SCS),[9] and was assigned to work in Middleboro, Massachusetts, a part of the world he had never seen, visited, or knew much about. But this was Clifford's first professional job and, adventurous as he was, he proceeded to meet the challenge. Although time would confirm that the Lord was in this transition, Clifford was not fully assured of this at the very beginning.

It was mid-February of 1970. This was the month of the year in which New England typically experienced its bleakest, coldest, snowiest, windiest, mid-winter weather, including legendary monster snowstorms known as Nor'easters.[10]

Massachusetts, and particularly the town of Middleboro, anxiously awaited this southern lad, Clifford Jones. He would be welcomed to this part of God's world with open arms. But for young Jones, traveling to Massachusetts in February he would soon chalk up as "a mistake." He had not researched the mid-winter conditions, so knew not what to expect. Possibly his move to there was ordained by God, which time seems to have confirmed.

Clifford Jones said "good-by" to his Mama and left Laurel, Mississippi with his best winter clothes, unaware that winter in Laurel was not anything like the winter in Middleboro, Massachusetts. He thus began his long bus ride northward.

The bus actually did encounter a *Nor'easter* snowstorm near New Haven, Connecticut, and it could not proceed any further. The roads beyond

Bus in a snowstorm
(Photo by Josh Hild from Pexels.com; file: pexels-josh-hild-2422497)

were closed, due to severe weather conditions. But trains were still running. Somehow, Clifford managed to get to the New Haven train station and boarded a train for the 121-mile trip to Boston. Next, at Boston, Clifford Jones had to walk from the train station to the bus station. Walking on fresh, wet snow is difficult, at best, for a seasoned New Englander. But for Clifford, it was an even greater, if not impossible, undertaking. He just had never walked

New Haven Railroad trains at Boston's South Station, Sept. 1965
(Roger Puta, "New Haven Railroad trains at South Station, September 1965." Retrieved from wikimedia.org)

Icy Boston streets on the morning after a blizzard (Feb. 1978)
[City of Boston Archives from West Roxbury, United States (https://commons.wikimedia.org/wiki/File:Boston_Police_Headquarters_on_Berkeley_Street_(16188352487).jpg), „Boston Police Headquarters on Berkeley Street (16188352487)", cropped by Stephen Robbins, https://creativecommons.org/licenses/by-sa/2.0/legalcode]

in these conditions, nor did he know how to do it. He smiles as he recalls that, along the way, he must have been picked up from the ground by at least five or six people. A movie of this would have been a great thing to get to his Mama, and amusing for his fraternity to view! Oh yes, and the bus that would have taken him the last twenty miles to Middleboro was grounded!

Massachusetts residents, and those living in other places north of the Mason-Dixon Line, are familiar with snow and the bleak, blustery and cold conditions that come with it during the winter months. But the morning after a snowstorm usually reveals a blanket of pure white, covering all the unattractive landscape that was polluted by man's exploits. Isaiah 1:18 notes that our sins "shall be as white as snow," describing one of Scripture's central themes.

Because Clifford had to sleep in the Boston bus station, he missed the 8 a.m. time to report for work in Middleboro. When he finally arrived there at 10 a.m., his understanding peers were somewhat amused at his story. Their understanding was appreciated and Clifford was warmly welcomed. Obviously, it would not have taken much for him to board the next-available southbound transportation for Laurel, Mississippi.

Fortunately, Clifford Jones remained in Middleboro for thirteen years, and was endeared in the community, in his church and in his employment. He became known and loved by the people of this town. Whenever Clifford walked along Middleboro streets, at his characteristic jaunty pace, automobile horns blew in recognition, people waved, shouts were exchanged, and he jubilantly *wove back*. Welcome Cliff! It was reported that sometime later, while on the job, Clifford Jones met a group of people at a nearby cranberry bog. Up to now, he had never seen cranberries growing, but their rich red color

(above:) **Cranberry harvest in Middleboro, Mass.**
[HalBrown (https://commons.wikimedia.org/wiki/File:Cranberry_Harvest_in_Middleboro.jpg), „Cranberry Harvest in Middleboro", edited by Stephen Robbins, https://creativecommons.org/licenses/by-sa/3.0/legalcode]

(below:) **Cranberries** *(Photo by Kristina Paukshtite from Pexels.com; file: pexels-kristina-paukshtite-139917. Cropped.)*

attracted his attention. During this meeting, Clifford reached down, gathered a handful of these beautiful, tempting berries, and chucked them into his mouth as if they were popcorn. Wow, he almost instantly learned why this was not a correct way to demonstrate the crop's goodness! At future meetings, he refrained from this demonstration!

Anyone from Massachusetts, and many from Wisconsin, are familiar with cranberries. New Englanders have to accept that Wisconsin has a competitive edge with its 21,000 acres[11] of cranberry bogs to Massachusetts' 14,000 acres.[12] However, cranberry farming began first in Massachusetts in 1816.[13]

Cranberry bogs are constructed on several-acre sites with sand layered over peat and clay, often with small streams passing around and through them. Conservationists like Clifford Jones have concerns with the cranberry bogs' soils makeup and water control, as both are precious natural resources.

At harvest time, the flowing water is dammed or pumped into the bog, to cover the growth. Because cranberries are light and airy, they naturally float to the water's surface, where they are harvested by scooping.

The growing and merchandizing of these pretty red berries are subject to the regulations of the United States Department of Agriculture, to ensure quality, safe handling, and grading standards.

Cranberries are a seriously healthy fruit, low in calories, high in fiber and contain lots of vitamin C and antioxidants. They are seldom eaten raw, because the natural taste is very sharp and sour. So, cranberries are usually cooked, with sweetener added, before consumption. The *bottom line* is: eating raw cranberries, other than one occasionally, is not an enjoyable or common practice.

In Middleboro Clifford Jones rented a room at the "Y"[14] for eighty dollars per month. For him, this was a fine place to live. He could use the gym

Clifford Jones rented a room at the Middleboro Y.M.C.A.
([post card] "Pub. by H. A. Dickerman & Son, Taunton, Mass. No. 4305"; postmarked 1914. Retrieved from digitalcommonwealth.org)

downstairs, play basketball here, and use the weight room. He also attended parties and functions at the "Y" and became acquainted with a host of people.

It appeared that skin color was hardly an issue in this rural community, and *discrimination* essentially nonexistent. Possibly because of his background, Clifford was conscious of being the only black person among an all-white crowd. During his tenure at Middleboro, he hopefully felt his welcome and acceptance. Everyone – well almost everyone – knew *Cliff* and held him in deserved high esteem. Some homesickness possibly tempted him at times, but he made the best of where he now found himself. His quick wit, humor, and exceptional southern congeniality soon made him a valued part of Middleboro's social landscape, and loved by all those he met.

Nevertheless, Clifford Jones' life at the "Y" emphasized that he was single. He often felt lonely and his thoughts all the time wandered back home and to *Lillie*, his college sweetheart.

Clifford now retells the story of how he met Lillie Mae[15] Stokes[16] on the campus of Alcorn State University, during his freshman year there:

Lillie *(courtesy of Clifford Jones)*

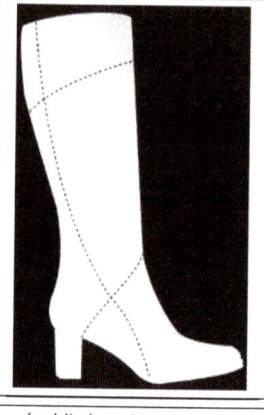

(publicdomainvectors.org)

> I saw her walking across the campus, in a pair of white ***go-go boots***.[17] I could spot her anywhere on campus and they were like a "magnet" or like honey drawing an ant – (smile) – and a smile that melted my heart. I told a friend of mine that I was

going to date her. Well, low and behold, we lived in the same apartment complex. My brother was employed by the University and I was living with him and his wife. Lillie was living with her cousin who was also a University employee, teaching mathematics. Ironically, these apartments were across the street from each other, meaning Lillie and I were across from each other. Although she really didn't want to have anything to do with me, I used to watch to see when she left to go on campus, and I had to leave at the same time to walk with her. I finally did enough for her and she began to soften up to me. She became a cheerleader and I was in the band, so I had the privilege of walking her home, protecting her after band trips. After a few walks home, I asked her to be my girlfriend. After about a month of asking, she finally said "Yes."

Because Clifford Jones was brought up attending church and had made a commitment to belong to Jesus at an early age, when he arrived in Middleboro one of his first concerns was to find an appropriate church where he could effectively fellowship. All of the churches "back home" in Mississippi were segregated, and the closest "black" church to Middleboro was twenty miles away in Brockton. But segregation based on skin color did not appear to be a factor in this new community, so Clifford began looking for a church in Middleboro.

After inquiring and visiting churches, Clifford quickly discovered Central Baptist Church,[18] pastored by Dr. Paul J. West. There were five or six African American families involved there; and they, together with the rest of the congregation and pastor, extended to him a warm welcome and a sense of comfort. In addition to Pastor West, Clifford notes several families in particular who warmly accepted him: Alan and Marge Demers,[19] John and Fran Russell, and this author and his wife with many kids! Several others joined in their appreciation for this young man who related so well and presented a wonderful testimony. The little-recognized town of Middleboro had acquired a delightful addition to its census! Welcome Mr. Jones!

Pastor Paul West
(author's collection)

Five-and-one-half years had elapsed since Lillie Stokes agreed to be Clifford Jones' girlfriend. During that time, Lillie had obtained her Master's degree in Remedial Reading from the University of Southern Mississippi. Clifford now convinced her to come North, which she did and nearly froze, in the Spring of 1970. After her arrival at Middleboro, Lillie Stokes was likewise welcomed into the church and community. She began teaching at the Mayflower Elementary School, and for the next thirteen years taught the fourth and fifth grades there.

On the day after Christmas, December 26th, 1970, Lillie Stokes became Lillie Jones. This also required Clifford to move from the Y into their first home.

The first home Clifford and Lillie Jones purchased was formerly a Unitarian Church parsonage, obtained for $12,000. A $500 down payment, loaned to them by the church, was repaid within the first year. Within three years, and after much remodeling, they sold this one for $26,000 and purchased a new home with five acres of land across town. Clifford planted a Christmas tree farm with three acres of Scotch Pine, but a move was made before he could harvest his crop with profit.

Again, in his own words, Clifford notes:

> The pastor and his wife, Dr. Paul and Edith West showed tremendous love toward Lillie and me. It was Pastor West who helped me to understand what it meant to have salvation. I attended and served my church in Mississippi, but had not fully given my life to Jesus Christ. At Central Baptist I gave my life fully to Christ.

Edith West
(author's collection)

Pastor West sensed that Clifford was being led of God to be in ministry, and gave him responsibilities in the church which he performed with great zeal and accomplishment. He taught Sunday school, became Sunday school superintendent, then youth director, and later director of Christian education. Clifford had a burning desire to know more about God and pursued that passion. And he was deeply loved by the congregates. These people will always

Cliff Jones *(right)* and Senator Edward Brooke of Mass. *(left)* at the U.S. Capitol building, Washington, D.C., 22 April 1975.
(courtesy of Karen Scofield)

remember Clifford singing "Amen" like no one

else, complimented by his dexterous body movements and infectious smile!

Clifford Jones was always involved in the sports interests of his peers. Young people thoroughly enjoyed being with him and playing sports with him in the schools, at church and at the "Y." "Cliff" (as the youth knew him) coached two of the author's daughters, Karen[20] and Diane,[21] on the girls' junior high basketball team. Karen shares her remembrances:

> Cliff dedicated time out of his busy schedule to coach some of Central Baptist Church's boys' and girls' basketball teams that competed in the Middleboro Sunday School Basketball League.
>
> The league was originally formed by Middleboro churches[22] to provide instructional and recreational opportunities for youth in town to compete in weekly basketball games. Each of the six or so member churches had their own teams in each age division. Games were held on Saturdays at the YMCA facility.[23]
>
> .... Since the league at that time functioned as the recreational league in town, lots of kids who wanted to learn to play, or wanted to play competitively, wanted to be on a team. But in order to play on a team, you had to be in that church at least once or twice a month.
>
> The Catholic church in town had the most teams in each age group, and they didn't need players. Also, kids found out they could get better playing time by *not* playing for the Catholic church! Therefore,

many kids wanted to play for Central Baptist, even when that meant they would have to come to church. There were a number of kids who came to church for that reason, and sometimes their families followed.

. . . . Cliff was a well-loved and respected coach who used the opportunity of sports to draw youth into church, since if you wanted to play on a church team, you had to attend that church.

. . . . Other than sports, what I remember most about Cliff was his smile and his characteristic chuckle/laugh.

This relation shows Clifford Jones' early commitment to the community, outside the church. He helped to increase the community's interest in church, which ultimately enhanced church attendance.

Clifford confesses that one of his interests was fishing, and especially deep-sea fishing. He did this from the bridges off Cape Cod. Raised in The South, the only fishing waters he had known were rivers and an occasional small lake. Now in Massachusetts, he was close to the great Atlantic Ocean and could appreciate its vastness. He loved what he saw and experienced.

A family who had befriended Clifford invited him to join them for overnight fishing trips on their house boat. Clifford was elated each time he could go. Sometimes the order of the day was jumping off the boat into the sea. Although he couldn't swim, putting on a life jacket was enough encouragement for Clifford to jump in and experience the good time for himself. One time, though, he became aware that he was drifting a distance from the boat and was unable to get back. His panicked screaming alerted his peers to get him and pull him back into the boat. Nothing was said about how many fish were caught that day, if any.

In wise counsel, and sensing Clifford's potential in the Lord's work, Dr. West convinced him to attend Gordon-Conwell Theological Seminary,[24] north of Boston, to further his education – not in agriculture, but in ministry. Along the way towards that goal, several new challenges appeared.

Despite Clifford Jones' government job, living expenses were such that tuition payments would not be possible. But through Dr. West's efforts, Jones was granted a full scholarship which would completely pay for his seminary classes.

The next challenge was that Clifford needed to continue his full-time employment. Fortunately, classes were offered at night! Even so, it was not easy to work eight hours daily, then drive seventy-five miles one way to the campus, three times a week, to attend classes from 6 p.m. to 9 p.m. But Clifford persevered with this tough routine for a total of six years! This testifies to his determination to follow the Apostle Paul's advice, as given to a young pastor-in-training, Timothy:

> 15 **Study to shew thyself approved unto God, a workman that needeth not to be ashamed, rightly dividing the word of truth.**
>
> *-2 Timothy 2:15 (King James Version)*

All the while, Clifford Jones faithfully continued in his church responsibilities, was a delightful friend to so many, and fulfilled his family roles as a husband and a father of two children.

Once most of Clifford's academic studies were completed, he still needed some courses that were not offered at night. He described his situation:

> I had a dilemma. I was employed with a government agency that had nothing to do with religion. I approached my State Conservationist and asked him if I could have a leave of absence to attend seminary classes. He first told me "No," then he asked me to show him how my degree from a seminary would benefit the agency. That was tough, but after I thought about it for a few days, I knew I was taking classes in preaching and public speaking. So, I went back to him about a week later and told him that my speaking classes would benefit the agency; as I made presentations to the public and different units of government, I would be more polished and precise in my presentation. He bought my explanation and allowed me to take a leave of absence, with no assurance that my job would be available when I came back. I took this challenge, believing if this was of God, He would work it out for my good. Three years later, I completed seminary with a Masters in Religion Education, and my fulltime job was still open, allowing me to return to my position as a soil conservationist.

Clifford Jones learned early that God was leading him all the way!

In 1979, Clifford Earl Jones was ordained at the Central Baptist Church in Middleboro, Massachusetts by the Conservative Baptist Churches. Dr. Paul West was extraordinarily supportive, guiding Clifford through this thorough and tough examination.

Of course, encouragement always came to Clifford from his mother, Geneva Jones, back in Mississippi. She supported her son in the best way she was able to do so. As Clifford dearly loved her coconut cakes, she would bake one for his birthday. She wrapped up the cake, along with a dozen eggs and other goodies, and sent the package through the mail – it arrived at Middleboro without an egg being broken! She must have been justly proud of her son's accomplishments.

Clifford remained in close contact with his Mom and family in Mississippi. He took vacation time to join his brothers for any necessary maintenance work on the family farm. One time, they even added another bedroom to mother Geneva's home. The Jones siblings especially directed their attention to fence repairs because, to the always-restless cows and horses, "the grass was always greener" beyond the fence!

The Jones children were proud of their Mom, and she of them. Following her death in 2009, four of the "kids" purchased the family home and

The Jones family's home in Laurel, Mississippi
(courtesy of Clifford Jones)

twenty acres, establishing an LLC (a limited liability company), so that it could always be a gathering place for the family and others. The LLC was named *GenIra16 Enterprises*, in honor of their parents. The name chosen for this organization combines "Gen" (the first three letters of mother Geneva's name) + "Ira" (father's name) + "16" (for the sixteen children). It was a matter of gratitude and pride to keep the land in the family.

For two more years Clifford Jones remained in Massachusetts, employed with the USDA-Soil Conservation Service. Meanwhile, he and Lillie adopted two children:

> *Clarinda Marie Jones*, born 4 April 1974;[25] and
> *Clifton Paul Jones*, born 16 July 1976.[26]

The Jones' desire grew for the children to be closer to grandparents. So, Clifford and Lillie made a decision to move back to the South. In March of 1981, Clifford Jones took a lateral transfer within the USDA-Soil Conservation Service, to Alabama. The events which followed over the next several years proved that this was indeed the leading of the Lord. Clifford and Lillie were brought to an eventual enlarging of the ministry for which he had so intently prepared.

Meanwhile, the Joneses had so endeared themselves to the people of Middleboro and Central Baptist Church that their departure felt bittersweet. They were dearly missed, especially by we who had savored Clifford's expertly-baked pecan pie (which, no doubt, he had learned from his Mama).

Rev. & Mrs. Jones *(courtesy of Clifford Jones)*

In June 1981, Clifford flew back to Middleboro, loaded his Toyota with their possessions, the children and the family dog, a Kerry blue terrier, and drove to Sylacauga, Alabama to their newly-constructed 2200-square-foot home. The Joneses lived in Sylacauga for the next three years while Clifford worked in Rockford as District Conservationist for Coosa County.

Sylacauga (pronounced "sill-uh-caw-guh") is located in a beautiful part of Alabama, with cascading waterfalls,[27] forests, caverns, parks, and a fascinating museum and arts center.[28] It is also known as the "Marble City" from its production of white marble. The Blue Bell Creamery makes ice cream in Sylacauga.[29] If the author remembers, ice cream was always Clifford's craving, so this alone may have brought him to Sylacauga! Best of all, especially for Lillie, no more snow and cold weather, or for that matter, cranberries! Challenges, however, did not go away!

Daughter Clarinda Marie Jones taught school for twenty-two years, then recently became Training and Organizational Development Manager for the City of Auburn, Alabama.[30]

Son Clifton Paul Jones, a graduate of Loyola School of Law in New Orleans, is employed by the Federal Emergency Management Agency (FEMA) of the U.S. Department of Homeland Security.[31] He was given the middle name of Paul in honor of Dr. Paul J. West, a fitting tribute.

With Clifford Jones' continuous desire to improve himself, he accepted a promotion to be the Soil Conservation Service Liaison at Tuskegee University, in Tuskegee, Alabama, about seventy-five miles from home. This was a most enjoyable position for Clifford. It was a rich experience serving a University founded by Booker T. Washington and scientist George Washington Carver. Always taking advantage of opportunities, Clifford received a Master in Personnel Administration degree and was an adjunct professor in the College of Agriculture at Tuskegee University. Not one to be content without always moving ahead, within two years

Professor Clifford Jones,
speaking at Southern Union State Community College
(courtesy of Clifford Jones)

he was promoted to be District Conservationist at Phenix City, Alabama. Moving from Sylacauga to Auburn was necessary, and it was only thirty-five miles from Phenix City!

Pleasant View Missionary Baptist Church in Salem, Alabama, about 17 miles and 20 minutes away, soon called Clifford Jones to be their bi-vocational pastor. Who was he to not accept a challenge like that? Clifford accepted the call to shepherd this church of about one-hundred members. In keeping with his "reach out to the community" philosophy, Reverend Jones began to establish ministries which positively impacted that rural congregation and community. Within three years, his programs increased the church membership to three-hundred souls. God was using an obedient Clifford E. Jones in a big way.

In 1993, Rev. Jones was "offered the privilege," as he puts it, to serve as pastor of the Greater Peace Missionary Baptist Church in Opelika, Alabama. Of course, he accepted. And Opelika was even close to the Jones' home in Auburn!

The Greater Peace church faced a daunting challenge. That may be exactly why the Lord sent in the fearless Pastor Clifford Jones. The church building had a maximum seating capacity of two-

Mrs. Lillie Jones and Pastor Clifford Jones
(church bulletin photo, courtesy of Clifford Jones)

hundred persons, which it had already outgrown. Also, being tucked into a residential community left it with little or no room to expand.

In Jones' coming, he was asked to lead the church into a building program. He remembered that, in seminary, he was taught to not rush into making changes too quickly – sound advice, *usually*. His initial plan, to wait at least eighteen-to-twenty-four months before moving on major changes, evaporated. The church sought *rapid* changes, and it was his responsibility to become ready!

A decision was reached that the church must build in a new location, which must have:

(1) adequate land for present expansion needs;
(2) ample space for future expansion needs;
(3) location in the immediate vicinity, in order to:
   (a) maintain recognized community presence;
   (b) allow many to keep walking to church.

The church was able to purchase ten acres nearby from the City of Opelika's Industrial Board. This was God's answer to prayer for a goal which had seemed almost impossible. Construction immediately began on a church of 15,000 square feet, including a sanctuary with a seating capacity for seven hundred persons. This project required a twenty-year mortgage, but with a stated expectation of full payment in only ten years. And this actually happened! The mortgage was completely paid in *nine years and ten months!* The mortgage burning was a great celebration and praise to the Lord for rewarding this people. It was proven to the membership that when a plan is properly put together, and implemented with their cooperation, many things can be accomplished.

With the worship center completed, there was now a desire to build a Family Life Center with a full gymnasium. Such a facility which could affordably host large events did not exist in the Opelika community; the alternative had been paying exorbitant prices to the big hotels. The structure was designed to match the new red brick worship center and to serve both the church and the community. Construction began soon thereafter. The completed Family Life Center is now being used as a vital part of this church's overall ministry. Pastor Jones believes strongly

Family Life Center, Greater Peace Missionary Baptist Church, Opelika, Alabama
(courtesy of Clifford Jones)

that the church has an important role in the community; otherwise, in times of peace, it could fast become irrelevant. The church should not lose its unique advantage, wherein it can instill positive change in a person's life. As in the early Pilgrim days, people should have their emotional and physical needs met, just as much as their spiritual needs are met. And where better to address and meet their needs than in their church! Jesus ministered to the people's physical needs and then addressed their spiritual needs.

"I believe the church has a responsibility and calling to impact the community around them" says Pastor Jones. He continues:

> The church is to be about developing outreach programs to make lives of people better, not only spiritually, but also physically. We have established over fifty ministries to do that. The preaching and teaching of the Gospel of Jesus Christ is priority, but people also need to be taught how to survive.

During a visit to Greater Peace Church, one readily witnesses much activity, especially within the Community Building. Many churches erect big facilities which see only limited use during the week. Not here! It is an exciting place with worthwhile happenings all week long!

Some of the ministries established within this church and its non-profit outreach include:

Senior Ministry – where senior saints come and do quilting and a variety of crafts, which are then given to nursing home patients, preschools and others in need.

Singles Ministry – where singles come together for fellowship, Bible study, workshops and retreats.

Couples Ministry – Marriages are strengthened as couples come together to share their concerns and problems in a safe setting, and to discuss ways for improvement. One outcome of this ministry was the formation of a couples Sunday school class.

STEM Ministry – An after-school program where students gather to focus on their schoolwork, and at the same time have a fun experience.

Summer Education Enrichment Program (SEEP) – Safe space is provided for students over the summer months. This program includes field trips. Resource people from Auburn University and other local leaders participate to enrich the lives of students, and to prepare them for entering school in the Fall.

Adult GED Ministry – Assistance is provided to adults who did not receive their high school diploma to now obtain their GED certificate. This program is offered to participants at no cost.

Men's Retreat Ministry – The men of the church annually take a three-day retreat to bond and grow spiritually, and prepare for greater service within the Body of Christ.

Mrs. Lillie Jones and Pastor Clifford Jones
(courtesy of Clifford Jones)

<u>Women's Retreat Ministry</u> – The church ladies spend three days away from the church to experience fellowship, spiritual enrichment, and yes – shopping!

<u>The Gymnasium</u> is in constant use, not only for sports, but also for assemblies and banquets.

The Greater Peace Church property is a very busy place, and is something which connects with the community for good. A natural result is that many are pointed to Jesus and added to the church body. I can imagine Clifford singing "Amen" as he walks around the campus.

Regrettably, probably a majority of churches in this era have become separated from the world surrounding them, then wonder why membership is stagnant or declining. They should take their cue from Rev. Jones and Greater Peace Church as to how successful church ministries are done.

We have previously discussed the importance of a pastor's involvement with the greater community surrounding the church in which he ministers. All too often, a "preacher" is too fully involved with his church- or denomination-sponsored meetings, seminars, and gatherings to participate in local programs and activities. Rev. Jones models a more positive and interactive approach. He devotes much of his time serving on local, state and national boards that he believes help make the community better. These include: Boys and Girls Clubs, American Red Cross, Auburn City Board of Education, Regional Bank Board, 100 Black Men of America, Auburn Chamber of Commerce, Alabama State Baptist Missionary Board, National Missionary Baptist Convention Board, Mid-South Resource Conservation and Development Board, Mercy Medical Clinic Board, and Salvation Army Board. Believing that a local church and its leadership have a responsibility to help impact and shape their community, Pastor Jones has served on these boards, and more, during his many years in ministry.

In 2000, citizen Clifford Jones became the president of the Auburn City Schools Board of Education, the first African American to hold that position in that school system. He was grateful to be accepted on the basis of what he was willing to, and could, contribute for the schools' betterment. With the Auburn City Schools system growing and many new schools built, Dr. Jones was excited to be involved in making it an "outstanding" system. He devoted over fifteen years to Auburn City Schools, with strong leadership and policies that rapidly moved them forward. Obviously, Clifford Jones was an outstanding member and participant in his community, while pastoring a large and vibrant church.

The *Jordan's Gate Housing Development* is a major and very successful initiative of Clifford Jones. The development's construction was the

(courtesy of Clifford Jones)

intentional result of his becoming founder and president of Greater Peace Community Development Corporation (GPCDC), and president of the Alabama Association of Community Development Corporations (AACDC). Application for affordable housing was presented to the Alabama Housing Finance Authority in Montgomery. GPCDC became, and is, a 501(c)(3) nonprofit organization which partnered with the Bennet Group of Auburn to do such a project together. With jointly-formed limited liability companies (LLCs), they

(courtesy of Clifford Jones)

purchased a twenty-five-acre plot of land from a group who had owned it for twenty-five years and were ready to divest themselves of it. The price for this tract was the amazingly low figure of only $100,000!

Major funding came through Enterprise Community Partners of Columbia, Maryland, whose primary purpose is to finance affordable housing projects. The Jordan's Gate Housing Development was built with tax credits over a fifteen-year span. After fifteen years, tenants would be able to purchase their homes and become a homeowner.[32] For each year a tenant occupies a home, a $5,000 credit is set aside for a down payment at the end of fifteen years. That set-aside is only applied if the tenant stays to the end of the period. Therefore, if a tenant stays for fifteen years, they will have $75,000 to apply toward a down payment for a fifteen-year mortgage. Dr. Jones says they project that what a tenant was paying for rent at the end of the fifteenth year would be approximately the same as a mortgage

(courtesy of Clifford Jones)

payment. Jones continues:

> We are in the thirteenth year of the project, and within six months, tenants will begin home ownership training to prepare them for all they need to know to purchase and maintain a home of their own.

Jones notes with some elation,

(images courtesy of Clifford Jones)

> I am excited to know that we had a hand in making it possible for forty-eight families to become homeowners. To God Be the Glory!

A few years ago, this author, a retired construction and engineering company president, toured Jordan's Gate Housing Development, close by the Greater Peace Church. The quality of the neighborhood impressed me. Active covenants are strictly enforced, and are noticeably accepted by tenants. Instilled with a desire to remain living within this important development, they take evident pride in maintaining each property, keeping up its value.

Rev. Dr. Clifford Jones is another very busy church preacher, and has come a long way from being a Sunday school teacher at Middleboro, Massachusetts in a snowstorm! Oh – also of note is his service as chaplain of the Lee County Sheriff Department, where he is often busy with counseling, consoling in times of tragedy, and conducting funerals for law enforcement officers. He also serves as an on-call chaplain for the East Alabama Medical Center Hospital.

Clifford Jones has been busy being about his Father's business. His training began way back in Middleboro where he simultaneously held a full-time position, was on his local church's staff, attended a university full-time, bought and updated a house, planted a tree farm, and totally engaged with the town's youth. All this was preparation for his current busy life and ministry. All of Clifford's accomplishments came to the attention of the Montgomery Bible Institute and Theological Center, which in 2002 conferred upon him a well-deserved Honorary Doctorate degree.

In his obedience to the Lord, and with the Lord's guidance, Rev. Dr. Clifford Jones has taken challenges and converted them into results which will last for eternity!

Not Just Any *Preacher,*
Clifford Jones

has earned a place in our list as
AN EXTRAORDINARY PREACHER !

(courtesy of Clifford Jones)

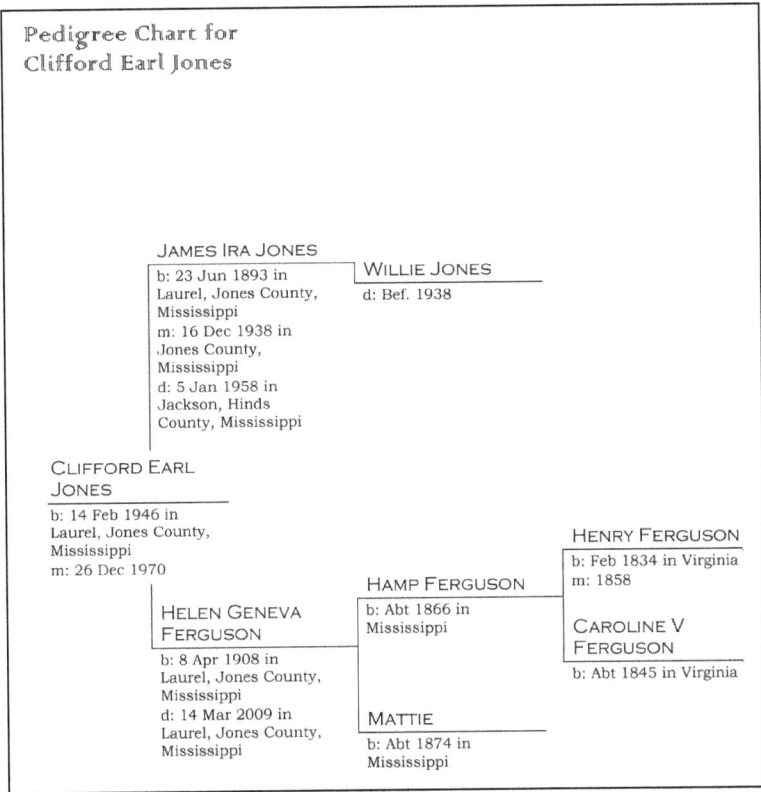

ENDNOTES

[1] "Clifford Jones' Reputation Profile," *MyLife*, MyLife,com, ©2020. Web: <https://www.mylife.com/clifford-jones/e409861624122>.
[2] "Laurel, Mississippi," *Wikipedia, The Free Encyclopedia*. Web: <https://en.wikipedia.org/wiki/Laurel,_Mississippi>. 61.3% in 2010; 55.08% in 2000.
[3] Ibid.
[4] "History: Historic District," *Laurel Main Street: Since 1907*. Web: <http://laurelmainstreet.com/about/history/>.
[5] Mississippi, County Marriages, 1858-1979 [database, familysearch.org].
[6] "Alcorn State University," *Wikipedia, The Free Encyclopedia*. Web: <https://en.wikipedia.org/wiki/Alcorn_State_University>.
[7] "Executive Summary [...] 2. What Every Alpha Should Know," *Alpha Protocol & Etiquette Manual*, (Baltimore, Md.: Alpha Phi Alpha Fraternity, 6 Dec. 2011, p. 8. Web: <https://issuu.com/apa1906network/docs/protocol_etiquette_manual/8>.

[8] "Alpha Phi Alpha," *Wikipedia, The Free Encyclopedia*. Web: <https://en.wikipedia.org/wiki/Alpha_Phi_Alpha>.

[9] The Soil Conservation Service (SCS) became Natural Resources Conservation Service (NRCS) in 1994.

[10] *Nor'easters* are storms along the East Coast of North America with winds generally from the Northeast, accompanied by heavy rain or snow, often bringing all travel to a halt.

[11] "Find out what cranberries can do for you!" *Wisconsin Cranberries*, Wisconsin State Cranberry Growers Association, ©2020. Web: <http://www.wiscran.org/cranberries/>.

[12] "How Cranberries Grow," *The Cranberry*, Cape Cod Cranberry Growers' Association, ©2020. Web: <https://www.cranberries.org/how-cranberries-grow>.

[13] "Where Tradition Meets Innovation," *The Cranberry*, Cape Cod Cranberry Growers' Association, ©2020. Web: <https://www.cranberries.org/history>.

[14] Young Men's Christian Association (YMCA).

[15] "Lillie Mae Jones Age 73 (Sep 1947)," *TruePeopleSearch* [database], TruePeopleSearch.com, ©2020. Web: <https://www.truepeoplesearch.com/>.

[16] Lillie M. Stokes was born 29 September 1947—["Lillie Jones' Reputation Profile," *MyLife*, MyLife,com, ©2020. Web: <https://www.mylife.com/lillie-jones/e409812518262>.

[17] Girls wore these classy fashion boots, usually white, which came up halfway up the calf. Go-go dancing, dance clubs, music and boots were fads begun in the mid-1960s. "Going to a Go-Go" was the title of a 1965 song by *Smokey Robinson and The Miracles*.

[18] Now known as Meeting House Church.

[19] Marge Demers was the then-church secretary.

[20] Karen is married to Carl Scofield; they still live in Middleboro. She notes, "In more current history, I served in various coach (1 year) or officer (6-7 years) positions with the Middleboro Sunday School Basketball League (can't recall the years, but from 2002 or 2003 through 2010 or 2011); so I'm familiar with the league itself and know that it's been around about 50-to-60 years."

[21] Diane is married to Pastor John Hooper, the preacher at Maple Street Church in Wolfeboro, New Hampshire.

[22] Karen Scofield continues: "The League is still in existence in Middleboro today (2020), although it is no longer run by the churches. . . . . [It is] one of the main recreational basketball leagues in town but churches really haven't been involved, so it's run independently, like a town sports league."

[23] What was formerly the Middleboro YMCA facility is now (2020) an apartment building.

[24] Gordon-Conwell Theological Seminary ranks as one of the largest seminaries in North America. With the help of Dr. Billy Graham, it was opened in 1969 as a merger between Gordon Divinity School of Gordon College, and Conwell School of Theology (a part of Temple University in Philadelphia). Harold John Ockenga was the first President. Other former Presidents (and who were known by this author) include Robert Cooley, Walter Keiser, Jr and Haddon Robinson.

Many former professors have also been a part of our lives. Dr. Barry Corey, who is now President of Biola University, Dr. Timothy Tennent, a noted American theologian was once a close neighbor of this editor, and their children played together. Dr. Tennent is currently President of Asbury Theological Seminary. (Now we add Rev. Dr. Clifford E. Jones to that list!).

[25] "Clarinda Perry's Reputation Profile," *MyLife*, MyLife,com, ©2020. Web: <https://www.mylife.com/clarinda-perry/e410103465486>.

[26] "Clifton Jones' Reputation Profile," *MyLife*, MyLife,com, ©2020. Web: <https://www.mylife.com/clifton-jones/e410331738480>.

[27] Kay, "Exploring Waterfalls: Easy Hiking Trails Near Me by Region," *Alabama Waterfalls* [blog], alabamawaterfalls.com, 9 May 2019. Web: <https://alabamawaterfalls.com/alabama-waterfalls/exploring-waterfalls-easy-hiking-trails-near-me>.

[28] "[Talladega County]," *Explore East Alabama*, TourEastAlabama.com. Web: <https://toureastalabama.com/counties/talladega/>.

[29] "Sylacauga, Alabama," *Wikipedia, The Free Encyclopedia*. Web: <https://en.wikipedia.org/wiki/Sylacauga,_Alabama>.

[30] "Clarinda Jones," *Linked in* [database], linkedin.com. Web: <https://www.linkedin.com/in/clarinda-jones-83428281>.

[31] "Clifton Jones," *Linked in* [database], linkedin.com. Web: <https://www.linkedin.com/in/clifton-jones-a2696b58>.

[32] Enterprise Community Investment, Inc., "Grand Opening of Jordan's Gate Creates 48 Affordable, Single-Family Homes for Families in Opelika, Alabama," *RealEstateRama*, 3 June 2009. Web: <https://alabama.realestaterama.com/grand-opening-of-jordan%E2%80%99s-gate-creates-48-affordable-single-family-homes-for-families-in-opelika-alabama-ID092.html>.

Howard B. Higgins Jr.
(photo courtesy of Robert Higgins)

Chapter 8

Reverend HOWARD BURTON HIGGINS Junior

"Be kind and compassionate to one another,
Forgiving each other just as in Christ God forgave you."
–Ephesians 4:32 (King James Version)

North of Boston, Massachusetts it can be very cold and unpleasant in the month of December. It was on one of these days, Monday, December 18th, 1916, and a week before Christmas, in the town of Danvers, that Howard B. Higgins, Junior was born.[1] Not that it was then important (or, for that matter, even now), but Betty Grable, destined to become a famous American actress, was also born on this date.[2] It was a leap year.

Howard was named after his father, Howard B. Higgins, Senior. Family history records that both his mother's and father's heritages had roots in eastern Massachusetts from the early 1800s. The family never strayed far from the Danvers vicinity; in fact, most of their graves can be found at the Walnut Grove Cemetery in Danvers.[3]

Howard grew up in Danvers and the neighboring town of Beverly, graduating from Beverly High School in 1934. Testimony has been given that he was a very quiet and bashful young boy in those years.

As a teenager, Howard became active in Christian Endeavor, a recognized youth organization, while attending the First Baptist

First Baptist Church, Danvers, Massachusetts, circa 1900

Church of Danvers. It was here that he accepted the Lord Jesus Christ as his Savior, and became a dedicated Christian. Howard indicated an interest in music and began singing the bass part in a male quartet. This group was soon well-known and popular throughout the area.

Yes, cold, especially after sundown, was not uncommon in the northeast corner of Massachusetts. Just as it was cold at Howard's birth in December 1916, it was also cold (in fact,

below zero) on a certain January night in the year 1939. That was when twenty-three-year-old Howard B. Higgins found his ice skates and went to Mill Pond for some exercise.

A local girl, by either coincidence or divine

nudging, elected to go ice skating on that same night and at that same pond. The rest is history!

About this same time Howard made friends with Clifford Hartman and Warren Harris who became Christians and were greatly influenced by the witness and testimony of Howard Higgins. In fact, both Clifford and Warren were a part of the youth group and both later went on to become pastors. Apparently, Clifford Hartman and Warren Harris were also witness to the newly-formed relationship between Howard and Mary Elizabeth Connors.

The year 1939 was, more importantly, when Howard dedicated himself to full-time Christian service. That fall, he enrolled at the Providence Bible Institute (PBI).[4]

Meanwhile, Mary Connors studied at Salem Teachers College. She and Howard kept "in touch" through letter writing (no iPhones then!).

These were days of intense study, but also a time for making long-lasting friendships with a host of other young people, who would remain treasured friends for the years that followed. Some of these became foreign missionaries, while others were pastors.

Howard Higgins in a graduation gown
(courtesy of Robert Higgins)

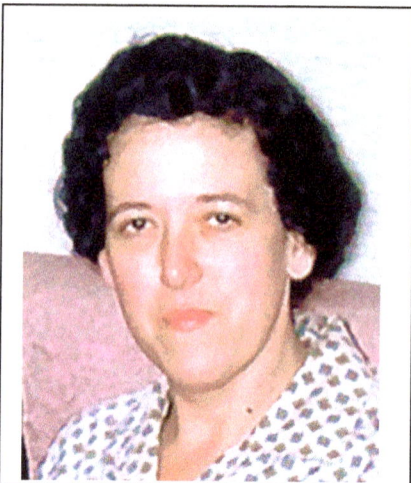

**Mary (Connors) Higgins
March 1959**
(author's collection)

**Baptist Church, Lebanon, Conn.
circa 1905**

Both Howard and Mary graduated in June of 1942. Marriage was most certainly a part of their expectations and plans. But first, their careers had to be consummated. This meant that their separation must continue for another year, after Mary accepted a teaching position in Danvers – where else? – and Howard responded to a call from the First Baptist Church of Lebanon, Conn.[5] This was his first pastorate, and where he served until July 1945.

A year as a busy pastor, living alone in a parsonage but staying in touch with Mary and planning a wedding, insured that time passed quickly. On Sept. 2, 1943 friends and family filled the home church, First Baptist of Danvers, Mass., for a 7:30 evening wedding. One of the hymns sung that night was the beautiful and meaningful, "O Perfect Love."

Marriage

675 PERFECT LOVE 11.10.11.10.   Sir Joseph Barnby, 1889

1 O perfect Love, all human thought transcending,
Lowly we kneel in prayer before Thy throne,
That theirs may be the love which knows no ending,
Whom Thou for evermore dost join in one. A-MEN.

2 O perfect Life, be Thou their full assurance
Of tender charity and steadfast faith,
Of patient hope, and quiet, brave endurance,
With childlike trust that fears nor pain nor death.

3 Grant them the joy which brightens earthly sorrow;
Grant them the peace which calms all earthly strife,
And to life's day the glorious unknown morrow
That dawns upon eternal love and life.

4 Hear us, O Father, gracious and forgiving,
Through Jesus Christ Thy co-eternal Word,
Who, with the Holy Ghost, by all things living
Now and to endless ages art adored.

Dorothy F. Blomfield, 1883.   Doxology (Rev. John Ellerton, 1875) added

"O Perfect Love"
(also known as "Marriage")

(Blomfield, Dorothy F. and John Ellerton [text]; Joseph Barnby [music]. *The Hymnal : published in 1895 and revised in 1911 by authority of the General Assembly of the Presbyterian Church in the United States of America : with the supplement of 1917*. (1921), p.884. [image online: <https://hymnary.org/page/fetch/THEH/884/high>])

Then it was back to Lebanon, a comfortable Connecticut farming village, northwest of Norwich.[6]

The area now known as Lebanon was first inhabited by the Mohegan, an Algonquian-speaking people. From 1663 to 1692 they sold these lands to white settlers from Norwich. Incorporated as a town in October 1700, it was given the name "Lebanon" by a parson's son due to "the height of the land and a large cedar forest" – the first Connecticut town to adopt a Bible name (see 1 Kings 7:2 and Ezekiel 31:3). History also notes Lebanon's significance during the Revolutionary War.[7]

Mary was warmly welcomed by the church members. A year later, on September 10, 1944 Howard's and Mary's first son, Robert Howard Higgins, was born at Windham Hospital in Willimantic, a small town just north of Lebanon. From somewhat obscure notes, it appears the trip to the hospital was in "The Green Hornet" (possibly the pastor's transportation). The church shared the Higgins' excitement, embraced their family and included them as true members of their church and community.

Sometime later, church members expressed enthusiasm for the Higgins' ministry. Flora William noted,

> Right from the first, your sermons were very inspiring and lucid. Some of us made outlines as you preached, and at our house we often discussed the sermons at the dinner table.[8]

Mary Parkhurst, the church organist, offered this endorsement:

> ... I believe the highlight of your years in the church was your introduction of Bible study such as we had never had before, bringing us to a new understanding of the Bible and our faith.[9]

Parkhurst speaks further about how they realized "afresh the influence your teaching and preaching has had on our lives."[10]

"This Is Your Life" programs,[11] done at various occasions, provide many remembrances about the Higgins family, especially about Pastor Higgins. These include how many *quahogs*[12] he got at one time, fishing trips in small skiffs that almost sunk in unexpected rain squalls, watching Friday night fights on a seven-inch television screen, clambakes, and making coffee with egg shells.

Digging clams at Camp Cole, Rhode Island, circa 1915.

Mention is made of the tomatoes he grew and supplied to members for canning.

On one New Year's Eve, the men made a trip to Boston to a Billy Graham rally and experienced a number of problems with the bus. It proved to be a night to remember with "our Pastor" who got them home at dawn. All the way back, the Pastor was joking and leading in singing. Somehow this earned him the fond title: "Jigger Higgins."

Leaving behind many memories and a fruitful work, a move to a larger church was made after Howard Higgins accepted a call to the First Baptist Church of Wickford, Rhode Island, in July of 1945.

First Baptist Church, Wickford, Rhode Island, circa 1910

The historic village of Wickford is a part of the town of North Kingstown, on the west side of Narragansett Bay. It appears much like an island, and is only a short walk to a fine beach.

Although Howard enjoyed swimming, there was little time for it. Two more children joined this family: a daughter, Nancy, was born on August 9, 1947; and another son, David, born September 26, 1949.

Travel back and forth to Gordon Divinity School, then located in downtown Boston, was a part of these years during which Howard earned a Bachelor of Divinity degree in 1950. In April of the same year, 1950, he was examined and ordained to the Gospel ministry, thus assuming the title of *Reverend* Howard Higgins. This event was noted in a *Providence Journal* article on April 28, 1950. Participants were Dr. Howard W. Ferrin, Rev. Norman S. Townsend, and Dr. T. Leonard Lewis[13] (with whom this author was acquainted).

In September of 1950, Reverend Higgins answered a call to the First Baptist Church of Hyde Park, Mass.[14] This transition from country life and resort village locations to city life was quite different and challenging. It was at Hyde Park that the Higgins children began their schooling. The old parsonage was sold and a new one purchased.

Pastor Higgins was effective in his manner of getting people to do things within the church. Someone was quick to notice how he could mentally note who was, or was not, at church on any given Sunday. As at previous locations, he made friends and was held in high

First Baptist Church, Hyde Park, Massachusetts, circa 1909.

esteem by parishioners and neighbors. He laughed and cried with the people, led many to the Savior, and helped others to grow in their Christian faith.

During Pastor Higgins' first year at Hyde Park,

> the church showed marked improvement in the general financial condition. Much was done in the way of property improvements, among which was the painting . . . on the building exterior" . . . . Approximately thirty new members were added . . . . many weddings . . . a memorable five years.[15]

Pastor Higgins also represented the church at the American Baptist Convention in Buffalo, New York and attended the State Convention in Worcester. Community religious classes were conducted for 4-to-6-year-olds and for grade 9, each week. Boston newspapers noted his presence at a licensing board meeting, to oppose the moving of a liquor store from Boston to Hyde Park.

After five full and rewarding years in Hyde Park, Pastor Higgins in July of 1955 was called by the First Baptist Church of Rockland, Massachusetts to become their new minister.

The Whitaker family moved in 1957 from Randolph to the second-oldest house in Rockland, at 925 Liberty Street. We attended the First Baptist Church in Rockland, became members, and soon were totally involved in this church and its ministry.[16] I recall Pastor Higgins' visit and his interest in our old house restoration project.

The parsonage, next door to the Rockland church at 210 Union Street, became the Higgins' new home. This was a large, three-story home,

(above:) **Pastor & Mrs. Higgins, March 1959**
(author's collection)

(below:) **First Baptist Church, Rockland, Mass., circa 1905**
(Dale Robbins collection)

containing not only living quarters but also a pastor's study and even some rooms used for meetings.

Later, a new parsonage would be acquired at 31 Crescent Street and the pastor's family relocated there. Then the old parsonage was used as overflow space for Sunday school, youth meetings, and other events. It was named "The Chipman House," after a man who helped begin this church.

Deacon George W. Chipman of Boston owned property in Rockland and spent time there. In 1854, he supported the establishment of a new Baptist church and donated the land on which the church and parsonage were built. The Church honored Chipman by giving this building his name.

I recall the church receiving the gift of an antique upright piano from an elderly church member. A group of church men, with me and my pickup truck, brought the piano to the back door and rear stairway of the Chipman House. We intended to locate the piano on the third floor, for use in youth meetings. After backing the truck to the fire escape stairs, someone noted the piano had a broken sound board. That meant it probably was not tunable – maybe worse. We had not been prudent enough to check the instrument's playability before moving it. The faulty piano's donors had successfully disposed of it – to us.

What could we do now? Our crew of six-to-eight didn't want to "lug" it up to the third floor, to be just an ornament. At 10 o'clock that night, we destroyed the piano on the spot, using a large sledge hammer which happened to be available.

Can you imagine what a loud noise that sledge hammer made on the old sound board? All this took place in the town center, surrounded by apartment houses. Amazingly, no one went to jail!

Fortunately, Pastor Higgins was far from the scene and unaware of our antics!

Pastor Higgins was a rather stout man and always wore a black robe in the pulpit, as was traditional at that time. This covered a well-worn Sunday suit which, eventually, the deacons quietly paid to replace.

Pastor Higgins, when speaking profound remarks to young people, folded his arms across his stomach and used his deep bass voice. This often elicited their laughter and made them scamper.

After Reverend Higgins began a sermon series on a different and

Pastor Howard Higgins
(courtesy of Robert Higgins)

particular sin each week, this author asked when he was going to get to the sin of gluttony. I remarked that if he did this, I would have to slip down and hide under the pew. My four- or five-year-old daughter nearby spoke up: "Dad you wouldn't fit!" She was the same one I had to take from a church service one Sunday morning because of her antics in the pew; as I carried her out, with one arm around her, she (facing the congregation), blurted out, "Pray for me!"

Interior of First Baptist Church, Rockland, Massachusetts
circa 1959 *(author's collection)*

First Baptist Church at Rockland was a vibrant church with a surprisingly large group of newly-married young people. This "home builders" contingent became the strength and backbone of this church. Many meetings, with many fun times accompanied by work or serious meditation, helped the church to grow both spiritually and in numbers.

In years past, my brother and I heard our Dad sing (in his monotone), "At the bar, at the bar, where I smoked my first cigar, and the burdens of the day rolled away . . ." while he drove us to our grandparents' farm in our big Nash automobile. This was supposed to be sung to the tune of the old hymn, "At the cross, at the cross, where I first saw the light . . ." On one Sunday, as Pastor Higgins announced this old hymn and the congregation began singing it, my brother Wayne (sitting across from me) reacted with a broad smile and the sound of clearing his throat, while glancing across the aisle at me. The pastor grinned; he knew what we were about!

It was always a challenge to serve on the deacon board of the church. One time, we received a complaint and question as to why our Baptist minister did not attend the local ministers' luncheons in town. When we inquired of our pastor, he said he preferred to have lunch with the priest, "because we have more in common than the ministers." Enough said! – and that matter went away.

However, as deacons who are expected to be humble, serious-minded spiritual leaders, we did have our "moments." Someone got the idea it would be nice for all the deacons to exchange our usual matching suit vests (worn in that day) for crimson red ones, and to present ourselves so-attired on the next Communion Sunday. And we did. But we were not sure how Pastor Higgins might react. We were pleasantly surprised when he asked if we would have red cardinal hats for the next Lord's Supper – and if so, to be sure we included one for him!

It was my privilege to occasionally assist as the "worship leader" for services. My training with Dr. Philbrook was put to the test. The Sunday morning worship was normally a formal, almost ritualistic program, with much dignity and reverence. (The *new* era had not yet dawned!).

Pastor Higgins once asked me to conduct the entire service for one Sunday, including the morning message (and I no longer remember the reason why).

My interest and curiosity were elevated by one cover sheet of Doctor Philbrook's many sets of sermon notes. In heavy red ink were the words, in quotation marks, "PLUS ULTRA" and a subtitle, "Sail On." And even more interesting was the date and location of his presentation: "Paterson, New Jersey" and "March 25, 1928." I have no idea why or where he was preaching in Paterson, New Jersey. However, additional dates had been added: "Everett, Mass., April 14, 1929 – Exchange with Rev. A. Judson Hughes." Other dates appear: June 23, 1941 at North Reading State Sanatorium; Randolph, Massachusetts, October 12, 1941; Columbus Day, Randolph, Massachusetts, October 12, 1947. Obviously, this was a popular sermon of the Reverend Doctor Philbrook. And, do you know what? It became a favorite sermon of mine as well. I often enjoyed using a message title that would catch one's eye and imagination, and usually it was more effective. On one occasion, but for a reason I do not recall, I was asked by the

Pastor Howard Higgins and Mrs. Mary Higgins

(courtesy of Robert Higgins)

pastor of the church we were attending, the First Baptist Church of Rockland, Massachusetts, to deliver the morning message. I chose this title, "Plus Ultra," and I think it got the attention of the Pastor, Reverend Howard Higgins. As I remember, he was obviously excited by my delivery, and even asked if I would share my notes with him! Bingo!

I was reminded recently, by one of that church's members then accompanying me, that I had costumed up to appear like Christopher Columbus on that date. And I entered the pulpit, just in time to speak, by proceeding down the center aisle, complete with a three-cornered hat and buckled shoes! I can assure you that my flair for getting attention did just that![17]

```
        CHRISTMAS SUNDAY MORNING WORSHIP SERVICE
December 21, 1969           9:30 & 11:00 A.M.
Miss Arleen Taft   Organist & Choir Director
     "Ye shall find the babe wrapped in swaddling
     clothes, lying in a manger."  Luke 2:12
Quiet Meditation and Prayer
Organ Prelude                         Miss Arleen Taft
          "The Holy Night"                      Buck
Call to Worship
*Processional Hymn
*The Invocation and The Lord's Prayer
*The Gloria Patri
***
The Responsive Reading
Morning Solo                 Mrs. John F. Brennan
     "How Beautiful Are The Feet"          Handel
The Scripture Lesson
Youth Choir   Direction of Mrs. John F. Brennan
     "Angels We Have Heard On High"  Old French Carol
Morning Prayer and Response
The Morning Offering
The Offertory                    Miss Arleen Taft
          "The Christ Child"              Hailing
*The Doxology and Prayer of Dedication
Church Announcements
Morning Anthem                      Senior Choir
          "Born A King"                  Peterson
Hymn of Preparation
The Morning Sermon      Mr. Albert Whitaker, Jr.
       "Peace On Earth, Farce, or Force"
*Hymn of Dedication
*The Benediction and Response
Postlude                                    Organ
          "Adeste Fideles"                  Buck

            RECEPTIONISTS FOR TODAY ARE:

      9:30 Service   Mabel Bryson
                     Ethelwyn Newcomb
     11:00 Service   Mr. & Mrs. Alexaner Millar
```

(opposite:) **Bulletin for the *Christmas Sunday Morning Worship Service*, First Baptist Church, Rockland, Mass. The author delivered the sermon.**

(below:) **Front page of the author's sermon notes for "Peace on Earth: Farce or Force?" He delivered this sermon on 21 December 1969 at First Baptist Church, Rockland, Mass.**

(author's collection)

PEACE ON EARTH: FARCE OR FORCE ?

SCRIPTURE
LUKE 2: 1-20

Whitman Baptist 12/7/69

12/21/69 Rockland MASS

1) Today our imagination go back two thousand years to that first Christmas when the world experienced three phenomena. First, there was the *star*. There were many stars in the sky, but none like this. This one shone with the aura and brilliance of another world. It was as though God had taken a lamp from the ceiling of heaven and hung it in the dark sky over a troubled world.

SECOND
2) And ~~third~~, there was *good news* — the good news that at last a Savior had come to save men from sin. "Thou shalt call his name Jesus: for he shall save his people from their sins" (Matthew 1:21). He was the central theme of that first Christmas. The star, the song, the gifts, the kneeling, the joy, the hope, the excitement — all were signs of him.

THIRDLY
3) ~~Second~~, there was a *new song* in the air. A world which had lost its song learned to sing again. With the coming of God in the flesh hope sprang in the heart of man; and led by angelic beings, the whole world took up the refrain, "Glory to God in the highest, and on earth peace, good will toward men" (Luke 2:14).

Christmas is a season that has always been celebrated in song.
Luke records some of these inspired songs, full of beauty and wonder.
   (a) in presence of her cousin Elizabeth, Virgin Mary sang "the Magnificat" (Luke 1:46
   (b) the song of the angelic host, Luke 2:14
      Gloria in Excelsis
About this song, recorded in Luke 2:14, we concern our thoughts today.
To many this song may seam like a FARCE - because to them it has never become a FORCE
Ever since the angelic host sang that wonderous chorus more than 1900 years ago, the world has know only restleness and war. Today the light of history gives no reason to hope that wars will ever cease.
In early times wars were waged on a small scale, between village and village: then between tribes and provinces: later between nations and groups of nations

At that time, it was customary to have a *revival* at least once a year. Usually, a dynamic, motivating personality was invited to speak for a three-day weekend, complete with a fellowship banquet or something unusual. Pastor Higgins had recommended (and the deacon board approved) an invitation to Pastor Perry F. Rockwood, a well-known radio evangelist from Halifax, Nova Scotia, Canada. His radio program, "The Peoples Gospel Hour" had been broadcast in our area since 1947. Upon talking with Pastor Rockwood, he agreed to come, but wanted to have services every night from a Tuesday through Sunday. As Pastor Higgins and I sat with him in my living room on that first Sunday night, Rockwood stated firmly that we should have meetings *every* night while he was here and not leave Monday night out. Pastor Higgins reluctantly agreed, responding to Pastor Rockwood's intensity. The meetings went well, were surprisingly well-attended and appreciated, and some *decisions for Christ* were being made.[18]

Another year came and, not knowing of any available evangelist, we turned to the monthly magazine, <u>Christianity Today</u>, to which I subscribed. It listed the names of three or four such speakers, and the first one was "Anderson" of Tele-Missions International. From what little was said about him, it was decided to ask him come to Rockland. We were almost surprised that he answered our invitation so quickly and positively. The show was on! Dr. Gordon Anderson was scheduled, came, and conducted one of the most successful revival campaigns the church had ever witnessed. This was also when my lifelong association with Tele-Missions International began.[19]

In September of 1969, Pastor Higgins completed fourteen years of service at Rockland. He then moved to Strafford, N.H. Of course, Mary Higgins, who had spent several years teaching in the Rockland school system, also relocated with her husband.

William "Bill" Atkinson, chairman of the board of deacons, conducted a farewell reception for the Higgins and noted the accomplishments during Rev. Higgins' tenure. The church school increased and there had been much growth among adults. A new parsonage was acquired, and a large amount of property adjacent to the church was purchased. Also at the reception were Rev. George Miller, a close personal friend of Rev. Higgins and pastor at North Abington Baptist Church, and Rev. Douglas Auld of Weymouth Baptist Church. Also, Rev. John Scheibly, representing Old Colony Baptist Convention, brought their best wishes. Rockland would no longer be the same community with the absence of its beloved Pastor Higgins.

The Higgins family relocated to Strafford, New Hampshire, a community just west of Portsmouth. This change, they hoped, would result in some slowdown of the pace they had been keeping. At almost 60 years of age, Rev. Howard Higgins was deserving of such. However, the Lord had other plans, and Higgins' ministry was yet needed.

Howard Higgins soon found himself pastoring not one, but three parishes: Third Baptist Church of Strafford, Bow Lake Baptist Church, and Crown Point Baptist Church. Howard's son, Bob Higgins, remembers that his Dad managed to conduct Sunday morning services at all three churches, every week!

At Bow Lake Baptist Church, Higgins engaged himself in adding a new classroom wing.

At Third Baptist Church in Center Strafford, he led in the construction of a new Christian Education Building. At the wooded grove beside the church, Easter sunrise services were held for several years. Here, a "Memorial Altar" was built in honor of Pastor Higgins following his passing.

In 1971, Rev. and Mrs. Higgins were invited to participate in a pulpit exchange with a pastor serving the Stuart Road Baptist Church in Liverpool, United Kingdom for a month.

For ten years they labored in this community. A newspaper article from the *New Hampshire Sunday News*, datelined January 6th [1979?], notes the following:

> In this rural area, which is more than 60 percent unchurched ... touching people is of great significance. ... under his leadership the churches have distinct and unique ministries. ... students at a nearby academy where he serves as friend and counselor ... correctional programs ... fine midweek Christian education program for youth and adults.[20]

Higgins' downplay of all of this, and in his "resonant but quiet" voice states,

> I am convinced that the laity are most influential in helping others come to Christ when they are excited about the church and their commitment with others.[21]

At the end of the year 1978, the humble minister, Pastor Higgins, was thrust into national attention when the National Board of American Baptist Churches selected him from about five thousand small town pastors to receive their annual Rosa O. Hall Award for outstanding work in the "Town and Country" church. Effectively, this award is acknowledging Rev. Howard Higgins as the best town and country Baptist pastor they could find in the United States. Congratulations to a well deserving preacher!

In 1978, Pastor Higgins, together with the former pastor of the First Baptist Church of North Abington, Rev. George Miller, who had also retired to Ossipee, N.H., together with Rev. Greta Dow, opened and made extensive repairs on the First Baptist Church of Ossipee, Wakefield and

First Baptist Church, Ossipee, N.H. - *[Image: John Phelan (https://commons.wikimedia.org/wiki/File:First_Free_Will_Baptist_Church,_Ossipee_NH.jpg), „First Free Will Baptist Church, Ossipee NH", cropped by Steve Robbins, https://creativecommons.org/licenses/by-sa/3.0/legalcode]*

Effingham. This building had not been maintained, and it sat unused for many years. Repairs were accomplished, including the reconstruction of its badly-deteriorated granite block foundation. They succeeded in having the building placed on the National Register of Historic Places. Worship was conducted there during the summer months.

Howard and Mary Higgins also continued restoring their farmhouse home to what it was in the 1800s. Alongside the house, they also tended their garden.

In April of 1979, Rev. Higgins resigned as minister of the three churches, completing ten years with them. Mary resigned from teaching English and language arts at the local elementary school. Their intent was to retire to their New Hampshire farm in Wakefield, a home built in the 1870s and now restored by them.

It has been said that good preachers never retire but only continue in ministry. One month following "retirement," Howard Higgins found himself "temporarily filling-in" at the New Hampton Community Church. Evidently, he enjoyed being back in

The New Hampton Community Church
New Hampton, New Hampshire

The Reverend Howard B. Higgins, B.D., Minister

Bulletin cover, New Hampton Community Church (N.H.)
(courtesy of Robert Higgins)

the pulpit preaching, as he accepted their invitation to be their official "part-time" pastor. This ministry Pastor Higgins fulfilled well, until the Lord *called him home* on the 14th of February in 1981.[22] Medically, the cause was an apparent heart attack, possibly brought on by his diabetes. His body was laid to rest in the family space at the Walnut Grove Cemetery in Danvers, Massachusetts.[23] Mary Higgins passed away on July 31, 2017, at 97 years of age.[24]

Rural New Hampshire (and rural New England, in general) sometimes seem almost forgotten corners of American civilization. Yet their people are vibrant with life and the desire to restore community life to the better way it used to be. These people are a part of the fabric which makes this a desirable area for many. Although "religion" for these souls often seems to be forgotten, ignored or just uninteresting, there are those like Preacher Higgins who calmly, yet directly, bring the "old fashioned" gospel back onto the scene.

Vacant churches, small churches, poor churches, run-down churches are not very attractive missions for many who have chosen ministry as a profession; instead, they aspire to lead mega-churches. Yet the call still comes –

"Send us a minister, any minister will do."

Pastor Howard Higgins

(courtesy of Robert Higgins)

Minister Higgins was not just *any* preacher, but a true and fruitful clarion of his Lord, and having a burden for the lost – the many rural souls along almost-forgotten by-ways.

At one of the "This Is Your Life" programs, the emcee closed with these words:

> We read in the Scriptures – we read in history – of men who have left their mark, their impression on people and society – that have been a testimony to others – and thereby affected another life. We have seen the life of one man oftentimes responsible for the salvation of many souls. We have seen the testimony of one man oftentimes influence the choice of life's work of another. The Scriptures say, "Let our life so shine that they may see your good works and glorify your father which is in heaven." Such has been, and is continuing to be, the life of Howard B. Higgins.[25]

A real man, yes, a remarkable man.
Not just *any* Preacher!

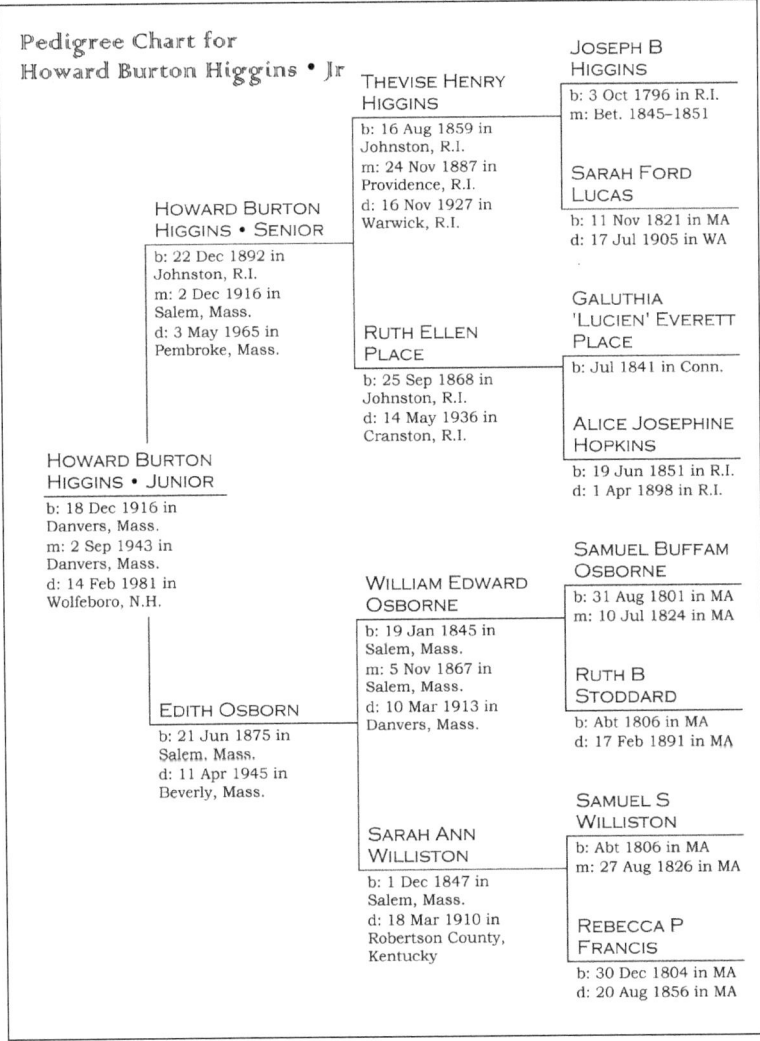

Pedigree Chart for
Howard Burton Higgins • Jr

Howard Burton Higgins • Junior
b: 18 Dec 1916 in Danvers, Mass.
m: 2 Sep 1943 in Danvers, Mass.
d: 14 Feb 1981 in Wolfeboro, N.H.

Howard Burton Higgins • Senior
b: 22 Dec 1892 in Johnston, R.I.
m: 2 Dec 1916 in Salem, Mass.
d: 3 May 1965 in Pembroke, Mass.

Edith Osborn
b: 21 Jun 1875 in Salem, Mass.
d: 11 Apr 1945 in Beverly, Mass.

Thevise Henry Higgins
b: 16 Aug 1859 in Johnston, R.I.
m: 24 Nov 1887 in Providence, R.I.
d: 16 Nov 1927 in Warwick, R.I.

Ruth Ellen Place
b: 25 Sep 1868 in Johnston, R.I.
d: 14 May 1936 in Cranston, R.I.

William Edward Osborne
b: 19 Jan 1845 in Salem, Mass.
m: 5 Nov 1867 in Salem, Mass.
d: 10 Mar 1913 in Danvers, Mass.

Sarah Ann Williston
b: 1 Dec 1847 in Salem, Mass.
d: 18 Mar 1910 in Robertson County, Kentucky

Joseph B Higgins
b: 3 Oct 1796 in R.I.
m: Bet. 1845–1851

Sarah Ford Lucas
b: 11 Nov 1821 in MA
d: 17 Jul 1905 in WA

Galuthia 'Lucien' Everett Place
b: Jul 1841 in Conn.

Alice Josephine Hopkins
b: 19 Jun 1851 in R.I.
d: 1 Apr 1898 in R.I.

Samuel Buffam Osborne
b: 31 Aug 1801 in MA
m: 10 Jul 1824 in MA

Ruth B Stoddard
b: Abt 1806 in MA
d: 17 Feb 1891 in MA

Samuel S Williston
b: Abt 1806 in MA
m: 27 Aug 1826 in MA

Rebecca P Francis
b: 30 Dec 1804 in MA
d: 20 Aug 1856 in MA

ENDNOTES

[1] "Massachusetts State Vital Records, 1841-1920," database with images, FamilySearch (https://familysearch.org/ark:/61903/1:1:23T5-K67 : 22 October 2019), Howard B Higgins, 18 Dec 1916; citing Birth, Danvers, Essex, Massachusetts, United States, certificate number 171, page 472, State Archives, Boston.

[2] "What Happened on December 18, 1916." *On This Day*. OnThisDay.com. Online: <https://www.onthisday.com/date/1916/december/18> ; accessed 25 Sep. 2020.

[3] "Walnut Grove Cemetery." [*Cemetery Register*].Legacy Mark. Online: <http://www.cemeteryregister.com/search.asp?id=MA_DANVERS> ; accessed 25 Sep. 2020.

[4] Providence Bible Institute later became Barrington College, which later merged with Gordon College.

[5] First Baptist Church of Lebanon, Connecticut originated in 1805—[<https://www.firstbaptistchurchlebanonct.org/church-history>].

[6] Author Albert Whitaker was born in Norwich, Connecticut.

[7] Wikipedia contributors, "Lebanon, Connecticut," *Wikipedia, The Free Encyclopedia*, <https://en.wikipedia.org/w/index.php?title=Lebanon,_Connecticut&oldid=979580356> ; (accessed 24 September 2020).

[8] Courtesy of Robert H. Higgins.

[9] Ibid.

[10] Ibid.

[11] Based upon a long-running television series of the same name, in which a guest was surprised, in a live and unrehearsed presentation before an audience, with their life story.

[12] A quahog *(Mercenaria mercenaria)* is a large edible clam found along North America's eastern coast and adopted as Rhode Island's official shellfish—[Wikipedia contributors. "Hard clam." *Wikipedia, The Free Encyclopedia*. Wikipedia, The Free Encyclopedia, 17 Nov. 2020. Web. 22 Nov. 2020].

[13] "Wickford Pastor To Be Ordained In Rites Tonight," *Providence Journal*, 28 Apr. 1950, p. 3. [image, GenealogyBank.com].

[14] "Pastor To Give Last Services At Wickford," *Providence Journal*, 03 Sep. 1950, p. 5. [image, GenealogyBank.com].

[15] Courtesy of Robert H. Higgins.

[16] In 1965, when we moved from Rockland to Bridgewater, we also moved our church involvement to Central Baptist Church in Middleboro (now known as The Meeting House Church). While we kept in touch with many Rockland friends, our contact with them became less frequent.

[17] Whitaker, Albert Preston Jr., Stephen Lee Robbins, and Levi Whitaker. *This Is My Story: A Story of the Whitaker Family*. (Brewer, Maine: North Wind Publishing; [Plant City, Florida]: [private distribution by Albert P. Whitaker, Junior], 2015, ©2015), p. 599.
[18] Recently, in 2008, at 91 years of age and yet to retire, Perry F. Rockwood went to be with the Lord.
[19] See Tele-Missions International: <https://telemissions.org/>. The author currently serves on the Presidents Council of Tele-Missions International. For more information on his involvement with this ministry, see his earlier books: (1) *This Is My Story* (op. cit.), p. 342-346, 411; (2) *OLIO: From Where I Sit*. (Brewer, Maine: North Wind Publishing; [Plant City, Florida]: [private distribution by Albert P. Whitaker, Junior], 2020, ©2020), p. 214-215.
[20] Courtesy of Robert H. Higgins.
[21] Ibid.
[22] "Find A Grave Index," database, FamilySearch (https://www.familysearch.org/ark:/61903/1:1:QVGY-GCXZ : 7 July 2020), Howard Burton Higgins, 1981; Burial ; citing record ID , Find a Grave, http://www.findagrave.com.
[23] Ibid.
[24] "Mary Higgins, July 31, 2017" [obituary]. Online: <https://www.edgerlyfh.com/index.cfm/obituary/mary-higgins?browse_on=desktop> ; accessed 23 April 2020.
[25] Courtesy of Robert H. Higgins.

Barry Grahl
(courtesy of Faith Spivey)

Chapter 9

Reverend BARRY LOWELL GRAHL

"17 . . . now I send thee, 18 To open their eyes, and to turn them from darkness to light, and from the power of Satan unto God, that they may receive forgiveness of sins . . ."
—*Acts 26:17b-18a (King James Version)*

In the 1600s, some Europeans desired a place to live where they could worship God in a Biblical way, which they felt had been corrupted in their homeland. Hoping to establish such a new home in North America, they endured the perils of travel by sail. A long trip through the often-angry North Atlantic seas was the only means of reaching their destination – the eastern coast of North America. Many Americans today proudly document their ancestry to passengers on the Mayflower, or on other similar ships.

During the 1700s, large groups of German people flooded into Philadelphia. Their reasons for seeking a new beginning in a new country are not entirely clear, but religious freedom was a factor. They also sought relief from the perennial ravages of conflict in Europe. This new land was reputed to offer a better life. Later, many German-Americans changed (Anglicized) their names, to avoid identification with their old homeland when it chose to be at war with America's allies.

There was an influx of Irish immigrants to the Boston area during the early 1800s, usually to escape the famine in Ireland and to seek a better life in a new country. They, too, were willing to endure the hardships accompanying such a migration.

Today, very large numbers of people from Spanish-speaking countries, like Mexico and others to the south, trek into the American Southwest to capture the better life they imagine is here. Their journey hardships, though not angry seas, are still many and dangerous, including the scaling of barriers along country borders, in desperate spurts toward a better land. Unlike Atlantic crossings, these often ignore the legal immigration provisions, which are mostly unenforced. Benefits available in the United States, far exceeding whatever they might receive elsewhere, are strong incentives for their efforts.

Our great country's advantages and benefits are like an enticing candy dish extended to the rest of the world, inviting all to come. Where once controlled with certain regulations and responsibilities, America's doors now seem open to all, regardless of how they arrive.

In researching our family's history, and the ancestry of others in which we take an interest, we are drawn back to immigrants' countries of origin. For the Grahl family, their roots are in Germany. Grahl was a Dutch-German name signifying "a maker (or merchant) of *graals* or drinking bowls."[1]

The Grahls came to America through the port of Philadelphia. While many remained in Philadelphia, others soon dispersed to more distant places. Rev. Barry Grahl's grandfather was among many others who migrated into the Upper Midwest.

Hermann Grahl, a widower, born in Germany June 13, 1862,[2] married widow Alwina (Kaschke) May, also from Germany, in Philadelphia on

> [handwritten: Alwina geb Kaschke]
>
> **The name of Alwina Kaschke**, as written in the baptism record for her son Max Carl Grahl, 25 Jan. 1900 at Tabor Evangelical Church, Philadelphia, Pa. [image: "Pennsylvania and New Jersey, Church and Town Records, 1669-2013." Ancestry.com. Ancestry indexed her name as "Aleycia Raffale" and the father's name as "Garmann Grall." Other records give more correct spelling and indexing.]

October 31, 1899.[3] They apparently remained in Philadelphia.

Their son, Carl Max Grahl, relocated to the Midwest, where he met and married Thelma Susanna Kastorff. Newly-wed and newly-ordained Rev. Carl Max Grahl became pastor of Zion Reformed Church in Freeport, Illinois in 1930, remaining there until retiring in 1970.[4]

Carl Max Grahl
(courtesy of Faith Spivey)

This church enjoyed immense growth while remaining a German-language church well into the 20th century, when 38 percent of the town spoke German. But by 2010, only 0.1 percent spoke German while 32.2 percent claimed German ancestry in the census.[5]

Freeport, in northwest Illinois and largely agricultural, hosted the 2nd Lincoln-Douglas debate of 1858.[6] It was also called "pretzel city" because its German bakery shipped pretzels across the entire Midwest.[7]

1932

Our story really begins on Saturday, July 9, 1932, shortly after the New York Stock Market had plunged to its lowest point ever, ushering in the *Great Depression*. Banks closed, companies cut jobs, unemployment grew, commerce nearly ceased.

The year 1932 was also a leap year. In May, Amelia Earhart flew across the Atlantic,[8] the first woman pilot to do so.

Also born on July 9th, 1932 was Donald Rumsfeld, who would later become a United States Secretary of State.[9]

Barry Lowell Grahl

Yet another person of significance was ushered into the world on this day – the 9th of July in 1932. Yes, even in those somewhat discouraging years, Barry Lowell Grahl was born.[10] While these

Grahl Siblings: Sylvia (left), Barry (center), Diane (right).

(courtesy of Faith Spivey)

years were not exciting for everyone, they were certainly thrilling to the Grahl family.

Two sisters later joined Barry in the Grahl home: Diane in 1934, and Sylvia in 1937.[11]

Barry spent his childhood in Freeport, Illinois, enjoying things most boys did, including playing "pick-up sticks" and "jacks" with his sisters. He spent time bowling and, best of all, fishing!

Barry Grahl graduated from Freeport High School in 1950. Soon after, he joined the Navy and went for basic training at Naval Station Great Lakes, on the shores of Lake Michigan in North Chicago, Illinois.

Barry as a young man

(courtesy of Faith Spivey)

Barry's "extra-curricular activity" led him to attend a Bible study group initiated by *The Navigators* and founded by Dawson Trotman. Trotman's Bible study emphasis was well-known throughout churches and Navy installations, for its Bible verse memory program. Here, Barry realized his need for the Savior and became a Christian. Another benefit for Barry was meeting the one who would later become his wife, Lt. Jr. Grade Ann Lemmond. She also became a Christian while attending this Bible study group.

In years to come, Barry often referred to his close association with Trotman, who ministered to many Navy groups, discipling sailors on a one-to-one basis, training them in Christian growth, Bible study and memorization.[12]

Soon thereafter, Barry was leading the Bible study at Great Lakes. He began to realize that he could dedicate himself to doing the Lord's work, while still in the Navy (and afterwards).

Here at Great Lakes, Barry became friends with another sailor, Cecil Murphey. Barry most surely had a lot to do with Murphey's conversion while at Great Lakes. Murphey became a prolific Christian writer, including for Dr. Ben Carson.[13]

Meanwhile, and after basic training, Barry was assigned to the *USS Los Angeles*,[14] a Baltimore-class heavy cruiser. After an overhaul and training, the ship re-deployed in October 1952, this time with (Seaman) Barry Grahl a member of the crew. They saw much active warfare by October, in heavy shelling of bunkers at Koji-ni and continual off-shore gunfire support of American ground operations. They cruised the Sea of Japan and participated in the bombardment of Wonsan early in 1953. They returned to Long Beach in May of 1953.[15] Barry was one of just over 1100 Navy personnel serving on this cruiser.

(right:) **Seaman Barry Grahl.**
(above:) **Barry in group photo of his ship's crew.**
(courtesy of Faith Spivey)

While aboard this ship, Barry was assigned duties as a dental technician after his instruction at the U.S. Naval Dental Technicians School at Great Lakes. He often enjoyed telling stories of his experiences. Sometimes Barry was questioned about his role, considering his ship was "at war." But everyone gets a toothache or broken tooth from time to time. And all require preventative maintenance. It is commendable that the military ministers to these needs. Barry's close attention to detail certainly enhanced the sailors' effectiveness in service.

(above:) **Barry's *Certificate of Instruction*** for successfully completing the Navy's "Dental Technician, Basic" training
(courtesy of Faith Spivey)

(below:) **Sailor Barry Grahl rests his sea legs in a foreign port**
(courtesy of Faith Spivey)

Being aboard ship was an enjoyable experience for Barry. He often told of how well he could sleep with the tossing of the sea. While he likely dreamed of casting a fishing line overboard, this would have been unrealistic on a ship engaged in warfare.

At times Barry would indicate his feelings about the official chaplain aboard the ship, then would conduct some Bible studies on his own. He felt the need to become a friend and counselor to some sailors. This was all valuable exposure and experience for his later role in the pastorate.

Ann Claire Lemmond

Ann Claire Lemmond was from Miami, Florida when she met Barry at Great Lakes. She was not in training but working in the Legal Office at the station.

Ann had graduated from Bessie Tift College,[16] in Forsyth, Georgia, 20 miles North of Macon, with a BA degree in 1951. Before joining the Navy as a commissioned officer, Ann taught at the Pisgah Forest School[17] in Brevard, North Carolina.

While in the Navy, Ann never served at sea. The closest she came to that was spending one day on a ship in Narragansett Bay, off the Quonset Point Naval Air Station in Davisville, Rhode Island, during a brief official visit there. One day!

Four generations back in Ann's family, on her mother's side, she could claim a real connection with the Civil War. Her great-great grandfather apparently owned a large farm in Abingdon, Harford County, Maryland, about 25 miles northeast of Baltimore. At that time, when Maryland was known as "a slave state," Benjamin F. Carroll had at least four slaves, according to the 1860 census.[18] It is believed these were housed and fed in exchange for performing farm duties.

Alarmingly, Ben Carroll's place was only seven miles away from the log cabin in Bel Air where John Wilkes Booth was born in 1838.[19] Booth, of course, was the well-known, wealthy and talented stage actor who assassinated U.S. President Abraham Lincoln in 1865.

On Ann's father's side, several generations were in Georgia. Her mother's side was part of the Philadelphia migration, moving to the Maryland area rather than the Midwest.

But God had His way in uniting the divergent paths when Barry L. Grahl married Ann Claire Lemmond on June 11th,[20] 1955 in Freeport, Illinois. Their courtship was unique in that the protocol of that time discouraged the fraternizing of officers with enlisted persons.

Barry and Ann often told many funny stories about how they managed to accomplish their courtship without causing any reprimands. Somehow, they made it work, possibly by not being in uniform when together. Love produces many innovations!

To some, their marriage in Barry's hometown, instead of in Ann's Miami, was an unusual breaking of tradition. To understand this, it needs to be noted that Barry's Dad was the natural one to officiate at the wedding ceremony.

Asheville Citizen-Times (Asheville, North Carolina), 11 March 1955, page 6. *[Newspapers.com]* (Used with permission from Asheville Citizen-Times.)

MISS ANN CLAIRE LEMmond, former faculty member of the Pisgah Forest School, is engaged to Barry Lowell Grahl, son of the Rev. and Mrs. Carl M. Grahl of Freeport, Ill. Miss Lemmond is the daughter of Mr. and Mrs. Millard G. Lemmond of Miami, Fla. The wedding is planned for June 11.

Reverend Carl Max Grahl seldom left Freeport, Illinois and probably would not travel so far away from his church, all the way to Miami. He was also well-known for his frugality, and would probably balk at spending the money to travel. The only exception to his tight financial fist was in his purchasing beef – the most expensive cuts – obtained at the local butcher shop. A former parishioner described him as staunch in his belief in reverence inside the church. That parishioner also described how Barry's father once – and from the pulpit – requested his wife to remove his young

Ann and Barry have a successful day of fishing
(courtesy of Faith Spivey)

son (Barry) from the service. This must have worked, as Barry became a pastor himself!

Grand Rapids Baptist Theological Seminary and Bible Institute {1955-1961}

After their wedding, Barry and Ann moved to Grand Rapids, Michigan where Barry could enroll in a five-year theology program at Grand Rapids Baptist Theological Seminary and Bible Institute.

Ann's former teaching experience helped her get a job teaching school in Grand Rapids while Barry was in seminary.

During his time at seminary, Barry also worked at several jobs. One was making furniture as an apprentice carpenter. He was also employed at Joppes Ice Cream[21] factory, where he often sampled the product! Many who knew Barry understood why he was a better "taster" than a carpenter!

Simultaneously, Barry and Ann began adding to their family, at the rate of one child per year:

    i. *Daniel Carl*, born October 6, 1956
    ii. *Faith Ann*, born December 15, 1957
    iii. *Timothy Gordon*, born November 7, 1958

Barry graduated from seminary in 1961. Now, with Seminary complete and three young children, it was time to become engaged in his chosen work as a pastor. This was the time to start that endeavor.

Laymen seldom understand the stress of this process, nor appreciate what excitement it can

Barry Grahl (in graduation cap & gown) with children, 1961.
(children, left-to-right:) **Faith Grahl, Timothy Grahl, Daniel Grahl.**
(courtesy of Faith Spivey)

foster. Tension mounts as one makes contact with churches having vacant pulpits and needing a pastor. Important considerations include:

- *why the previous minister left, and*
- *circumstances of the exit;*
- *the opportunity for growth;*
- *where one might take up residence;*
- *the interview and selection process;*
- *salary, and a host of other things.*

How many contacts, interviews, "test sermons" and investigations that were involved for Barry Grahl may never be known. Would the candidate be chosen from a list of other candidates?

Green Corners Baptist Church, Belding, Michigan
{1962-1964}

The *bottom line* was this: In 1962, the Grahl family were issued and accepted a call to the Green Corners Baptist Church in Belding, Mich. This had to be excitement in the *first degree*, but it also carried a very humbling responsibility. It is recognized that pastors learn more by doing than by all the seminary study they had in preparation. This was about to happen.

Belding, a town of about six thousand souls, is about in the center Michigan's lower peninsula, or in the "palm" of its mitten-like shape. It lies about twenty- five miles

Barry Grahl
(courtesy of Faith Spivey)

Grahl Family in winter

(courtesy of Faith Spivey)

northeast of Grand Rapids. In the late 1800s, Belding was a major silk manufacturing town.[22]

The Grahl's left Green Corners Baptist Church in 1964, when Barry accepted a call to the Broadway Baptist Church in Muskegon, Mich. He ministered there for the next five years.

Broadway Baptist Church, Muskegon, Michigan {1964-1969}

While at Muskegon, Barry used a borrowed boat to take each of his three children fishing, one at a time. Daughter Faith recalls going outside the night before with a flashlight, looking for "nightcrawler" worms for bait. Equally memorable was watching her father clean the newly-caught fish, preparing them for mother to cook for their dinner. As a pastor, Barry never neglected giving much attention to his family.

(above:) **Barry Grahl holds a big one that *didn't* get away**
(below:) **Barry, Ann and three kids**
(courtesy of Faith Spivey)

Near the end of his Muskegon assignment, in 1969, Barry was able to make a never-to-be-forgotten trip to the Holy Land. Anyone, especially those who preach, need to spend some time in the very place where Jesus walked. Here, one experiences the very essence of the Scriptures and can more effectively relate Jesus' life. Barry was overjoyed to have had such experience.

Windsor Village Baptist Church, Indianapolis, Indiana {1969-1979}

For the next ten years, 1969 to 1979, the Grahl family accepted the challenge of pastoring the Windsor Village Baptist Church in Indianapolis, Indiana.

Indianapolis, affectionately called "Indy," is the capitol of Indiana, likely because it is in the central part of the state. It is known for its auto racing, the "Indy 500," and as home for Fortune 500 companies such as Eli Lilly. "Indy" also boasts the world's largest children's museum. It is also the birthplace of TV journalist Jane Pauley, late-night television show host David Letterman,[23] and former U.S. Vice President Dan Quayle.[24]

The Amazing Roger Smith[25]
{15 June 1930 – 26 October 2020}

Early in his ministry at Windsor Village, Barry and his son Dan slipped into a dark church one night, assuming they were the only ones there – until they heard organ music filling the air. Bewildered, Barry went to the sanctuary where the music rang out in full volume within the dark auditorium. Only then did he make out the form of one gleefully playing the instrument – but with no light of any description. Then, when these two men met face-to-face – only then did Barry realize that the very capable master organist was totally blind. Roger Smith became Barry's long-time associate and friend, appreciated for his education and talent in serving his Lord. Books could be written about Roger's career and his innovations in instruments that serve the sightless.

About 2002, I met Roger Smith in Warsaw, Indiana at a church attended by my daughter, Dale[26] and her husband, Steve Robbins (this book's editor). As soon as Roger learned that Plant City, Florida was our abode, he promptly inquired for the Grahls. We were pleased to relate that Barry Grahl was our current Sunday school teacher in Dover, Florida. It is amazing how people are brought together over the years, causing a repeat of the expression that *"It's a small world."* We attended Roger's teaching of a large Sunday school class and witnessed a knowledgeable, capable and scholarly presentation. His Bible reading was as though he could see normally. A short, barely-heard signal was noted, about two minutes before closing time, which prompted Smith's closing remarks. This was almost an unbelievable experience. Friendships cultivated by those in ministry often continue into the future,

K. Roger Smith
(15 June 1930 – 26 October 2020)
(courtesy Mrs. Carol Smith)

and long after the pastor moves on to another assignment.

Calvary Baptist Church, Bellefontaine, Ohio {1979-1994}

In 1979, Barry accepted a call to the Calvary Baptist Church, in Bellefontaine, Ohio, about forty-five miles northwest of Columbus. This church, chartered April 1st, 1931 and in its fourth building, was already planning a large expansion.

Bellefontaine, meaning "beautiful spring" in French, is correctly pronounced as "Bell-Fountain." The city's largest employer is Honda, making motorcycles. Here, in 1891, the first concrete street in the nation was placed. The renowned author and preacher, Norman Vincent Peale, had his first pastorate here, at First United Methodist Church. Investment banker Edward Jones, Sr., founder of Edward Jones Investments, had his first brokerage here.[27]

In October 1986, Barry was given a surprise party in honor of his twenty-

June 1980 – Party for the Grahl's 25th wedding anniversary. Ann Grahl feeds cake to Barry.
(courtesy of Faith Spivey)

five years in the ministry. Several tributes were received and read, noting the high esteem in which he was held by many.

One such tribute was received from the Dady family,[28] associated with Word of Life Fellowship, Inc. It noted,

> You are the best pastor I have ever had. The reason why you are the best is because you have the balance of in-depth Bible teaching, an evangelist's heart, and an exhorting spirit with love.[29]

From the Grand Rapids Baptist Seminary came this tribute: "It was always a delight to have him in class," wrote a former professor, Victor Matthews. Some remembered him as the tall, lanky man that wore a "trench-coat" and walked fast![30]

In 1989 Pastor Grahl, together with the former pastor of Calvary Baptist Church, John Wood, and the mayor of Bellefontaine, Richard Vicario, celebrated the payment of the church's indebtedness by burning the mortgage on Sunday morning, November 5, 1989. This was also the beginning of additional construction and remodeling of the facilities. This was to accommodate the growth and development of the church's ministries, under Barry Grahl's leadership.

Again, Barry never lost sight of his family responsibilities. Daughter Faith remembers well his taking them bowling on a Friday afternoon, after advising his secretary: "Don't call me today or tomorrow unless somebody dies." She adds, "I felt so special to have my Dad's uninterrupted time!"

(above:) **Barry & granddaughter Heather Glerum gardening.**
(below:) **Surprise 60th birthday party for Rev. Grahl at his office on 9 July 1992.** *(photos courtesy of Faith Spivey)*

When, in 1994, Barry Grahl felt the Lord had other areas to challenge him, he and Ann retired from Bellefontaine and moved to Plant City, Florida. Other considerations also helped in making that decision. Barry and Ann wanted to be nearer to their children and grandkids, who had migrated from the Midwest to Georgia and Florida. And they were responding to the call of warmer weather.

First Baptist Church, Dover, Florida {1994-2016}

The Grahls soon found fellowship at the First Baptist Church at Dover, Florida, and Barry filled-in at several area churches for a time. He accepted a position to teach the adult mixed Sunday School class. Barry's class quickly became popular, and he taught it masterfully.

This church had an outreach ministry at "The Oaks," an extensive mobile home park nearby; services were conducted there each Sunday. When an associate pastor, who had been ministering there, decided to retire, Barry assumed the position. For many years, Preacher Grahl was The Oaks' beloved pastor, even to its winter residents of other faiths. He was kept busy as an associate pastor at Dover, as minister at "The Oaks," teaching Sunday school, and visiting sick and shut-in folks.

This real Preacher would often preach on *forgiveness*, as his daughter recalls. Possibly in the Grahl household that may have been a requirement!

When Barry was asked to fill-in for the regular minister on occasion, his sermons were notably well-prepared, and deliberately presented by a divinely inspired and seasoned professional. Barry would spend more than an hour each morning, alone with his God, in study of the Scriptures and in prayer. If you knew Barry, or were in any way a part of his world, you could be sure you were included in his intercession with his Lord.

Extended Grahl family, 15 October 2011 at Dover, Florida. *(left-to-right:)* **Rev. Barry Grahl, Faith (Grahl) Spivey, David Spivey, Hunter Spivey, Ann Grahl, friend Norma (Smith) Whitaker, Karen Grahl, Tim Grahl.** *(author's collection)*

While keeping as busy in his retirement, one of Barry's relaxing diversions was assembling large interlocking picture puzzles. Puzzle pieces were almost always spread across the dining room table. At any time on any given day, Barry could pause to put another piece in place, on his way by, between the kitchen and his lounge chair in the living room and his "snappy-nappie."

Barry Grahl's puzzle-solving passion becomes even more interesting, because he insisted that he was color blind. This meant he had to fix these "broken pictures" mainly by shape, not by color.

Despite his color-blindness, Barry was cleared to serve in the Navy. He often told of how, when he joined the Navy, he managed to pass a certain color vision test, which is used to detect color blindness. It was likely the Pseudoisochromatic Plate, or PIP test, where one had to correctly identify the colors on 12 of 14 plates to pass. Somehow, Barry had obtained a copy of that test in advance. He memorized it by order so that, when actually given the exam, he correctly identified enough colors to be accepted for ship duty.

Barry noted that, although his color-blindness was an inconvenience at times, he usually "got along fine." Because present-day computer-based vision testing is far more reliable, he might not have succeeded in qualifying today.

Over the years, Barry Grahl had apparently learned "colors" by other physical characteristics. The identification of birds he mastered by shape, movement and markings; traffic lights, by position; automobile colors, by who drove them! It was apparent that Ann most often "laid out" his clothing so that he would avoid a mis-matched pair!

Barry always knew the color yellow when served a lemon merengue pie, or red for strawberries. But a red velvet cake might confuse him! He completed puzzles rapidly, then it was on to another one. Some problems occurred when guests were invited to dinner and the table had to be set. Apology necessary? Oh yes – Barry's sometimes-discarded shoes had to be retrieved from under the table. His children often noted that he only required four pair of shoes: one black, one brown, one tennis and one work shoe. Many times, he simply wore his stockings when home, likely discarding shoes during puzzle-solving.

Barry was neither a very good, nor qualified, *handyman*; he usually had others do this type of thing around his home or automobile. His boys, and even his daughter, were sometimes called upon to do many of the simple mechanical tasks.

Credit has to be given for Barry's grand effort to paint the exterior of their retirement house. There was some discussion about the paint color which he had purchased and applied. Only a couple of years later, Ann insisted in selecting a more appropriate paint color for another application. With this, Barry also performed well, even to the manipulation of the ladder. No bucket of paint was upset, as far as anyone knew.

During Barry's retirement years, he often viewed *National Geographic* television documentaries, paying close attention to any about the ocean (and fishing!).

Because Ann's Navy career and Barry's sailing on the great oceans had instilled within them a thrill and love of the seas, they made time very often to take cruises to many places. They enjoyed at least fifty-two vacation cruises and met a host of people from several countries, some of whom became lifelong friends. The pastor in Barry was evident as he sought out, and talked with, many a traveler. And he loved the rocking of the waters!

A walk around his Plant City neighborhood was part of Barry's daily routine. Along the way, he spoke to all he saw, and stopped to talk with others. Barry was the chaplain of the community, often responding to spoken problems or family concerns. As he always did, he walked with long strides and freely swinging arms, head high and not expecting to miss anything. Once back home, Barry rested in his lounge chair and fell asleep eating his favorite popcorn. Often the small family dog found fellowship in his lap. Then, when it was time to assist Ann with "supper," he set up his grill to prepare some fish fillet or steak – only real charcoal please; no gas flames to spoil the flavor. After dinner had settled, a big bowl of ice cream, please!

Here was a pastor-preacher who really enjoyed life, thankful to his God for every experience. Even when some experiences were less-than-enjoyable, especially during tragedy within his own family, Barry Grahl's unwavering trust in the sovereign will of God prevailed, helping him to comfort and strengthen those involved.

This author was impressed when, together with Barry, we had almost daily hospital visits with a Sunday school class member who was spending his last days on earth. Barry always approached the patient's hospital bed in an encouraging and upbeat manner, saying "I have good news for you." Barry then read a carefully-selected Bible verse printed on a small piece of paper, which he then left at the bedside. Barry's prayers were strong, forward-looking, and encouraging; they were obviously appreciated very much by this suffering gentleman.

Attending Busch Gardens, or other theme parks, was another of Barry Grahl's enjoyments. He loved the thrill of riding a roller coaster. Not many years before his passing he rode on a rather large roller coaster, which "disgusted" his wife, Ann. But at the same time, he never ignored an opportunity to witness for his Savior. Barry lived his faith to the fullest, and we know he was welcomed into Heaven with "Well done, good and faithful servant." That time came in his eighty-third year, on a Monday, April 25th, 2016.[31]

Among Pastor Barry Grahl's good and lasting friends were the Rev. and Mrs. Rolla Utley. Polly,

Plant City, Florida friends, 8 August 2008
(left-to right:) **Al Whitaker, Norma Whitaker, Rev. Rolla Utley, Polly Utley, Ann Grahl and Rev. Barry Grahl.** *(author's collection)*

as she often did for others, wrote a special piece of poetry to be read at Barry's funeral (see Appendix F). Also, an interesting letter, written by Barry's physician, Dr. Christopher M. Berchelmann, M.D., is included in Appendix G.

A preacher? God produced an outstanding one in the person of Barry Grahl. His family, his churches, his friends, his community, and even his personal physician appreciated his outstanding life and testimony.

Please all stand!

The first "home" of the First Baptist Church, Dover, Florida, completed and dedicated 28 June 1914.
[First Baptist Church (Dover, Fla.). *History of First Baptist Church: Dover, Florida ; 1904-1988*. (Dover, Fla: The Church, 1988), p. 46. Image: eBay.com; edited.]

Pedigree Chart for Barry Lowell Grahl • Reverend

BARRY LOWELL GRAHL • REVEREND
b: 9 Jul 1932 in Freeport, IL
m: 11 Jun 1955 in Freeport, IL
d: 25 Apr 2016 in Plant City, FL

- **CARL MAX GRAHL • REVEREND**
  b: 3 Oct 1900 in Philadelphia, PA
  d: 28 Apr 1980 in Freeport, IL
  - **HERMANN GRAHL**
    b: 13 Jun 1862 in Germany
    m: 31 Oct 1899 in Philadelphia, PA
    d: 13 Jan 1915 in Philadelphia, PA
  - **ALWINA KASCHKE**
    b: 10 Aug 1873 in West Prussia [Germany]
    d: 31 Jan 1955 in Philadelphia, PA

- **THELMA SUSANNA KASTORFF**
  b: 13 Jul 1899 in Eden, WI
  d: Apr 1989
  - **MAX KASTORFF**
    b: 25 Mar 1859 in Germany
    m: 27 Mar 1883 in Fond du Lac County, WI
    d: 23 Sep 1945 in Fond du Lac, WI
    - **JOACHIM "JOSEPH" KASTORFF**
      b: 1831 in Germany
    - **FRIEDERICKA TIEDEMANN**
      b: 1833 in Germany
      d: 1922 in WI
  - **PAULINA FINDLING**
    b: 6 Feb 1864 in Theresa, WI
    d: 11 May 1947 in Fond du Lac, WI
    - **PHILIP FINDLING**
      b: 1828 in Germany
      d: 1912 in Bonners Ferry, ID
    - **SUSANNA JAEGER**
      b: 1827 in Germany
      d: 1877 in Dodge County, WI

ENDNOTES

[1] "Last name: Grahl," *The Internet Surname Database,* Name Origin Research, ©2017. Web: <https://www.surnamedb.com/Surname/Grahl> ; accessed 29 Sep. 2020.

[2] This date is probably from private family papers. His death certificate gives a birth date of 24 June 1865—["Pennsylvania, Philadelphia City Death Certificates, 1803-1915," database with images, FamilySearch (https://familysearch.org/ark:/61903/3:1:S3HT-67B3-ZR2?cc=1320976&wc=9FRM-T38%3A1073208301 : 16 May 2014), 004009402 > image 370 of 567; Philadelphia City Archives and Historical Society of Pennsylvania, Philadelphia.]

[3] "Pennsylvania Civil Marriages, 1677-1950," database with images, FamilySearch (https://familysearch.org/ark:/61903/3:1:S3HT-6QYR-CC?cc=2466357&wc=QDNG-MP7%3A1588753668%2C1588753697 : 30 January 2017), Philadelphia > Marriage licenses, no 118200-118699, 1899 > image 201 of 1686; citing the Register of Wills Offices from various counties.

[4] "Rev. Carl M. Grahl" [obituary], *Register Star* (Rockford, Illinois), Wednesday, 30 Apr. 1980, p. 3. [Image, GenealogyBank.com]. "... pastor of Zion Church, Freeport, until retiring in 1970 ..."

[5] "Freeport, IL Demographic Data," *neighborhoodscout.com*, Location, Inc., ©2020. Web: <https://www.neighborhoodscout.com/il/freeport/demographics>; accessed 29 Sep. 2020.

[6] "History of Freeport," *City of Freeport, Illinois*, City of Freeport, ©2005. Web: <https://cityoffreeport.org/about/freeporthistory.htm>; accessed 29 Sep. 2020.

[7] Wikipedia contributors, "Freeport, Illinois," *Wikipedia, The Free Encyclopedia*, Wikipedia, The Free Encyclopedia, 27 Jun. 2020. Web. 26 Sep. 2020.

[8] "What Happened on July 9, 1932," On This Day, OnThisDay.com, ©2020. Web: <https://www.onthisday.com/date/1932/july/9> ; accessed 29 Sep. 2020.

[9] Ibid.

[10] "Barry Lowell Grahl" [obituary], *Plant City Times & Observer* (Plant City, Florida), Friday, 06 May 2016. [Image, GenealogyBank.com]. Includes birth date: "July 9, 1932."

[11] Carl Grahl household, 1940 U.S. Census, Freeport, Stephenson County, Ill., p. 8b, [image, FamilySearch.org]. Sylvia K. (Grahl) Seagrin is now living in Grand Junction, Colorado.

[12] Trotman died attempting to save another in a boating incident on Schroon Lake in June 1956.

[13] After the Navy, Murphey became pastor of a church in Atlanta and a volunteer hospital chaplain for ten years. Murphey followed this with missionary service for six years in Kenya. Thereafter, Cecil Murphey developed a brilliant and prolific writing career, which has included most of Dr. Ben Carson's many books, as "the man behind the words."

During Barry Grahl's future years in ministry, he also enjoyed fellowship with other well-known Bible expositors, including James T. Jeremiah (father of Turning Point's Dr. David Jeremiah) and Warren Wiersbe.

[14] The *U.S.S. Los Angeles* was built in Philadelphia and originally commissioned 22 July 1945. In 1948, the ship was decommissioned and entered the Pacific Reserve Fleet. For the next four years, it was in operations along the Korean Peninsula with its heavy guns engaged against enemy coastal positions. It had also engaged in operations at Guantanamo Bay, Cuba and along the coast of China. The USS Los Angeles was returned to the States for overhaul and training early in 1951.

[15] Wikipedia contributors. "USS Los Angeles (CA-135)." *Wikipedia, The Free Encyclopedia*. Wikipedia, The Free Encyclopedia, 27 Jun. 2020. Web. 26 Sep. 2020.

[16] At the time, Bessie Tift College was one of the nation's oldest women's colleges. It closed in 1986. Since 2010, it is headquarters for the Georgia Department of Corrections.

[17] "Miss Ann Claire Lemmond," *Asheville Citizen-Times* (Asheville, N.C.), Fri., 11 Mar. 1955, p. 6.

[18] Benjamin F Carroll 1860 U.S. Federal Census - Slave Schedules, Abingdon, Harford County, Maryland, p. 6. [image, Ancestry.com].

[19] Wikipedia contributors. "Harford County, Maryland." *Wikipedia, The Free Encyclopedia*. Wikipedia, The Free Encyclopedia, 20 Sep. 2020. Web. 27 Sep. 2020.

[20] "Miss Ann Claire Lemmond," *Asheville Citizen-Times*, op. cit.

[21] Now known as Buth-Joppes Ice Cream Company.

22 "Belding Museum and City History," *City of Belding*, City of Belding, Michigan, ©2020. Web: <https://belding.mi.us/museum_history.php> ; accessed 29 Sep. 2020.

[23] Wikipedia contributors. "Indianapolis." *Wikipedia, The Free Encyclopedia. Wikipedia*, The Free Encyclopedia, 27 Sep. 2020. Web. 29 Sep. 2020.

[24] "J. Danforth Quayle, 44th Vice President (1989-1993)," *United States Senate*. Web: <https://www.senate.gov/about/officers-staff/vice-president/VP_Dan_Quayle.htm> ; accessed 29 Sep. 2020.

[25] K. Roger Smith, born 15 June 1930 in Wabash, Ind., son of Russell & Helen (Coblentz) Smith. He m. (1st) Mary Jo (   ) on 22 Aug. 1955 [she d. 1993]; Roger m. (2nd) Carol (Easter) 6 Aug. 2002. Roger d. 26 Oct.

2020 in Warsaw, Ind.—["K. Roger Smith." [obituary], *Times-Union Online* (Warsaw, Ind.), Tue., 27 Oct. 2020, 5:16 PM. Web: <https://timesuniononline.com/Content/Obituaries/Obituaries/Article/K-Roger-Smith/75/337/129667>. ; accessed 28 October 2020.]

[26] Dale also played the organ at the Pleasant View Bible Church in Warsaw, Indiana.

[27] Wikipedia contributors. "Bellefontaine, Ohio." *Wikipedia, The Free Encyclopedia*. Wikipedia, The Free Encyclopedia, 27 Jul. 2020. Web. 29 Sep. 2020.

[28] Ken Dady is currently the "International Coach for Word of Life to Missionaries and Local Churches"—[" Get to Know the Dady Family," *Word of Life*, Word of Life Fellowship. Web: <https://give.wol.org/kdady> ; accessed 27 Sep. 2020.

[29] Courtesy of Faith (Grahl) (Schmitt) Spivey.

[30] Ibid.

[31] "Barry Lowell Grahl" [obituary], *Plant City Times & Observer* (Plant City, Florida), Friday, 06 May 2016. [Image, GenealogyBank.com].

Chapter 10

Reverend WILLIAM HOWARD STONE Senior

"And we know that all things work together for good to them that love God, to them who are the called according to his purpose." —Romans 8:28 (King James Version)

Have you ever heard of "Northeast Overshoe"? This expression, used by some old-timers, denoted an obscure place, vaguely somewhere, which they'd never visited. But they'd assign "Northeast Overshoe" as the place of origin for someone else they came across.

It is probably true that the majority of people living in New England, and likely in Massachusetts, have never heard of the village of Montague City, Massachusetts. Some would recognize "Montague" as descriptive of gold mines in Nova Scotia, Canada. Others with a more scientific background might remember it as a minor planet or asteroid orbiting the sun.

Actually, Montague City is one of five villages within the town of Montague, founded way back in 1792 when the small village split from Sunderland and began with a grist mill. It had been settled by some enterprising German immigrants. A series of canals and locks were developed to access the Connecticut River for northerly commerce. Great expectations were short-lived and Montague City never achieved the success it had anticipated. By 1885, it became well-

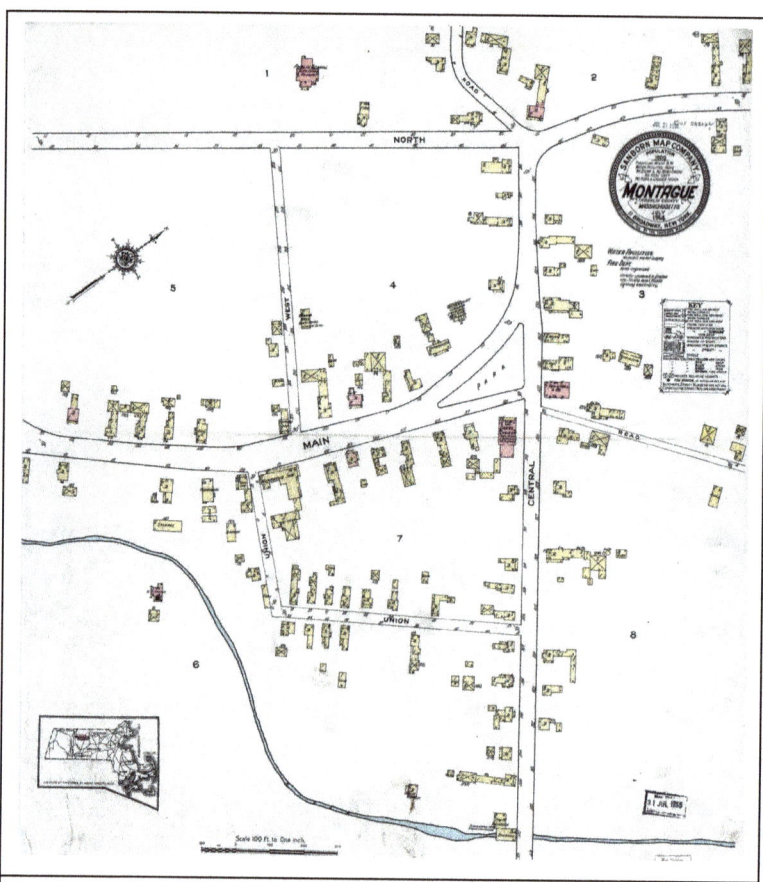

Bill Stone's home village, Montague City, Mass., July 1914
<u>Sanborn Fire Insurance Map from Montague, Franklin County, Massachusetts</u>. (New York, N.Y.: Sanborn Map Company, July 1914. [Map]. *(Retrieved from the Library of Congress, https://www.loc.gov/item/sanborn03797_001/ . Edited)*

known as the home of Montague Rod and Reel Company, makers of the world-famous split bamboo fishing rods. This city was thought to be the place where a stately maple tree inspired Joyce Kilmer to pen the famous poem "Trees", during a time he visited Farren Hospital.[1] Today, a hydroelectric generating facility, Cabot Station, and the well-known Northeast Anadromous Fish Research Center are located in this obscure village.

On November 24th, 1940, just days after Franklin Roosevelt was re-elected President, Dorothy (Hillock) Stone gave birth to William Howard Stone [Senior], to the delight of her husband Howard Stone, at Farren Hospital, in the

**Bill Stone's birthplace –
Farren Memorial Hospital, Montague City, Massachusetts**
(post card, circa 1910; ebay.com; edited)

village of Montague City. "Bill" was the first of what would become a family of six, born to Howard and Dorothy Stone. Did they give any thought at that juncture as to what young "Bill's" life would be like? If typical of most births, such future thinking was not the immediate consideration of the day. Looking back over "a life well-lived", we can report that his life has left an indelible mark on multitudes of people, including many who are, or will become, eternal inhabitants of Heaven. Bill Stone became God's messenger, faithfully heralding the message which God called him to *preach.*

That specific "call" to serve his God, wherever He led, came fifteen years later. Because a devastating fire had destroyed his family's farm, the house and seven other buildings, Bill was spending the night at Northfield with pastor Paul Bubar, who was in the process of planting the Northfield Baptist Church. That fire prompted local churches to provide housing, clothing and food for the displaced Stone family. Thus, it was to the Bubar home that Bill had been directed. The fire – its traumatic events and totality – along with this Providence Bible Institute[2] student pastor's compassionate leading, combined to influence Bill's decision, which he made upon his knees at the couch in the Bubar

Northfield [Mass.] Baptist Church, 2010
[Doug Kerr (https://commons.wikimedia. org/wiki/File:Northfield,_Massachusetts_ 9.jpg), „ Northfield, Massachusetts 9", cropped by S. Robbins, https://creativecommons. org/licenses/by-sa/2.0/legalcode]

home. Here, Bill Stone dedicated his life to full-time Christian ministry.

All of this occurred just two weeks before Bill was to leave for Hampden DuBose Academy in Zellwood, Florida for his high school education. Obviously, the Stone family was unable to pay the tuition, so that debt had to remain until Bill was married and in the working world.

While at DuBose, Bill had the privilege to meet leading evangelists and Bible teachers, including Vance Havner, Dr. M. R. DeHaan, Ruth Graham and Redd Harper.

Ewell Hall, Hampden Dubose Academy, Zellwood, Florida, circa 1942
(Retrieved from Florida Memory.com; ID n044937; edited)

During Bill's senior year at DuBose, his roommate was Don Wyrtzen,[3] the son of evangelist Jack Wyrtzen who had founded the Word of Life ministry.

When Christmas break came, and Bill's finances prevented his travelling home to Massachusetts, the school's president, Dr. Pierre DuBose, gifted him with a leather-bound *Scofield Reference Bible*.[4]

1917 ed. *(wikimedia.org)*

After Bill's graduation in 1960, and with the aid of Don Wyrtzen, Bill received an invitation from Chris Williams, chief of staff at Word of Life Camps, to work the summer there as a camp counselor. This was located on a 90-acre island in Schroon Lake, high in the Adirondack Mountains in upstate New York, and far from Florida.

Together with three other high school boys, and Chris Williams, Bill occupied the only winterized building on the grounds. The four young men formed a quartet which sang in local churches. Bill became an assistant business manager, working with Paul Keller, Fred Scharman, plus Jack Wyrtzen and Harry Bollback. Thereafter, Bill traveled to and from Orange, New Jersey seasonally, to move the Word of Life Bookstore to and from Schroon Lake. Each spring, Bill worked at Harry Norman's nursery in Connecticut, preparing the plants used to beautify the Word of Life Inn.

Since there was no gospel-preaching church in Schroon Lake at that time, on Sundays the young men traveled about eighteen miles with Chris Williams, to attend the First Baptist Church of Ticonderoga.

Ticonderoga, located at the north end of Lake George, and with a portion of Lake Champlain, has much historical significance as the setting for historical battles of the French and Indian Wars (and the construction of Fort Ticonderoga), and the American Revolutionary War. In the early 1800s they began graphite mining, later providing No. 2 HB pencil lead. Another item of interest to

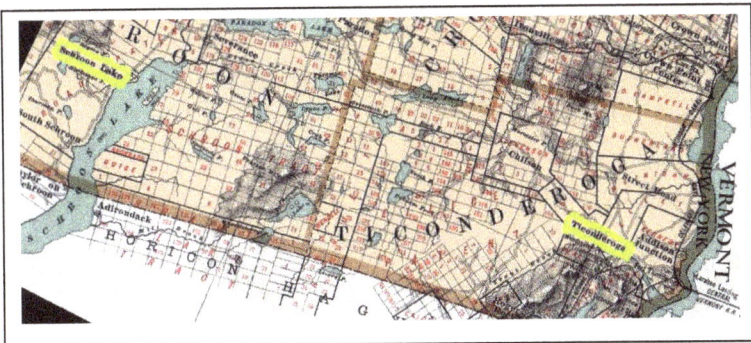

Bill from Schroon Lake met Betty in Ticonderoga, 1961
(Detail from: <u>Essex County</u> [NY] [map]. New York: Julius Bien & Company, ©1895. davidrumsey.com; edited)

our story is the separation of Ticonderoga from the town of Crown Point in 1804.

It was at this church, in 1961, that Bill first met Betty LaTour of Crown Point, New York. Possibly it was Betty's trumpet playing that first alerted Bill to her? Her sister-in-law helped make arrangements!

They became engaged the next year, and both attended the Bible Institute of New England in Hartford,

First Baptist Church of Ticonderoga, circa 1905
(oldpostcards.com; edited)

Vermont, which moved to St. Johnsbury the next year.

In Hartford, the school occupied an old New England home, a three-storied building with

Hartford, Vermont, circa 1913   (post card, ebay.com; edited)

beautiful carved woodwork. Bill worked nights at Cross, Abbott Company's, Red and White food warehouse.

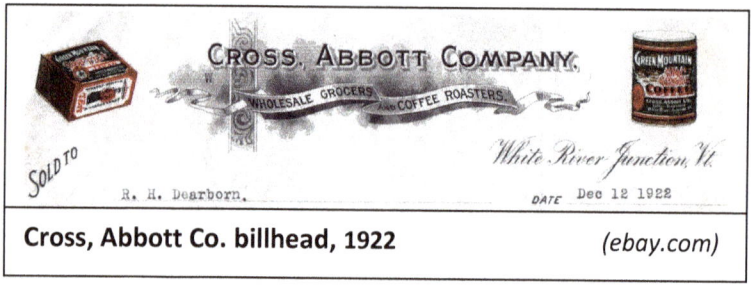

Cross, Abbott Co. billhead, 1922   (ebay.com)

On June 8, 1963, Bill and Betty were married at the **First Baptist Church of Ticonderoga**. They chose, as their lifetime Bible verse, Romans 8:28 and had it inscribed in their wedding bands.

The driving time between St. Johnsbury, Vermont and Ticonderoga, New York was about three hours. To provide financial support, Bill then worked at the A & P grocery store in St. Johnsbury.

Wedding of Betty LaTour & Bill Stone,
First Baptist Church of Ticonderoga,
June 8, 1963
(courtesy of Bill & Betty Stone; edited)

Bill continued to serve as "practical work director", and to represent the school as part of a quartet. Locally, he served on the board of "The Fold", an orphanage in Lyndonville, Vermont.

On November 22, 1963, news spread quickly of the assassination of president John F. Kennedy, shocking all at the A & P Store, and Betty at home as she hung clothes on the clothesline. The Stone's first son, Billy (William, Junior) Stone,[5] was born in St. Johnsbury, Vermont on March 12, 1964 during Bill's final exam week.

Upon his graduation in 1965, Bill Stone became the first pastor of the newly-formed Community Baptist Church in Hinesburg, Vermont. He

Hinesburg, Vermont, August 1941
(Delano, Jack, photographer. The town of Hinesburg, Vermont. *Aug. 1941. [Photograph]. Retrieved from the Library of Congress, https://www.loc.gov/item/2017795989/ . Edited)*

explained that the church could only afford a salary of $22.50 per week. To accommodate this, the Stones moved into some small rooms on the second floor of the Old Shelburne Inn, and they also worked for Dr. Goldsboro, an ear, nose and throat specialist.

Bill and Betty then moved to a mobile home in Hinesburg, and later in a two-room apartment attached to a widow lady's home. To access this apartment, one entered through a shed and passed the toilet which was under the stairs. Baths were taken in a portable copper tub.

The Community Baptist Church met in the big New England home of Dick and Myrtle Kimball.

(left-to-right:) **Betty, Bill Junior, & Rev. Bill Stone. Community Baptist Church first met at the Kimball's home, Hinesburg, Vt.** (photo dated Oct. 1965; courtesy of Bill Stone; edited)

Baptisms took place in Lake Champlain, where Bill baptized his mother-in-law, Lena LaTour.

Bill also drove bus for the Champlain Valley High School.

Champlain Valley Union High School, Hinesburg, Vermont, established 1964 (photo 24 Aug. 2006)
[User:Dismas (https://commons.wikimedia.org/wiki/File:CVU_Hinesburg_Vermont_USA.jpg), „CVU Hinesburg Vermont USA", edited by Stephen Robbins, https://creativecommons.org/publicdomain/zero/1.0/legalcode]

Soon, the Stone's second son, Bernard Daniel Stone was born on February 18, 1966 in Burlington, Vermont.

Community Baptist Church, Hinesburg, Vermont
(photo dated June 1968; courtesy of Bill Stone; edited)

By 1968, the Community Baptist Church in Hinesburg had outgrown the Kimball home. So, the congregation obtained new piece of land, erected an A-frame church building with attached parsonage, and dedicated this in 1968.

By now, Bill's pastor salary had increased to $45.00 each week. Two couples added to the Stone's monthly support, and their family helped to find clothing for their sons. Christine Sears,[6] who had assisted in building the church, has since been a missionary in Germany more than fifty years.

During the Stones' time at Hinesburg, and because Bill always enjoyed eating and fellowship, a family in the church prepared a Sunday dinner for the pastor's family every week. This was how God provided their big meal of the week. Oh yes – and another lady made them a pie every Sunday!

Bill Stone likes pie
(editor's collection)

Bill was ordained to the Gospel ministry on November 16, 1968, back at his home church in "Northeast Overshoe" –

**Stone Family portrait on their 1968 Christmas card.
Community Baptist Church, Hinesburg, Vermont**
(courtesy of Bill Stone; edited)

Turners Falls (one of the five villages within the town of Montague, Mass.).

Along the way, Betty Stone graduated from a one-year business course offered by Bob Jones University. Later, she attended The Bible Institute of New England for a year.

Baptist Church, Montague, Mass. Bill Stone's *home church*, where he was ordained 16 November 1968
(post card, circa 1910; ebay.com)

If we could "fast forward" over the next fifty-plus years, we would witness many persons, young and old, whose lives were changed for the better through Reverend Stone's ministry. Of these, a number of young people accepted the challenge to enter full-time ministry, often in far-away countries "at the ends of the earth."

In 1969, the Stones felt the call to go to Oneida, New York and start a church. But before getting there, it was the Stone family's vacation time. For a month, Bill and Betty, with sons Billy (age 5) and Dan (age 3), traveled across the country with a pop-up camper. A truck camper accompanied the Stones, carrying Betty's brother Jack, his wife Beulah and their three kids. They all got to take in the Grand Canyon, Salt Lake City, Yellowstone National Park and Mount Rushmore.

Back in Oneida, New York, the old Methodist Church building was purchased, together with a parsonage – a new home for a newly-organized congregation, the Community Bible Church. Reverend Stone's preacher salary was now $10.00 per week. This church had a large pipe organ but no one able to play it. So, the people sang without accompaniment. To help with finances, Bill drove a bus for the school district. He also began a radio program on a local station. And the Stone's large vegetable garden was of much help. And again, family provided food showers. The Stone family was thankful for the Lord's provision.

Methodist Church, Oneida, N.Y.
This became Community Bible Church about 1969
(post card, circa 1910; ebay.com)

In 1969, the Stones moved to their first established church, The First Baptist Church of Goffstown,[7] New Hampshire, located in the village of Grassmere. Bill also became chaplain of the Hillsborough County Farm, a nursing home, senior citizens home and a jail. As Bill became engaged in the community and did a lot of home visitation, this church grew substantially.

In 1971, Rev. Harold Duff[8] recommended that Bill look into four Maine churches which needed a pastor. Bill candidated at each of them. When arriving at one, he saw that some people were standing up on the pews while men were chasing a mouse with a broom!

The Stones accepted a call to the Boothbay Baptist Church later in 1971. Upon their arrival,

Boothbay [Maine] Baptist Church, interior view.
(courtesy of Bill Stone; edited)

the church provided a huge housewarming event. This supplied many needed items such as towels, sheets, a broom, a clock and many other necessities. Betty exclaimed, "Again, the Lord provided!"

Out of a new Bible study group conducted by Pastor Bill, still another new church was planted – the Victory Baptist Church of Monmouth, Maine.

From 1979 to 1988, Reverend Stone served on the board of the Conservative Baptist Churches of Maine, taking leadership as their president for three years. This position required travel to Wheaton, Illinois, and even to special meetings at Portland, Oregon. Bill was their representative at many ordination councils, and he moderated at others.

The Stones' ministry flourished at Boothbay. With ladies providing food, enthusiastic church

Boothbay Baptist Church, Boothbay, Maine
(courtesy of Bill Stone; edited)

members helped a contractor erect a new wing designed to seat three-hundred-and-fifty persons. This addition was also necessary to accommodate the forty or more seasonal visitors attending each summer. Monday night work parties were held to complete the interior finish work. Church ladies provided supper for the men. The completed structure was dedicated in 1975.

Boothbay Baptist Church became a busy and active assembly. Two buses were acquired and a bus ministry began. Both *Word of Life* and *Good News* clubs were instigated. Other activities included Bible clubs, taking kids to "The Basketball Marathons," Super Bowls and talent competition, singing, instrumental groups, storytelling, etc. Betty organized a church orchestra of teens who played for Sunday evening services. The ladies held picnics for people over fifty years old, at various homes throughout the summer.

Pastors are called upon to do baptisms, funerals, and weddings during the normal course of their pastorates. For all the importance of properly observing these life events, even the best arrangements and most detailed preparations can be susceptible to unforeseen last-minute changes. This became all too real for Pastor Bill Stone at one 1970s wedding he was prepared to conduct in Boothbay, Maine. Pastor was properly attired with

a black bow tie, had his little black book of notes in hand, and stood at the head of the church aisle. The wedding march was set to be played.

Everything appeared to be in order. Even the flowers looked happy. But the rites seemed to be delayed. The people stood, first on one foot, and then on the other. An intense quiet filled the air. Then it was realized that the groom had not yet arrived at the church. Did he get "cold feet?" Was the poor nervous bride about to be to be jilted?

The organist played on – for thirty minutes – until she ran out of music. Pastor Stone then had no choice but to dismiss all those who had gathered, promising to call them back when the groom was located.

(trade card; ebay.com; edited)

Thirty more minutes passed while the guests milled about, discussing the situation. Then suddenly, in comes the groom, tripping into church but still in full stride. All awaited his explanation.

The groom lived some distance away, in the town of Bath. His planned route to Boothbay crossed Carlton Bridge. This vertical-lift drawbridge was drawn upwards and open, every bit of the thirty minutes, for a tall ship to lazily navigate up the deep Kennebec River channel. We should be reminded that, in the 1970s, there were no cellphones to advise of his delay.

Carlton Bridge *(right)*, between Bath and Woolwich, ME, over Kennebec River. Opened in 1927, replaced in 2000 by Sagadahoc Bridge *(left)*.

(Highsmith, C. M., photographer. "Bridges, including the now-incomplete Carlton Lift Bridge over the Kennebec River in the ship-building town of Bath, Maine." *13 Sep. 2017.* [Photograph] Library of Congress, https://www.loc.gov/item/2017882599/ . Edited.)

Pastor Stone resumed the ceremony. However, the groom was so nervous that he could hardly breathe. Once again, the pastor had to stop the ceremony. The groom was instructed to pause a bit and take several deep breaths, very slowly, until he recovered. After all that, Pastor Stone finally solemnized the marriage. And all the guests took a deep breath. That was one wedding which Reverend Stone will never forget!

Many baptisms were a part of this ministry. One winter, Pastor Stone scheduled the use

Waldoboro Baptist Church's baptismal tank. The first baptism candidate who stepped into the water reacted almost in shock. The custodian had forgotten to heat the water in the tank. Even so, several candidates were baptized, including some from the Monmouth Bible study group. Although the candidates were in the frigid water only briefly, Pastor Stone emerged with very cold and numb feet! – a hazard of his profession! Later, when the Boothbay church built an addition, they installed a new, automatically-heated baptismal tank. At its inauguration, twenty-one persons were baptized. The pastor didn't get "cold feet" this time!

Impressive Easter sunrise services were conducted on the coast in Bayville, at Boothbay Harbor. Betty Stone recalls that "It was always chilly, with the sound of the waves and the sea gulls in the background." As she played the

View from Bayville Landing, Boothbay Harbor, Maine
(post card, circa 1910; ebay.com; edited)

rousing hymn "Up from the Grave He Arose"[9] on her trumpet, the sound of the singing carried all the way to the Bayville Inn, a vintage hotel owned and operated by church member Jessie Roberts. At

Bayville Inn, Bayville, Boothbay Harbor, Maine
(post card, circa 1915; ebay.com; edited)

the service's conclusion, the celebrants migrated to Jessie's establishment for a delicious breakfast.

The Boothbay church joined with Barters Island Baptist Church to form Mid-Coast Christian School, with Bill Stone as its administrator. At the dedication of the school, with a full church and a special speaker, school administrator Bill Stone had to rather pointedly request an unruly woman to cease her commotion or leave. The woman's husband reluctantly led his inebriated wife out before she escalated her antics. Oh yes – she was a member of the church, and also the mother of a Christian school student!

These were busy, eventful days in the ministries of Bill and Betty Stone. Their full story could fill many pages – all a testimony of a successful pastor and pastor's wife team, fully involved in their community. There is little doubt that many people's lives have been impacted by their witness and leading. A chorus in Heaven possibly now sings their praise.

In 1972, while still at Boothbay, the Stones bought a camp at the Vassalboro Union Camp Meeting Association, the first home they owned

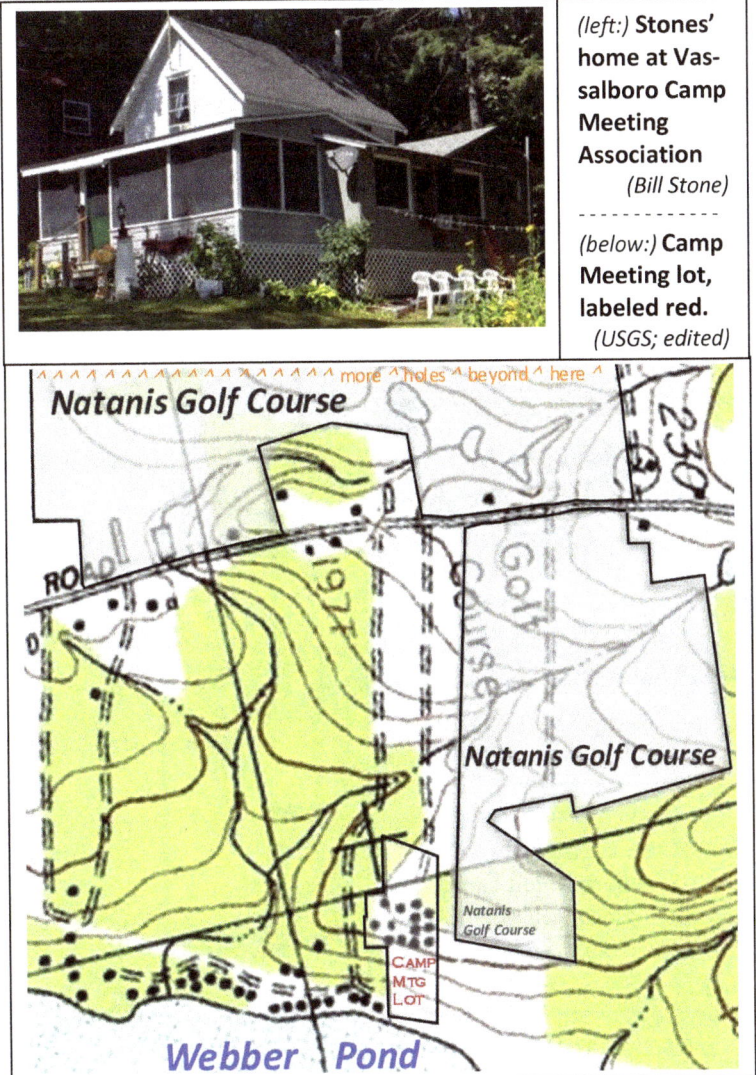

(left:) **Stones' home at Vassalboro Camp Meeting Association**
(Bill Stone)

(below:) **Camp Meeting lot, labeled red.**
(USGS; edited)

despite many years in the pastorate and living in parsonages. Bill has served this group many years as president and trustee; presently (2020) Bill is vice-president of this twelve-cottage Christian camp association, owned by pastors, missionaries and Christian leaders. An annual meeting is held during the summer to elect officers and set assessments which maintain the water well,

(above:) **Camp Meeting sign**
(Gerald Robbins 16 Sep. 2004; edited)

(right:) **Rev. Stone's home is one of the cottages on lot 51 (the Vassalboro Union Camp Meeting Association's land).** (Vassalboro (Me.). Assessor. [Tax map 7]. 2019. <http://www.vassalboro.net/property_tax_maps/Map 6.pdf>; edited)

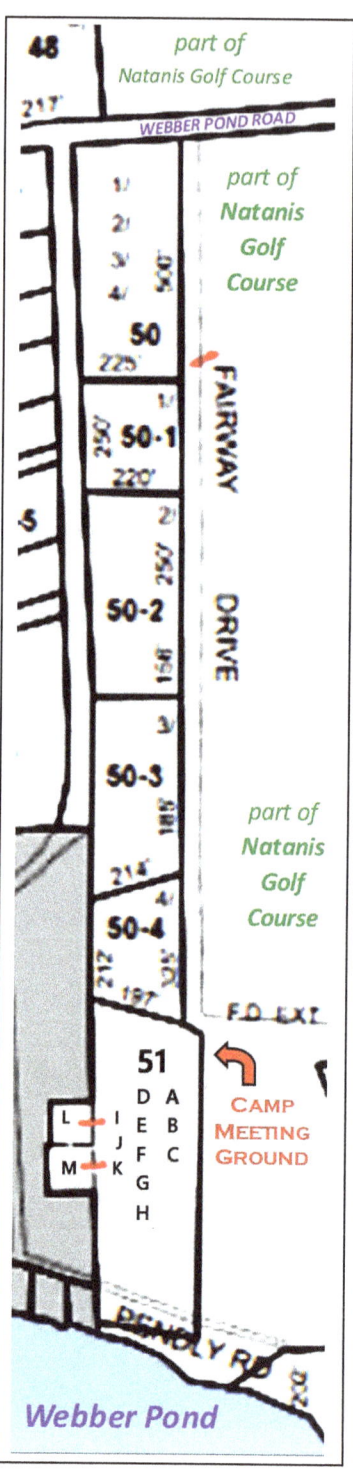

the central restrooms and the grounds. The Tabernacle is a multi-purpose building used for meetings, recreation and storage.

In the past, various Christian organizations held children's summer camps here, including the Advent Christian Church,[10] the American Mission for Opening Closed Churches,[11] and the American Baptist Convention.[12] But the dining hall / girls dormitory was removed in 1980.

On the grounds of Vassalboro Union Camp Meeting
(above:) **Memorial Chapel** **(also called the Tabernacle)**
(below:) **Several cottages**   *(Gerald Robbins, 16 Sep. 2004; edited)*

The camp meeting site, a three-and-one-third-acres "little clump of oaks, maples and elms"[13] on the knoll overlooking Webber Pond,"[14] first known as Robbins Grove, came out of Fairview Farm, owned by editor Steve Robbins' great-grandparents Ira and Lucy Robbins. Steve speculates that camp meeting founders George H. Pope and Rev. Mark Stevens[15] first spied this property about 1910, while riding the recently-built Lewiston, Augusta & Waterville Street Railway.

View to Webber Pond from Vassalboro Union Camp Meeting grounds. The utility poles, seen crossing the end of this field, follow the former electric trolley right-of-way.

(Gerald Robbins, 16 Sep. 2004; edited)

It was only in November 1908[16] that this electric trolley had begun its route along Webber Pond's western shore. The rails ran through Fairview Farm, skirting Robbins Grove. Pope and Stevens, imagining this picturesque spot's potential, signed a purchase agreement with owner Ira Robbins on 12 April 1911, for $1,050. Cottages were built or moved onto the plot, and families came by trolley from Augusta (9.5 miles) or Waterville (11.7

miles)[17] to spend weeks there in the summertime. Alma Robbins recalled,

> *"There was a large circus tent for inside Meetings in bad weather, and under Mr. Stevens' direction an amphitheater was built, with rows of seats under the trees facing down the little slope to the Pond and the covered pulpit where the preacher and the organ held sway. Often there were large crowds on a pleasant Sunday afternoon.[18] The older people could listen to the sermon and the children could be happy playing among the trees."* [19]

In the fall of 1980, the Stones transitioned to Calvary Baptist Church at Sherman Station, Maine, so that Pastor Bill could become

Calvary Baptist Church, Sherman Station, Maine.
(courtesy of Bill Stone; edited)

administrator and principal at Calvary Christian Academy in Patten, Maine. To better perform his new duties, Bill went to Dallas, Texas for Accelerated Christian Education training. The Stone's two sons, Billy and Dan, graduated from this school. They traveled with thirty of the

Billy Stone *(left)* **and Dan Stone** *(right).* **Both graduated from Calvary Christian Academy, Patten, Maine.** *(courtesy of Bill Stone; edited)*

student body on many field trips, including a memorable one to Kings Landing, a recreated living history village at Lower Prince William, New Brunswick, Canada. While ministering at Patten, Maine, Bill and Betty also taught courses at the New Brunswick Bible Institute in Victoria Corner, New Brunswick.

Patten is located in the heart of Maine's logging and potato country. From their parsonage the Stones could view impressive Mount Katahdin. Sometimes, Bill would get up at three o'clock a.m. to ride a logging truck with a church member.

Snowmobiling was one of the Stone family's experiences, often involving a troublesome machine deep in the woods and in deep snow.

The Stones once traveled a section of the "Golden Road", a 100-mile gravel road through the wilderness between Millinocket, Maine and Québec. While camping along the way, Bill and

Betty inspected various pieces of logging equipment and observed multiple moose – as many as eighteen on one trip!

Often, and with permission from the landowners, Bill and Betty Stone "gleaned" left-behind potatoes in the already-harvested fields.

When dining out, Pastor Bill usually orders baked or mashed potato, and asks the waitress to assure they'd be *Maine* potatoes. Yes, Bill makes this same request even in Florida! One memorable reply was: "I don't know, but you can assume anything that makes you happy!" Most New Englanders know that Maine potatoes have the best flavor; they are certainly in demand for making the best-tasting potato chips.

In the fall of 1983, churches in the Patten area united to hold evangelistic services, featuring a well-known Canadian evangelist, Barry Moore. Weldon Smith's potato house in Hodgdon, Maine was the "auditorium." For those unfamiliar, this

Smaller potato house, near Caribou, Maine, October 1940.
(Delano, Jack, photographer. "Potato storage barn on a field near Caribou, Maine. The earth is built up around the sides to provide a more even temperature throughout the year." October 1940. [Photograph] Retrieved from the Library of Congress, https://www.loc.gov/pictures/item/2017792134/ ; edited).

would not be unusual. Potato houses, built partly underground in the northern Maine countryside, have the largest open interiors of any local structure.

In 1984, Calvary Christian Academy's girls volleyball and boys basketball teams won state championships in the Christian school league.

As often happens to preachers, a possible move to another field presented itself. In 1984, the Stones relocated to Bowdoin, Maine in order to pastor the Bowdoin Center Baptist Church.

Bowdoin Center [Maine] Baptist Church, outside *(above)* and inside *(below)*. *(photos courtesy of Bill Stone; edited)*

In the spring of 1986, Bill and Betty Stone traveled to Israel with their good friends, Ken[20] and Pat Dutille. For a pastor, this opportunity to "walk where Jesus walked and talked" was the experience of a lifetime – simply awesome!

Pastor Bill also took on responsibilities for leading the South Monmouth Baptist Church, at Monmouth, Maine. Here he conducted and preached at both morning worship services and weekly prayer meetings. This was accomplished, in part, by fast travel between the two churches. And, yes – Bill also taught their adult Sunday school classes!

Son Billy Stone was instrumental in constructing a new church with steeple, along with – yes, even an outdoors "baptismal pool." All this was necessary to replace the old church which sat at the road's edge and lacked a septic tank, a water supply, and parking room. Generous church members donated both the land and pine boards.

In October of 1986, the Stones accepted a call to the Calvary Baptist Church in Newport, Maine.

Calvary Baptist Church, Newport, Maine

(before 1987, when the front entrance was moved to the rear).

(courtesy of Bill Stone; edited)

This was not one of the century-old churches typically found in rural Maine. Rather, it had been founded about thirty years previous. The building was originally constructed and occupied in 1965. An existing home, adjacent to the church lot, was acquired for use as the parsonage.

At one point, a unique Dumont wood boiler system was installed in an out-building (a garage-shed), from which heated water was piped into both church and parsonage. The pastor and the men of the church had to cut and split a delivered truckload of logs into stove-size firewood. It was one more responsibility for pastor and his wife – keep the boiler fire fueled and burning!

While at Newport, Pastor Bill produced devotionals for the *Open Door* television program on Bangor's Channel 5 (WABI). He also served on the town of Newport's budget committee.

The Stone family actively supported their missionary friends abroad. Overnight, on September 17-18, 1989, Hurricane Hugo destroyed the home and church of missionaries of Clif and LeEllen Bubar on the island of St. Croix in the U.S. Virgin Islands. The winds, up to 168 miles per hour, destroyed about ninety percent of the island's buildings. Son Billy Stone went there to help the Bubars rebuild. Pastor Bill and Betty Stone also took time to visit there.

Pastor Bill traveled to South Korea with a group of pastors in the spring of 1994. The next year (1995), Pastor Bill went to Bulgaria to teach extension Bible classes sponsored by missionary Richard Walden of Send International.

The Newport church celebrated its fortieth anniversary in 1997. The guest speaker was one of Betty Stone's former pastors, Rev. Robert Becker, who came all the way from New Jersey. Other special guests at this occasion were chalk artist Rev. Ding Teuling, evangelist Wendell Calder, and various southern gospel music groups.

During the Stones' eleven years of service at Newport, Maine, the fellowship continued to grow. It became necessary to plan and build an addition to the facility. In our previous book, *This Is Olio!*, we related some of why this transpired:

A True Shepherd[21]

It has been said, the best pastor is one who is a pastor to the people, evidenced by his compassion and concern for all in his congregation. Some years ago, a local minister[22] was visiting with us. Our talk centered around many things of common concern, as well as church matters.

Then the telephone rang and interrupted our conversation. It was my son in a neighboring town calling. He sought immediate help gathering a field's worth of bailed hay into his barn, noting an approaching thunderstorm. And it was Sunday.

In the past, more rigid Christians refrained from all work on the Sabbath – a strict observance of Old Testament law. However, in the New Testament, Jesus made it clear that, while the principal rule is still valid, the infrequent opportunity to do good deeds on the Lord's Day was sometimes necessary and sanctioned. Jesus understood, and He was practical. Work, whether undone or done, was not the important thing in unlocking the means to Heaven. Jesus' words are quoted below in red:

> 5 **Then He answered them, saying,** "Which of you, having a donkey or an ox that has fallen into a pit, will not immediately pull him out on the Sabbath day?" 6 **And they could not answer Him regarding these things.**
> —*(Luke 14:5-6 New King James Version)*

> 27 **And He said to them,** "The Sabbath was made for man, and not man for the Sabbath."
> —*(Mark 2:27 New King James Version)*

Out the door I raced, with the pastor close behind me. "I'm coming with you," he shouted, as we made haste to get to our son's farm field. My suggesting there was no need for him to do this would not deter him. To him, assisting people, especially when needed, went beyond preaching itself. After all, hard work had always been a part of his constitution; helping others was a part of his calling to ministry.

During this pastor's tenure, the little church's attendance increased – a testimony of the townspeople's appreciation for him. Their pastor had demonstrated that he was not above assisting them with manual tasks. Pastor was real and, just like Jesus, appreciated the reality of human existence. He was putting his Christianity into practice. After all, *What would Jesus do?*

Calvary Baptist Church intentionally integrated its people and activities with the local community. Cooperating with other churches, it hosted "Law Enforcement Banquets", and helped provide meals and programs for these events. This church, with three others, presented annual Easter and Christmas cantatas. Calvary Baptist also participated in a SHARE food distribution program. The church also held monthly men's breakfasts, hosted *Awana* and *Word of Life* clubs, and entered floats in local parades.

Bill and Betty Stone enjoyed a thrilling whitewater rafting trip down the West Branch of the Kennebec River with son Billy and his wife Cecelia. Along the way, Bill noticed an old tractor for sale,

(above:) **Cecelia and Billy Stone.**
(below:) **Bill Stone & 1955 Farmall tractor (Super C, wide front end).**
(photos courtesy of Bill Stone; edited)

resting and rusting in a barn at Solon, Maine. He could not resist taking a closer look. This vintage machine, a 1955 Farmall tractor (model Super C with wide front end), turned out to be just what Bill had been wanting! After enlisting a knowledgeable church member to closely inspect this mechanical horse, Bill brought it home – a new prized possession. Getting the tractor into working condition required Bill's hard (but enjoyable) labor.

In the fall of 1999, pastor Bill accepted a call to the Clifton United Baptist Church, in Clifton, Maine. This rural town is situated on Route 9, also

Clifton United Baptist Church, Clifton, Maine
(courtesy of Bill Stone; edited)

known as "The Airline" – a scenic wilderness route between Bangor and Calais, Maine. Bill and Betty ministered at Clifton until his retirement in 2005. The Clifton church served monthly lunches at the Salvation Army in Bangor. The church's men participated in a greater-Bangor area dart-ball competition. The Stones occupied the parsonage, grateful to have a sizable garden plot there.

Bill's treasured tractor, although well-used, was no longer needed, either for his garden or to pull parade floats. Bill sold it to a friend who appreciated its worth.

Bill Stone's Farmall tractor, restored and well-used
(courtesy of Bill Stone; edited)

Bill supplemented his Clifton pastor's salary by driving a bus for School Administrative District 63, until 2001. Then Bill began driving an Island Explorer shuttle bus in Acadia National Park,

Bill Stone drove these *Island Explorer* shuttle busses for visitors to Acadia National Park, Mt. Desert Island, Maine.
(courtesy of Bill Stone; edited)

which he enjoyed doing for the next fourteen years. Bill also became an unofficial chaplain for the Park's eighty bus drivers; and the friendships begun there have continued to the present.

After retiring, Pastor Bill served from 2006 to 2013 as a supply preacher for Inter-Church

Ministries, nearly every Sunday during summer months, for some of Maine's forty-two member churches.

Since then, the Stones have spent their winters in St. Cloud, Florida. From November through April, Bill pastors at Central Park II Chapel in Hanes City, Florida. Then, the Stones spend their

The Stones' winter home at St. Cloud, Florida
(courtesy of Bill Stone; edited)

summers at Vassalboro, Maine. From May through October, Bill pastors the Northport Community Church in Northport, Maine.

The more stylish shirts of this day are without a pocket in which many men used to carry eyeglasses, a pen, and something on which to write notes. Ink stains inevitably appeared, from pens left uncapped or not retracted. But Preacher Bill always has pockets in his shirts to conveniently carry those usual items. His shirt pocket also holds a sheet of printed stories, jokes and adages, which he often retrieves near the end of a conversation.

Betty and Bill Stone, ministering at Northport Community Church, Northport, Maine in the summer of 2019.

(courtesy of Bill Stone; edited)

Thus, he leaves you smiling – accomplishing a "lasting impression" very well.

Over their lifetimes, Bill and Betty Stone have served in rural hamlets and communities, in both full-time and temporary pulpit-supply preaching positions. They have willingly answered the calls for a minister wherever there was a need – when

. . . not just ANY minister will do,

but one like pastor Bill Stone – an energetic, people-minded person who, in his own way, desires above all else to have a person come to know his Lord. And this Bill most effectively accomplished by becoming *one of them*, being engaged in their daily lives. The same may be said of Betty Stone, a dedicated, supportive pastor's wife who contributes her own assistance, encouragement and trumpet!

Betty and Bill Stone
(author's collection; edited)

Pedigree Chart
for
Reverend
William Howard Stone
Senior

William Howard Stone •
Reverend •
Senior
b: 24 Nov 1940 in Montague City, Mass.
m: 8 Jun 1963 in Ticonderoga, N.Y.

Howard Harland Stone
b: 4 Jan 1914 in Rowe, Mass.
m: 1939 in Montague, Mass.
d: 25 Oct 2000 in Vernon, Vt.
Burial: Leverett, Mass.

Delbert Leon Stone
b: 4 Jun 1886 in Whitingham, Vt.
m: 25 Feb 1913 in Whitingham, Vt.
d: 30 Oct 1952 in Charlemont, Mass.

Frederick Eugene Stone
b: 23 Sep 1857
m: 1 Dec 1882
d: 28 Jan 1936

Nella Alice Starks
b: 13 Oct 1864
d: 28 Nov 1954
Burial: Rowe, Mass.

Musa Adella Cutting
b: 6 Jun 1886 in Whitingham, Vt.
d: 10 Feb 1972 in Greenfield, Mass.
Burial: Whitingham, Vt.

James Franklin Humes Cutting
b: 18 Dec 1848
m: 15 Oct 1884
d: 25 Apr 1928

Della Oliva Fairbanks
b: 18 Oct 1857
d: 23 Feb 1935

Dorothy May Hillock
b: 2 Mar 1919 in Leverett, Mass.
d: 20 Sep 1995 in Turners Falls, Mass.
Burial: Leverett, Mass.

George Richard Hillock
b: 10 Jan 1892 in Winchendon, Mass.
m: 24 Dec 1914 in Montague, Mass.
d: Sep 1967 in Northfield, Mass.
Burial: Leverett, Mass.; Plain View Cemetery

George H Hillock
b: 16 Feb 1854
m: 10 Feb 1889
d: 7 Jul 1925

Marietta Peed
b: 24 Sep 1861
d: 25 Feb 1942
Burial: Groton, Mass.

Daisy Viola Black
b: 10 Feb 1897 in Leverett, Mass.
d: 9 Feb 1950 in Leverett, Mass.
Burial: Moore's Corner, Leverett, Mass.; Pleasant View Cemetery

John James Black
b: 28 May 1876
m: 18 Apr 1894
d: 10 Nov 1955

Rose Alice Carey
b: 23 Feb 1879
d: 3 Sep 1912

How the Parson Broke the Sabbath [23]

On the grave of Parson Williams
  The grass is brown and bleached.
It is more than fifty winters since
  He lived and laughed and preached.

But his memory in New England
  No Winter snows can kill;
Of his goodness and his drollness
  Countless legends linger still.

And among those treasured legends
  I hold this one a boon.
How he got in Deacon Crosby's hay
  On a Sunday afternoon.

He was midway in a sermon,
  Most Orthodox, on grace,
When the sound of distant thunder
  Broke the quiet of the place.

Now the meadow of the Crosbys
  Lay full within his sight,
As he glanced from out the window
  Which stood open on his right.

And the green and fragrant haycocks
  By the acre there did stand;
Not a meadow like the Deacon's
  Far and near in all the land.

Quick and loud the claps of thunder
  Went rolling through the skies,
And the Parson saw his Deacon
  Looking out with anxious eyes.

"Now, my brethren," called the Parson,
  And he called with might and main,
"We must get in Brother Crosby's hay,
  'Tis our duty now most plain!"

And he shut the great red Bible,
  And he tossed his sermon down,
Not a man could run more swiftly
  Than the Parson in that town.

And he ran now to the meadow,
  With all his strength and speed;
And the congregation followed,
  All bewildered in his lead.

With a will they worked and shouted,
  And cleared the field apace,
And the Parson led the singing,
  While the sweat rolled down his face,

And it thundered fiercer, louder;
  And dark grew east and west;
But the hay was under cover,
  And the Parson had worked best.

And again in pew and pulpit
  Their places took compose;
And the Parson preached his sermon
  To "fifteenthly," where it closed.

            — H. H., in the N. Y. Independent.

3 Stone generations *(l-to-r:)* **Bill, Dan, Matt** *(Bill Stone; edited)*

ENDNOTES

[1] Now known as Farren Family Care Center, which now specializes in psychiatric care.

[2] Later known as Barrington College.

[3] Don Wyrtzen became a gospel hymn composer and Christian musician. His talents were recognized with a Dove Award from the Gospel Music Association in 1981.

[4] Scofield, C I. *The Scofield Reference Bible: The Holy Bible, Containing the Old and New Testaments: Authorized King James Version, with a New System of Connected Topical References to All the Greater Themes of Scripture, with Annotations, Revised Marginal Renderings, Summaries, Definitions, Chronology, and Index, to Which Are Added, Helps at Hard Places, Explanations of Seeming Discrepancies, and a New System of Paragraphs*. (New York: Oxford University Press, ©1945).

[5] Billy Stone, Junior unfortunately passed away on Monday, 19 October 2020, due to a massive stroke.

[6] Christine Sears is a graduate of the Bible Institute of New England.

[7] In December 1995 this church changed its name to Goffstown Christian Fellowship—["First Baptist Church Of Goffstown, N.H." OpenCorporates.com. Updated 6 Nov. 2020. <https://opencorporates.com/companies/us_nh/93274>; accessed 24 Dec. 2020.]

[8] Reverend Harold C. Duff (1922-2013), an itinerant preacher, was president of Glen Cove Christian Academy and Bible College at

Rockport, Maine. He also directed Fair Haven Camps, a Christian summer camp for children, located in Brooks, Maine and operated by Central Maine Bible Conference.

[9] Written by Rev. Dr. Robert Lowry in 1874 and first published in 1875, this popular Easter hymn has also been titled "Low in the Grave He Lay" and "Christ Arose".

[10] Also known as the Advent Christian General Conference, with headquarters in Charlotte, North Carolina.

[11] Now known as the American Mission for Opening Churches (AMOC), with headquarters in Olcott, New York.

[12] Now known as the American Baptist Churches USA (ABCUSA), with headquarters in Valley Forge, Pennsylvania.

[13] Bill Stone's comment (May 2020): "There are no elm trees now, only oak, maple and pine".

[14] Robbins, Alma P., *History of Vassalborough, Maine, 1771-1971*, [Lewiston, Maine : Twin Cities Printery], 1971, page 35.

[15] George H. Pope was a member of Vassalboro Monthly Meeting of Friends (Quakers). "Elder" Mark Stevens, an Adventist minister, lived in Wolfeboro, New Hampshire. Both Pope and Stevens were also members of the China Camp Meeting Association, on China Lake in China, Maine.

[16] Cummings, O.R., *Lewiston, Augusta & Waterville Street Railway*, [Manchester, New Hampshire: O. R. Cummings, 1963], page [13].

[17] Distances to the Robbins Grove stop are measured from each city's "Waiting Room" stop. Mileage data is taken from a chart in Cummings, *op. cit.*, page [48].

[18] Including Ira Robbins who liked to sing with them.

[19] Robbins, Alma P., *op. cit.*, page 35.

[20] Rev. H. Kenneth Dutille was pastor at Swan's Island Baptist Church in Maine.

[21] "A True Shepherd". In: Whitaker, Albert Preston, Jr. with Stephen L. Robbins. *This Is Olio: From Where I Sit*. (Brewer, Maine: North Wind Publishing, ©2020). Pages 321-322.

[22] Rev. Bill Stone, Calvary Baptist Church, Newport, Maine.

[23] H.H. "How the Parson Broke the Sabbath." *Daily Globe* (St. Paul, MN), 23 Feb. 1879 (v.2, n.40, p.3, col.1). Web: Chronicling America: Historic American Newspapers. Library of Congress. <https://chroniclingamerica. loc.gov/lccn/sn83025287/1879-02-23/ed-1/seq-3/>; view 11 Oct. 2019.

Harvey L. Cossaboom
December 1959

(author's collection)

Chapter 11

Reverend HARVEY LEE COSSABOOM

Do you recall your junior high school and high school years? Maybe you would rather concentrate on something else? But those were formative years, important for a boy's growth into manhood. In addition to the routine of school and extra-curricular activities, it was during those years that one's future life began to develop, and lasting friendships were nurtured, interspersed with some shenanigans.

In the mid-1940s and 1950s, the Christian Endeavor youth program at First Baptist Church of Randolph, Massachusetts was well-attended, active and a real part of teenagers' lives, including this author and my best friend Harvey Cossaboom.[1] Christian Endeavor was vital to our growing into adulthood as fine Christian people. Skills developed in these meetings and activities would shape our existence for a long time, which we realized even more as life went on.

Ethel Powers, an exceptional leader, directed our Christian Endeavor group, usually assisted by a Gordon College intern.[2]

Although I remember many of those in the group, their journeys through life were soon forgotten once college and the wider experiences of life came into view. Research into how each one's life turned out would likely be interesting but, at this point, it may not be so important or inspiring. One can only hope and trust that their genuine Christian testimonies and experiences had continued with them throughout their lives.

As often happens, some associations formed during youth do endure across one's lifetime. Close friendships seemingly interweave with our lives forever. Harvey Cossaboom and I became best friends and *buddies* (and co-conspirators) during those years and for several years thereafter.

Harvey was three months older than I, but a year behind me in school, because I was allowed to start school a year early. When my folks purchased our home at 536 North Main Street in 1947, Harvey's house was only about a mile down the street from me. We walked or rode bicycles back and forth between our homes many times.

Harvey (born 1933) lived at 178 Liberty Street with his family: father, Omar Glendon Cossaboom (a uniformed Randolph police officer); mother, Sarah Gertrude

Above: **Omar Cossaboom** *(courtesy of Randolph [MA] Police Dept.)*
Below: **Gertrude (Cook) Cossaboom**, Dec. 1959
(author's collection)

(Cook) Cossaboom; Sterling Cossaboom (born 1944); and step-grandmother, the widow Florence E. Cook.[3]

Sterling Cossaboom Dec. 1959
(author's collection)

Harvey's older sister, Ruth (born 1920), lived nearby. Her husband, Ashley A. Smythe, was also a police officer. I remember Ruth as a local telephone operator. If I picked up the telephone to call Harvey, she would not only ask, "Number, please?" – but when I spoke Harvey's phone number, she told me whether he was home or where else he might be! She was a great news source for events in the town, which she would freely relate (depending upon how busy her switchboard was). Do you remember when there was a *real* telephone operator on the phone line?

Both Harvey and I were active members of the First Baptist Church in Randolph, Mass. We were also co-students of

First Baptist Church, Randolph, MA *(courtesy of JoAnn Randall)*

Rev. Dr. Eugene S. Philbrook
(courtesy of First Baptist Church, Randolph, Mass.)

the Reverend Doctor Eugene S. Philbrook, who trained us in public Scripture reading (from an un-microphoned pulpit), and in the art of sermon preparation and delivery.

Frequently, Pastor Philbrook would usher Harvey and I into the church sanctuary to practice Bible reading or message delivery at the pulpit, while he sat in the last row and coached us in proper elocution and reading. I can still hear him, in his quiet professional demeanor, give encouragement to read *slowly*, with careful *enunciation* and distinct sounds, never dropping the last word or syllable, effectively *projecting* our God-given ability and voice strength. There were no microphones or sound systems then, just the acoustics of the room and our natural voice power. Over and over again, we practiced until Doctor Philbrook felt we had mastered the lesson.

The skills learned there have proved to be extremely useful during my lifetime of speaking opportunities. From Dr. Philbrook, I think that both Harvey and I got a lot of exposure to what being in ministry was like.

Together, Harvey and I were leaders in the Christian Endeavor youth group for many years. But that's not all. We also engaged in some things with our peers that did not necessarily meet with our elders' approval. One incident in particular my mind can recall very well. The youth director, a Gordon College student named Donald R. Donica, drove a small Volkswagen that we usually ignored – that is, until one Sunday afternoon. We (not me? or Harvey?) decided that, together, we could all lift that vehicle up the church's front steps and leave it on the platform near the entry doors. By the time that Mr. Donica discovered it, we had all disappeared! I honestly don't remember how the Volkswagen was returned to the driveway – but it was not there the last time I checked!

Harvey Cossaboom, July 1958
(author's collection)

Harvey's father, policeman Omar Cossaboom, was also a well-known and entertaining magician.

While off-duty, Mr. Cossaboom performed throughout the area, mystifying his audiences with an extra-ordinary personality.

Omar Cossaboom
(1897 – 1947)

(images courtesy of Randolph [Mass.] Police Department; used with permission; edited by Steve Robbins)

Unfortunately, while Harvey and I were in Stetson High School, Mr. Cossaboom suffered a heart attack while on duty and died in his Randolph police cruiser, on September 19th, 1947. I stayed by my close friend Harvey throughout this unforgettable experience.

Sometime afterward, Harvey, thinking about his father's magic shows, sought out the "equipment." From recalling his father's performances, Harvey decided he could learn the art of "magic" and use it to illustrate Bible teachings.

After checking out the living room floor from the basement of his house, we noted what was left of some "rigging" where Harvey's father had once made a piano disappear during a family gathering! This only further intrigued Harvey, who over the next several months "played" with the discovered props, and worked up his act. Much practice was required to effectively accomplish the necessary *sleight of hand*, but he did it!

Some of the props Harvey acquired and used, at first, were simple things. Like the one time when an expected guest came to Sunday dinner at the Whitaker home. Nearly every week we would

Whitaker home at 536 North Main Street, Randolph, Mass.
(author's collection)

have one or two guests at our table, such as the youth director or a special speaker at the church.

Nobody noticed when Harvey slipped out of church early, went next door to our house and placed a little flat rubber balloon under the plate where the guest was to sit. This inflatable piece was attached to a thin rubber tube run beneath the

Dinner with guests at the Whitaker home, Dec. 1959
(left-to-right:) Mrs. Cossaboom, Dave Brown, [unidentified girl], Al Whitaker Sr, Minnie Whitaker.

(author's collection)

tablecloth. The other end of tube attached to a squeeze bladder, placed where Harvey usually sat. You can imagine the guest's reaction as his plate, every once-in-a-while during dinner, rose up then settled down as he ate! And then, there was the dribble glass and the collapsing spoon!

Amongst Harvey's pocket of "tricks" was some black substance which first appeared as ink, but after a short time it would neutralize to a clear liquid. One time, he placed a bubble of this "ink" onto Mother's fine white linen tablecloth, looking as if it had spilled from an overturned ink bottle. Mother almost had an attack! – if only an attack

Mrs. Minnie Whitaker
Mother, in 1945
(author's collection)

aimed at Harvey's head (or backsides). It is needless to say how relieved she was when that spot dissipated, leaving no damage to the tablecloth! And Harvey was spared, yet again, from any consequences.

Harvey's performances were billed as "Gospel Magic," and his rather unusual and mystifying "tricks" often carried a Gospel illustration. As he began filling engagements, he enlisted me to be his assistant. I accompanied him to these "shows" and acted as an accomplice (often planted as an in-audience co-conspirator).

Harvey's accomplice, Al Whitaker Jr., about 1940
(author's collection)

We performed all around our area and in several church "gigs," usually concluding with a strong Gospel message. A local newspaper described one such show:

> RANDOLPH, Jan. 28.—Town Hall was filled to capacity last evening when Stetson High school students presented a minstrel show....
>
> "Now You See It, Now You Don't" were a series of magical tricks expertly executed by Harvey Cossaboom. Laughs galore followed the act in which the youthful magician literally pulled out practically everything from a hat lent for the occasion by George Crimmins, member of the High school faculty.[4]

Of course, such activity lent itself well to the possibility of embarrassing a church's pastor or youth leader. Many times, Harvey would have the pastor get his felt hat (they wore them in that day!) and show everyone that there was nothing inside it. – Until . . . – Harvey waved his magic wand over the hat as it was placed, with its brim up, on his table. He then proceeded to remove a host of interesting things from the pastor's hat, in full view of the audience. Out came cans of vegetables, soup, socks, keys, miscellaneous and sundry things – enough to fill a bushel basket. Then the question was asked: "Pastor, why do you carry all of this in your hat?" Finally, he would call the pastor back to return his hat and, as he came, in full view of all, Harvey would produce, from this pastor's hat, some unmentionable women's undergarments! The pastor's face would glow with a red blush seldom ever seen on a proper Reverend's face. I cannot remember what the moral of this story was; perhaps I was so intent on watching the pastor that I missed the application.

Somewhere in his house, Harvey discovered an accordion. He taught himself to play this "belly organ" or "squeeze box" (as we named it). Harvey played this instrument in youth group and in churches every time the occasion allowed. This accordion was always as a part of Harvey's magic performance repertoire. Accordionists were as uncommon then as they are now – except for Myron Floren, "the happy Norwegian" on *The Lawrence Welk Show* from 1950 onward.[5]

During these high school years, Harvey and I, together with one Dave Brown, formed *The Gospel Crusaders* group. We traveled around to various youth groups and conducted meetings, using the accordion, magic and speaking. Actually, we must

```
                                              GOSPEL CRUSADERS
                                              Randolph, Massachusetts

       "So faith comes from what is heard, and what is heard comes
        by the preaching of Christ." ... Romans 10: 17  (RSV)

            Once again we of the Gospel Crusaders are happy to greet you in the precious
       name of our Saviour and Lord, Christ Jesus. Another year has come and gone and at
       this time the churches are beginning to make plans for the coming season. We trust
       that it will be your theme as you do this, to exalt the name of Christ and with us
       of the Crusaders, to preach Christ, and Him crucified, risen and coming again.

            A little over two years ago three young men of the Randolph First Baptist
       Church, under the able advisorship of their pastor, and with the prayers of
       interested church members and friends, began what was then known as the Randolph
       Gospel Crusade. The first year was one of constant struggle, difficulty, and
       discouragement; but we adopted as our motto Philippians 4: 13, "I can do all things
       through Christ which strengtheneth me", and we pressed on. The next season was a
       truly great one in the Lord, and now we greet you at the outset of our third. The
       Lord has been good to us. We believe it is His holy will that we, even as young
       people, should continue to preach His gospel.

            Following are the names of those who preach this glorious gospel of Christ:

       Harvey L. Cossaboon, President, accordianist, song leader, preacher,
            student at Emerson College, Sunday School teacher, Recreational Chairman
            of the Brockton Christian Endeavor Union.

       Albert Whitaker, Jr., Vice President, song leader, preacher, student at
            Boston University College of General Education, Sunday School teacher,
            Vice President of the Brockton Christian Endeavor Union.

       David H. Brown, Treasurer, agriculturist, leader in youth work at the
            Randolph Baptist Church, graduate of Norfolk County Agricultural School.

            These are the charter members of the Gospel Crusaders. For the meetings
       which we hold in the various churches, we draw talent from a long list of well
       qualified young people, including vocalists, violinists, pianists, trumpeters,
       and others. We consider ourselves fortunate to have a staff of advisors, headed by
       our Pastoral Advisor, Dr. Eugene S. Philbrook, Pastor of our home church.

            We of the Gospel Crusaders covet your prayers that God will direct our paths,
       that He will open the doors of churches where we may preach the gospel and also
       open the doors of men's hearts that many souls may be won for Jesus Christ and His
       church.
                 ("..... and the Lord will answer." Isa. 58:9.)

            If you would like to have the GOSPEL CRUSADERS in your church, either for
       young peoples or evening services, write now for the date you desire. If you are
       in Brockton, write to our representative, Arthur Wilbur, 60 Market Street, Brockton.
       Anyone may write for information to either of our offices: 536 North Main Street,
       or 178 Liberty Street, Randolph, Massachusetts.

                                              Yours in His service,

                                              The GOSPEL CRUSADERS
```

The Gospel Crusaders handbill
(author's collection)

**Dave Brown
December 1959**
(author's collection)

admit that David's contribution was his vehicle, a green Pontiac "woody" station wagon.

Harvey had the male lead role in the play "Mother Is a Freshman," presented by the Junior Class of Stetson High School on 16 December 1949.[6]

Later that school year, Harvey was the understudy for the star – or lead role – in the play "Grandma Pulls the String." This was the Stetson High School Dramatic Club's "first venture .... an evening of one-act plays" scheduled for 17 March 1950 at 8:00 p.m. Then the unexpected happened, when

Stetson High School, Randolph, Massachusetts
(Dale Robbins collection)

> ... Thomas Schneider, leading man, was stricken with an acute attack of appendicitis two hours before curtain time and was rushed to the Quincy Hospital for an emergency operation.
> Harvey Cossaboom, after less than two hours preparation took to the footlights and gave a remarkable performance.[7]

By becoming comfortable before audiences of any size and complexion, Harvey seemed a natural one to undertake a career in the arts. This, more than anything, may have prompted his application and acceptance at Emerson College in Boston, where he could study performance besides expanding his skills in radio work. Harvey enrolled at Emerson College for the 1951 fall semester. However, the Lord obviously had other plans.

The Korean War had begun in June 1950.[8] As United States' participation intensified, Congress extended the selective service system draft by new legislation in June 1951.[9] Students were fast being drafted from academia. With a potential Selective Service "draft" looming, Harvey began to rethink his future. During the summer, he applied to Gordon College for its ministry studies program, and was accepted. This, had it been necessary, would have deferred him from military service because he was now a full-time ministerial student.

Gordon College, then located in downtown Boston, was very familiar to Harvey, because our church and its youth groups had a strong relationship with that school. In fact, our youth

Harvey's friend, Al Whitaker Jr., in 1950
(author's collection)

pastor at that time, Donald R. Donica, a was a full-time student at Gordon. Harvey and I had participated in Don's wedding (about 1951), and we had spent time auditing classes at Gordon. This was an additional incentive to apply to Gordon.

Although Harvey had not appreciated the study of Latin and German in Stetson High School's college preparatory program, he persevered because they were prerequisites for graduation. Surprise! – At Gordon College, Harvey actually *excelled* in Greek, Hebrew and language studies! By following the Lord's leading, the languages became much more enjoyable and practical.[10]

Faithful is he that calleth you, who also will do it.
--1 Thessalonians 5:24 (King James Version)

During those early 1950s, I was studying at Boston University and my close friend Harvey was, at the same time, attending Gordon College and preparing himself for the ministry. I can recall the many hours we spent, on weekends, in *bull session* debate on various subjects related to our beliefs and their promulgation. I remember being somewhat alarmed on learning that, even in his preparation for the pastorate, Harvey was not required to take a course in public speaking. I wondered out loud what other vital study was being overlooked.

In those days (and still today) in New England, there were few *large* churches. Most often, the pastor alone comprised the entire church staff. In almost every case, a pastor had (or has) no formal education in any part of business administration, accounting, management, finances and such. Yet the pastor was expected to do it all, oftentimes even including the janitorial functions! My college experience exposed me to all these business-related topics (but not to religion-related or ministry-related topics). I soon questioned why my friend Harvey was required to undertake only courses in theology and religion. Was it because good public speaking skills and good business practices were considered unimportant tools for a minister?

Meanwhile – besides Harvey's better interest in the languages, his attention was also drawn toward one particular female student. Dorothy "Dottie" Etta Emery became his full-time "associate," resulting in their marriage shortly after graduation. The wedding took place in Kingfield, Maine on June 12, 1955.

'*Dottie*'**in Dec. 1959**
(author's collection)

About sixteen months later, Harvey and I learned that our beloved former pastor and

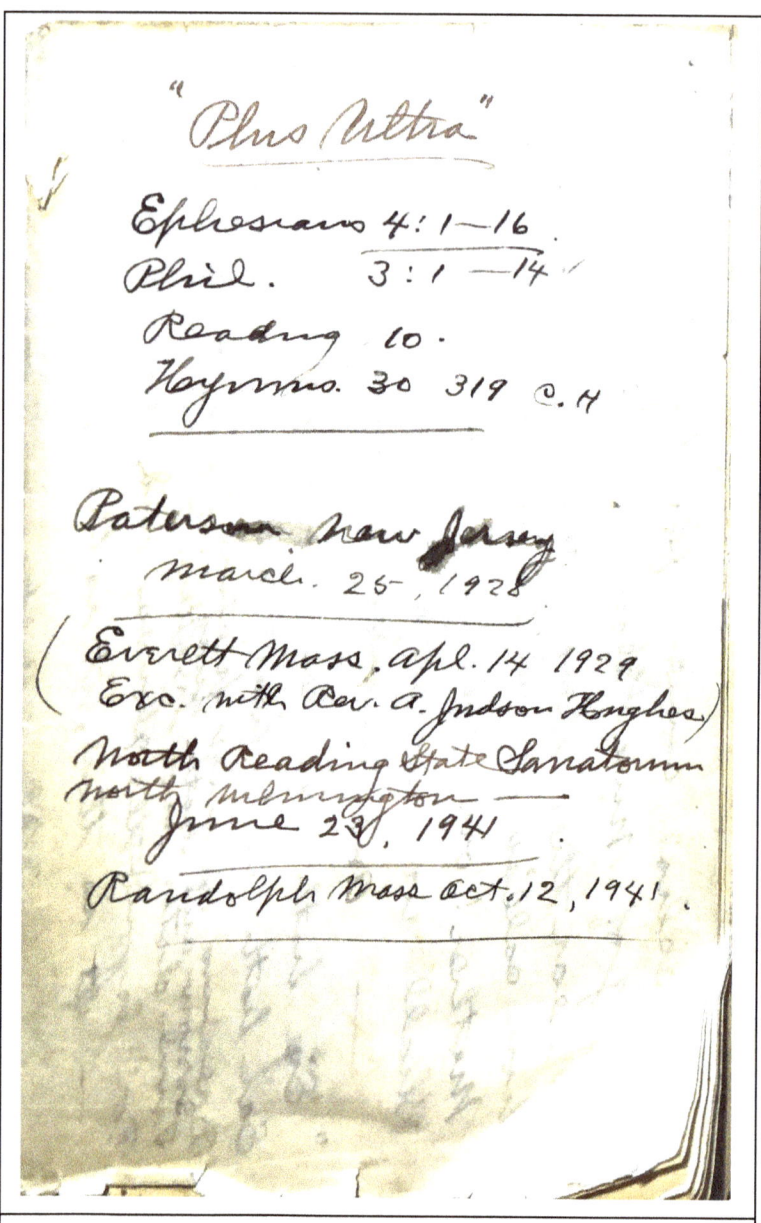

Dr. Philbrook's sermon: *"Plus Ultra."*
(Above:) Scripture references, dates and places where delivered.
(Opposite:) Dr. Philbrook's handwritten sermon text. *(author's collection)*

> "Plus Ultra".
> Truth is absolute and eternal but its discovery has been long and difficult and often painful. Fragments have been detected here and there through the ages and placed in the mosaic of philosophy. A bit of truth appeared minted in a Spanish coin near the close of the fifteenth century. This truth was expressed in the form of a Latin motto with just two words, "Plus Ultra", meaning "More Beyond."

mentor, the Reverend Doctor Eugene Philbrook, had passed from this life to his eternal home on October 24th, 1956. Soon afterward, his widow Bessie gave to Harvey and me a file cabinet of her husband's sermon notes. These were handwritten on letter-size paper, sometimes accompanied by various newspaper or magazine clippings, or other notes. Each sermon's material was folded halfway (lengthwise) into a neat package. On a facing side appeared the sermon title and often a Scripture reference, along with places and dates where Dr. Philbrook had used this prepared message. The outlines were handwritten with an ink pen, in an older script style, and underlined where emphases were warranted. Harvey and I went through these files and divided them according to our own interests.

Pastor Harvey Cossaboom's first pastorate was at the First Baptist Church in Danville, New Hampshire. I still have my original sermon notes for one of the times I preached for Harvey at Danville; I delivered a Sunday morning message on October 20th, 1957, titled "Help Wanted! No Experience Necessary!"

Page *one* of author's sermon notes, 20 Oct. 1957, preaching for Harvey Cossaboom at First Baptist Church, Danville, N.H.

(author's collection)

Obey His Command
God's way — "Lord I'll Come if my way turns"
Argument of Naaman v 1 & 2

4. Have Faith
   Faithful Servants — Persistent Parents etc.
   Change of Heart — Testing of Faith
   Persecution — Faith it will work —
      Faith in family doctor.

5. Accept free gift of His love
      Naaman tried to pay — Hard to understand
      that it is free — free cure
   God's desire: that we come to Him
   Be Customer of God — not Satan.
   Rejoicing in Heaven — Happy reunion
   Simple yet would make it hard. Believe & thou shalt be saved.

III. Duty of Believer — must SELL
   Good to consider just first 2 points
   — then relax says Christian.
   Our invigorating duty as little girl
      to tell others. God's Workmen.
   "Tell desperate lost sinners the way
      To know Christ & Make Him known"
   How about this church?
   Being Christian called to Full time Service
   Paul looked, Converted — went to Preach
   1. Life greatest testimony — as Blind
      man — one thing I know — now I see
   (?) lapel button — People ask — tell them
      Be always ready to give reason for hope in you.
   2. Tell others.
   3. Every Talent & will bring
      Reward in heaven — Harvest is white
   How about you? Release us when work to be done?

Page *two* of author's sermon notes, 20 Oct. 1957, preaching for Harvey Cossaboom at First Baptist Church, Danville, N.H.
(author's collection)

Having gained valuable experience at Danville, N.H., Harvey next moved on to a double pastorate

FREE BAPTIST CHURCH, DANVILLE, N. H.

Harvey Cossaboom's first pastorate was at this church in Danville, N.H.
(post card, mailed in 1906; ebay.com)

– two associated Maine churches: one at Waterboro and another at Alfred. He soon stood for ordination and assumed the well-earned title of "Reverend," which was conferred by his *home church*, First Baptist at Randolph, Mass.

Pastor Cossaboom at First Baptist Church, Danville, N.H. in 1958
(author's collection)

Dottie recalls an episode during one of Harvey's pastorates that especially revealed his Christian maturity:

> ... I was thinking about Harvey and an incident that happened in one of the churches. . . . Probably the people involved are all gone now but, just to keep it anonymous, I won't say which church.
> There was a disagreement, and [sometime] afterward someone remarked that Harvey was *a real Christian* because he stayed calm, and used logic, and did not get angry. Evidently, [some more] recent pastor or pastors had not reacted that way. I can't remember the details. Anger only shows weakness of argument.[11]

Dottie and Harvey Cossaboom had six children, born during his somewhat brief ministry years:

i. *Stephen Mark*, born November 4, 1956.
ii. *Philip Omar*, born March 16, 1958.
iii. *Elisabeth Ann*, born July 6, 1960.
iv. *Deborah Joy*, born July 8, 1962; died July 12, 1962.
v. *Nathan Andrew*, born August 15, 1963.
vi. *David Lee*, born January 9, 1965.

Dottie and Harvey Cossaboom with baby Stephen August 1957 *(courtesy of the Cossaboom family)*

In 1965, Reverend Harvey Cossaboom and his family heard a call from the Lord to join Wycliffe Bible Translators (remember his interest in languages). Harvey applied. He resigned his Maine pastorate and prepared to move his family to Norman, Oklahoma. There, Harvey would enter Wycliffe's training program at their Summer Institute of Linguistics. This was a big and bold move, taken on faith in the Lord's leading, and with unknown financial implications and many young children. Dottie remembers:

> As we were leaving town to go to Oklahoma, we stopped by the church and he went in and stood in the pulpit one last time. I still get a lump in my throat thinking about it.¹²

Wycliffe required a complete physical exam, then recommended open-heart surgery to correct a problem Harvey had long known about. He underwent the operation at Maine Medical Center in Portland, Maine.

Although Harvey appeared to have responded well to the surgery, post-procedure hemorrhage problems developed. Unfortunately, Harvey did not survive. Reverend Cossaboom's untimely death occurred on the 6th of April, 1965, at the age of only 32 years. He was interred at New Portland, Maine in the East New Portland Cemetery, where his monument is inscribed:

> "LIVING FOR HIM ON EARTH WAS
> EXCHANGED FOR LIVING WITH HIM
> IN HEAVEN"

A surgery, unfortunately, also prevented me from attending Harvey's funeral. I underwent abdominal surgery to remove a diseased gall bladder, remove an inflamed appendix, and have a colon resection. But a memorial service was held later at the Randolph church, in which I gladly participated.

The loss of my long-time best friend Harvey was difficult for me – especially knowing that my own heart problem would eventually require a surgery similar to his. Another thing – I would no longer have an opportunity to occupy Harvey's pulpit, something I had really enjoyed doing from time to time.

Harvey's young widow, Dottie, with their five young children, moved "back home" to her parents' farm at East New Portland, Maine. Sometime later, Dottie became the Town Manager.

As this occurred thirty-some years before there were any e-mail or texting, it meant that my contact with the Cossaboom family would essentially be lost.

– And the magic was gone –

Then, about 2015, I became aware that our son Keith had assisted a church in Solon, Maine with some construction engineering problems, and a part of that church was a youth pastor named Glen Cossaboom.

I then contacted Glen Cossaboom and learned that he is a son of Philip and a grandson of Harvey Cossaboom. Glen noted what each of Harvey's and Dottie's "kids" were then doing (Stephen, David, Nathan, Philip, and Beth).

Glen's grandmother (and Harvey's widow), Dottie, had married Vernon E. Meldrum on October 18th, 2008[13] and was living in Farmington. It is notable that all five of Harvey's and Dottie's children and their families are still in Maine, very close to their Emery grandparents' home at East New Portland, where they were all raised after Harvey's untimely death. It is also commendable (and with special credit to Dottie) that they apparently are all either in ministry or involved in Christian churches.

A look at grandson Glen Cossaboom's Facebook web page shows his continuing involvement in ministry. Since June 2020, Glen is the owner of Timber Yard Services in Madison, Maine, doing landscaping and other yard services. And since June 2020, he is also an "Independent Missionary" whose organization, named "Back Woods Gospel," he describes as

> A vibrant Ministry seeking to fellowship and connect back woods outdoorsmen for the Gospel of Jesus Christ.[14]

Glen shared this recent update with the editor:

> We are now . . . independent home missionaries. And my wife and I are taking classes to become online missionaries, as this is a new and growing field. We work through local school sports teams, coaching and reaching children and families. We are also Sunday school teachers at our church for the middle school group. I was a youth pastor and involved in youth ministry for 15 years.
>
> I can say I wish I had known my grandfather, as I have always felt that I was supposed to carry on after him. His legacy still carries on today in our family, and my grandmother has done great to continue to be a rock for our family's faith.[15]

Glen Cossaboom is carrying forward his grandfather Harvey Cossaboom's legacy. To this, grandfather would surely offer a hearty "Amen!"

However short his ministry, Reverend Harvey Cossaboom emerged as a giant in his Christian witness and life. I was privileged to be among his close associates.

He was a Pastor,

but not just ANY pastor.

**Harvey with Stephen and Philip
July 1958** *(author's collection)*

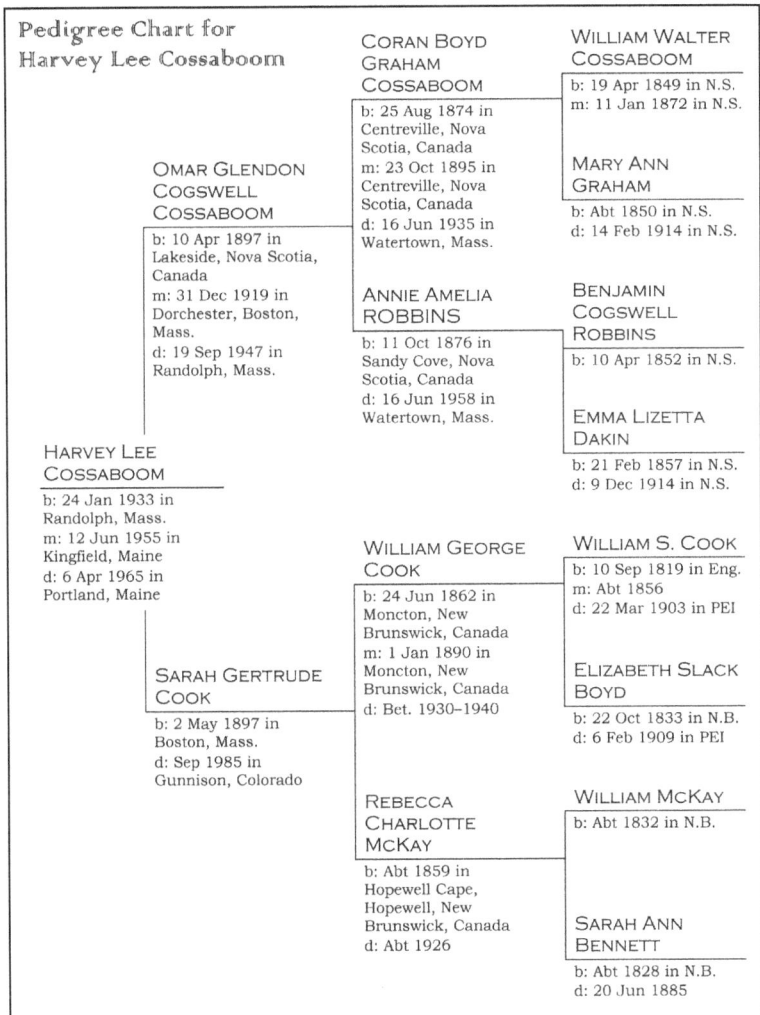

ENDNOTES

[1] In 1949 and 1950, some of the "kids" involved in Christian Endeavor at Randolph were: Harvey Cossaboom, Albert Whitaker Jr (myself), Richard Thorne, Robert Preble, Fred McKeeman, Gerald Eagles, Ronald Koski, Claire Dockendorff, and Dorothy Boynton. Whereabouts of these, except for Harvey, quickly vanished from my view after I went off to college and was no longer a part of this group.

[2] Ethel Powers was also an accomplished pianist.

[3] Harvey's biological grandmother, Rebecca (McKay) Cook had died about 1926. Grandfather William George Cook then married Florence

E. (????). Florence was a tenant at 536 North Main Street when that residence was purchased by the Whitakers.

[4] "HS Students Present Show" [unidentified newspaper clipping, in a "Randolph" local news column. Datelined "Randolph, Jan. 28."]. Image is by courtesy of Dorothy (Emery) (Cossaboom) Meldrum. The original clipping appears to be mounted in a scrapbook.

[5] Wikipedia contributors. "Myron Floren." *Wikipedia, The Free Encyclopedia*. Wikipedia, The Free Encyclopedia, 9 Oct. 2020. Web. 20 Oct. 2020.

[6] "Rehearse for Annual Play" [unidentified newspaper clipping, in a "Randolph" local news column. Datelined "Randolph, Nov. 29 [1949]."]; "Seniors [sic] Plan Annual Play" [unidentified newspaper clipping, in a "Randolph" local news column. Datelined "Randolph, Dec. 16 [1949]."]; also, a partial image of the event's printed program" "Junior Class, Stetson High School presents *Mother is a Freshman* by Perry Clark." All images are by courtesy of Dorothy (Emery) (Cossaboom) Meldrum. The original items appear to be mounted in a scrapbook.

[7] "Rushed Into Leading Role" [unidentified newspaper clipping, in a "Randolph" local news column. Datelined "Randolph, March 20."]; also, a partial image of the event's printed program, dated 17 March 1950 at 8:00 P.M. Both images are by courtesy of Dorothy (Emery) (Cossaboom) Meldrum. The original items appear to be mounted in a scrapbook. Of two more one-act plays presented that evening "before a capacity audience," Harvey had a role in at least one of them: "A Good Girl in the Kitchen."

[8] Wikipedia contributors. "Korean War." *Wikipedia, The Free Encyclopedia*. Wikipedia, The Free Encyclopedia, 17 Oct. 2020. Web. 20 Oct. 2020.

[9] Wikipedia contributors. "Military Selective Service Act." *Wikipedia, The Free Encyclopedia*. Wikipedia, The Free Encyclopedia, 20 Mar. 2019. Web. 20 Oct. 2020.

[10] "He and Sterling used to play *Scrabble* in Latin"—[Dorothy E. (Emery) (Cossaboom) Meldrum to Albert P. Whitaker Jr., e-mail, 28 Nov. 2020.

[11] Dorothy E. (Emery) (Cossaboom) Meldrum to Albert P. Whitaker Jr., e-mail, 29 Aug. 2020.

[12] Dorothy E. (Emery) (Cossaboom) Meldrum to Albert P. Whitaker Jr., e-mail, 25 Nov. 2020.

[13] "Maine Marriages, 1892-1966, 1977-1996" [database], Maine Genealogy. Web: <https://www.mainegenealogy.net/individual_marriage_record.asp?id=977018> : accessed 21 Oct 2020; entry for Vernon E. MELDRUM and Dorothy E. EMERY, Saturday, 18 Oct. 2008, citing Maine Vital Records.

[14] "Glen Cossaboom" [Facebook web page]. Facebook.com. Web: <https://www.facebook.com/GlenCossaboom> ; accessed 20 Oct. 2020.
[15] Glen Cossaboom to Stephen Robbins, Facebook Instant Messages, 28 Nov. 2020.

Haddon W. Robinson
(photo courtesy of Discovery House, Our Daily Bread Ministries)

Gordon-Conwell
Theological Seminary

130 ESSEX STREET
SOUTH HAMILTON, MA 0198
508 468-7111

November 22, 1993

Mr. and Mrs. Albert Whitaker, Jr.
141 Rhode Island Road
Lakeville, MA 02347

Dear Al and Norma,

From the depths of my heart, I want to thank you both for your generous hospitality to me while I was at your church last Sunday.

You made me feel right at home in your home. The dinner was delicious and the setting was warm and inviting. Most of all, I enjoyed getting to know both of you.

I enjoyed being in your congregation for the morning service. The folks who worship there at Central Baptist Church are warm and affirming. Thank you for making my visit possible.

May God continue to use as you serve him here in Massachusetts and in Florida.

An object of grace,

Haddon Robinson

Chapter 12

Doctor HADDON WILLIAM ROBINSON

Serving on the President's Advisory Council at Gordon-Conwell Theological Seminary during the 1990s afforded me the opportunity to become acquainted with many distinguished people within Christian circles. This included the Seminary's presidents Dr. Robert C. Cooley and his successor, Dr. Walter C. Kaiser, Jr. These two men, and other preachers too numerous to mention in this volume, were invited and spoke at the Central Baptist Church in Middleboro, Massachusetts. However, any book about preachers must make room for Dr. Haddon W. Robinson. His accomplishments alone in the area of preaching could fill an entire book.

Haddon Robinson, a native New Yorker, was born on 21 March 1931.[1] Somehow, after losing his mother at age ten, Haddon survived growing up in Mousetown, a poor, rough and unsafe tenement neighborhood in Harlem, which *Reader's Digest* then named as "the toughest neighborhood in the

Harlem Apartment House, May 1943
(photo by Gordon Parks. Library of Congress; no known restrictions)

country." Haddon joined a gang and carried an ice pick to protect himself.

Because young Haddon and his cousin wanted to play on the Broadway Presbyterian Church's basketball team, they reluctantly agreed to attend the Sunday school three times a month. And that is where Haddon became a Christian when he responded to the Gospel presentation of his caring teacher, John Mygatt.[2]

Broadway Presbyterian Church
4 August 2014

[Beyond My Ken (https://commons.wikimedia.org/wiki/File:Broadway_Presbyterian_Church.jpg),<https://creative commons.org/licenses/by-sa/4.0/ legalcode>.]

Upon completing his undergraduate studies at Bob Jones University, Haddon not only received his Bachelor's degree,[3] but was also honored with the school's "Outstanding Preacher Award."

Miss Bonnie Vick became Haddon Robinson's college sweetheart at Bob Jones University, despite almost being expelled "for making 'cow-eyes' at him in the lunch room." Haddon and Bonnie got married just two weeks before moving to Dallas, Texas, where Haddon would begin graduate studies.[4] The marriage took place at Albany, Oregon on 11 August 1951.[5] Two children were eventually born to Haddon and Bonita "Bonnie" (Vick) Robinson:

i. **Vicki Ann**, born 12 Apr. 1955 in Dallas, Texas.[6]
ii. **Torrey William**, born 2 June 1957.[7]

Haddon's offspring would ultimately judge their father's lifetime priorities, and put forth their verdict in his obituary: "Despite the great demands on his time, his family always felt he put them first."[8]

Haddon Robinson pursued his love for learning to earn advanced degrees at Dallas Theological Seminary (Th.M., 1955), Southern Methodist University (M.A., 1960), and the University of Illinois (Ph.D., 1964).[9]

In addition, both Gordon College and McMaster Divinity College awarded Dr. Robinson with honorary degrees. His growing reputation also earned him the following honors:

1996 – listed on "12 Most Effective Preachers in the English-speaking World" by Baylor University.
2006 – listed in top 10 on "25 Most Influential Preachers of the Past 50 Years" by *Christianity Today*.
2008 – received the "E.K. Bailey Living Legend Award" by E.K. Bailey Expository Preaching Conference.
2010 – listed on "25 Most Influential Preachers of the Past 25 Years" by *Preaching Magazine*.[10]

Haddon Robinson also edited the *Christian Medical Society Journal* and wrote articles for various publications.[11]

Among Dr. Robinson's several books about preaching, one in particular has achieved an almost classic status: *Biblical Preaching: The Development and Delivery of Expository Messages* [Grand Rapids, Mich.: Baker, 1980; 3rd ed., 2014]. This title, a widely-recognized work on expository preaching, has long been used as a primary text in more than 140 Bible colleges and seminaries worldwide."[12]

Boston Globe featured Haddon Robinson in an article on 7 July 1996. He was aligned alongside other preaching giants: Billy Graham, John R. W. Stott, Lloyd John Ogilvie and Charles Swindoll.

Education isn't filling a pail with information; it's lighting a fire in the spirit of a learner — Dr. Haddon W. Robinson

---

Dr. Robinson spoke regularly in pulpits and schools around the world.

After teaching homiletics at Dallas Theological Seminary for 19 years (about 1960-1979), Dr. Robinson served 12 years as Denver Conservative Baptist Seminary's president (1979-1991) and shortened its name to Denver Seminary.

Then, beginning in Spring 1992, Haddon Robinson taught preaching for 21 years at Gordon-Conwell Theological Seminary before his retirement about 2013.[13] Except for 1 year when he served as "interim president" (2007-2008), Dr. Robinson filled the honored chair: "Harold John Ockenga Distinguished Professor of Preaching." And during this same time Dr. Robinson was also the senior director of the Doctor of Ministry (D.Min.) program.[14]

A former colleague, Dr. David A. Currie, describes Haddon's pioneering educational innovations in Gordon-Conwell's D. Min. program:

Working with his colleague, Alice Mathews, Haddon reconfigured the program from being course-based . . . to cohort-based with specialized tracks. This approach creates a mentored learning community, focusing on a shared passion for a particular area of ministry among the same group of students and faculty over the course of three years. Students learn with and from one another, sharing life as well as learning. . . .

[T]he result has lit fires in the spirit of learners ever since, fulfilling his own definition: "Education isn't filling a pail with information; it's lighting a fire in the spirit of a learner." D.Min. programs around the world increasingly have adopted this cohort model . . .[15]

On November 21, 1993, Dr. Haddon Robinson was the special Sunday morning speaker at Central Baptist Church, Middleboro, Mass., where it was my pleasure to introduce him to the

```
            MORNING WORSHIP SERVICE
               Central Baptist Church
                  Middleboro, Mass.
                  November 21, 1993

        Today's service will be videotaped and
        shown on local cable stations.

Piano Prelude
Hymn #111   "Come, Ye Thankful People"
Invocation Prayer
Welcome and Announcements
Duet by Ruth and Judy "Praise God", accompanied
Tithes and Offerings            by Cynthia Carver
Choral Anthem   "Fully Alive"
Doxology and Dedicatory Prayer
Pastoral Prayer
*Hymn #110   "Thanks to God!"
MESSAGE:  Special Speaker:  Dr. Haddon Robinson
Closing Hymn #430   "Count Your Blessings"
```

congregation as my special friend. He graciously enjoyed dinner with our family in Lakeville, where he shared many of his experiences with us.

Author A. P. Whitaker's home, Lakeville, Massachusetts

After 2013 and during his four short retirement years, Haddon Robinson lived at Willow Street, in Lancaster County, Pennsylvania (not far from some of his peers and former students).[16] From there, at age 86 years, he "went to be with the Lord on July 22, 2017 after a prolonged battle with Parkinson's Disease."[17]

Dr. Haddon W. Robinson was one preacher from whom you not only learned, but did so in full enjoyment of his manner and delivery. I remember Haddon as a master storyteller, noting that he was following the example of **Jesus, the Master Storyteller**. It was an honor to know this distinguished preacher.

. . . NOT JUST ANY MINISTER !
but the EXPERT !

Pedigree Chart for Haddon William Robinson

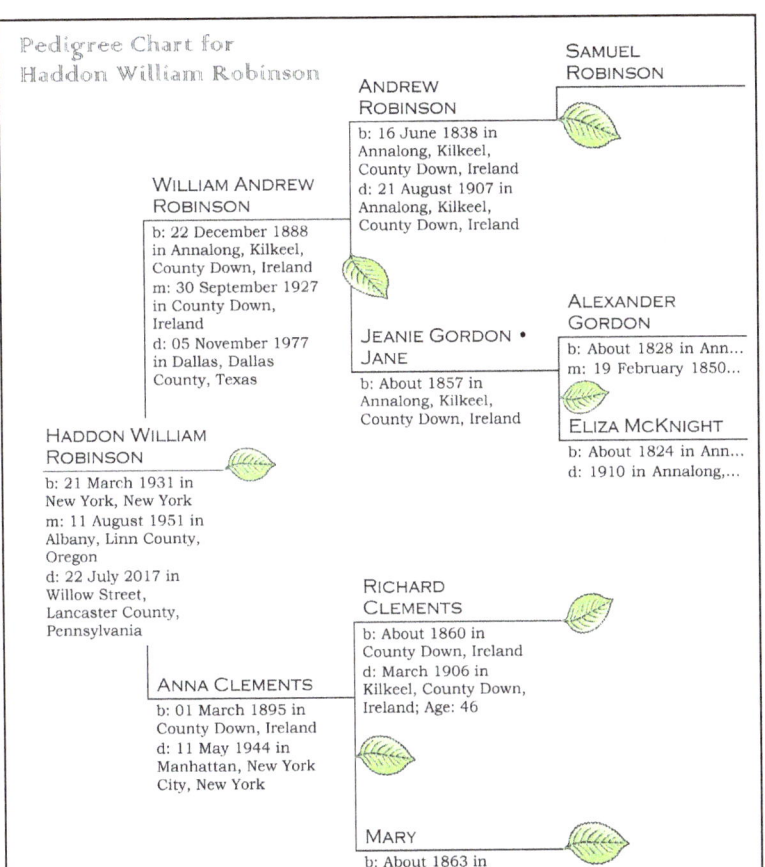

HADDON WILLIAM ROBINSON
b: 21 March 1931 in New York, New York
m: 11 August 1951 in Albany, Linn County, Oregon
d: 22 July 2017 in Willow Street, Lancaster County, Pennsylvania

WILLIAM ANDREW ROBINSON
b: 22 December 1888 in Annalong, Kilkeel, County Down, Ireland
m: 30 September 1927 in County Down, Ireland
d: 05 November 1977 in Dallas, Dallas County, Texas

ANNA CLEMENTS
b: 01 March 1895 in County Down, Ireland
d: 11 May 1944 in Manhattan, New York City, New York

ANDREW ROBINSON
b: 16 June 1838 in Annalong, Kilkeel, County Down, Ireland
d: 21 August 1907 in Annalong, Kilkeel, County Down, Ireland

JEANIE GORDON • JANE
b: About 1857 in Annalong, Kilkeel, County Down, Ireland

RICHARD CLEMENTS
b: About 1860 in County Down, Ireland
d: March 1906 in Kilkeel, County Down, Ireland; Age: 46

MARY
b: About 1863 in County Down, Ireland

SAMUEL ROBINSON

ALEXANDER GORDON
b: About 1828 in Ann...
m: 19 February 1850...

ELIZA McKNIGHT
b: About 1824 in Ann...
d: 1910 in Annalong,...

361

ENDNOTES

[1] "Dr. Haddon W. Robinson" [obituary], Charles E. Snyder Funeral Home & Crematory. Web: <https://snyderfuneralhome.com/obituary/dr-haddon-w-robinson/>; accessed 22 October 2020.

[2] Smith, Steve, "Truth Poured Through Personality: Dr. Haddon W. Robinson." *DTS Voice*, Dallas Theological Seminary, 9 January 2017. Web: <https://voice.dts.edu/article/truth-poured-through-personality-smith-steve/>; accessed 23 October 2020.

[3] "In Memoriam: Haddon Robinson: Remembering the Legacy of Former President and Harold John Ockenga Distinguished Professor of Preaching," Gordon-Conwell Theological Seminary, ©2018. Web: <https://archive.gordonconwell.edu/Haddon-Robinson.cfm.html>; accessed 23 October 2020.

[4] Smith, Steve, "Truth Poured Through Personality: Dr. Haddon W. Robinson." op. cit.

[5] "Oregon, State Marriages, 1906-1966" [image, ancestry.com].

[6] "Texas, Birth Index, 1903-1997" [image, ancestry.com].

[7] Minnesota Department of Health. "Minnesota, Birth Index, 1935-2000" [database on-line]. Provo, UT, USA: Ancestry.com Operations Inc, 2004.

[8] "Dr. Haddon W. Robinson" [obituary], op. cit.

[9] Last.fm contributors, "Haddon Robinson: Biography." Last.fm, 15 May 2009. Web. 23 Oct. 2020.

[10] "In Memoriam: Haddon Robinson: Remembering the Legacy of Former President and Harold John Ockenga Distinguished Professor of Preaching," op. cit.

[11] Last.fm contributors, "Haddon Robinson: Biography." op cit.

[12] Smith, Steve, "Truth Poured Through Personality: Dr. Haddon W. Robinson." op. cit.

[13] Hollinger, Dennis, David A, Currie and Scott M. Gibson. "Remembering the Legacy of Our Friend and Mentor, Dr. Haddon W. Robinson," *Blog*, Gordon-Conwell Theological Seminary, [blog post 28 July 2017], ©2020. Web: <https://www.gordonconwell.edu/blog/remembering-the-legacy-of-our-friend-and-mentor-dr-haddon-w-robinson/>; accessed 22 October 2020.

[14] Wikipedia contributors. "Haddon Robinson." *Wikipedia, The Free Encyclopedia*. Wikipedia, The Free Encyclopedia, 7 Jan. 2020. Web. 22 Oct. 2020.

[15] Hollinger, Currie and Gibson, op cit.

[16] Robinson's peer and contemporary, Dr. Lloyd M. Perry, also retired to Willow Street, Pa. (in 1985), living at Willow Valley Communities until his death in 1998. Similar to Robinson, Perry had "published many books about preaching, taught homiletics for years at Trinity Seminary

[i.e. Trinity Evangelical Divinity School] in Deerfield, IL, and was one of the most influential preaching professors of the last forty years"— [Pritchard, Ray, "Lloyd Perry's Benediction," *Ray Pritchard's Blog*, Keep Believing Ministries, 24 October 2006. Web: <https://www.keepbelieving.com/lloyd-perrys-benediction/>; accessed 23 October 2020].

Perry's books, *A Manual for Biblical Preaching* and *Biblical Preaching for Today's World*, were also used as textbooks.

During his 13-year retirement, Dr. Perry taught at Lancaster Bible College, where the editor was head librarian and had the privilege of sharing offices with him.

[17] "Dr. Haddon W. Robinson" [obituary], op cit.

Hudson T. Armerding
{Courtesy of Special Collections, Buswell Library, Wheaton College (IL)}

Chapter 13

Doctor HUDSON TAYLOR ARMERDING[1]

Do you remember when Sunday night church services and young people's meetings had a *testimony time* every week? I can recall one night in the 1950s when our youth group at First Baptist Church of Randolph, Massachusetts attended Trinity Baptist Church in Brockton. Three of us were asked to come up on the platform to give our testimonies. At that time, the Brockton church's pastor was Dr. Hudson T. Armerding. We often attended there after our own Christian Endeavor meetings, because our church at Randolph did not always have a regular Sunday evening service.

I have often thought about this. I remember standing there and giving a testimony, but I cannot remember anything I said – not one word! Since then, I have wondered several times what the congregation thought. *Testimony time* is seldom done at churches anymore.

For many years, another traditional activity in Protestant churches was the annual *Roll Call Supper*. This event in our church's heritage was exciting and well-attended. It was usually held on, or near, the date of the church's founding, to celebrate that happening. All church members were expected to attend. It was normally a large, formal dinner, practiced somewhat like

Thanksgiving, where the congregation praised God for their assembly and its mission.

The meal was characteristically a full-course turkey dinner complete with all the *"fixins,"* including homemade country-style pies made by the women. Sadly, the *traditional* home-baked (i.e. *from scratch*) pie has *gone by the wayside.*

Following the eating, and for those still awake, a *Roll Call* commenced. As the church clerk read through the membership roll, an appropriate response from attendees was quoting a Bible verse. Another response, possibly more important to the leadership, was a commitment pledge to support the church's ministry.

Sadly, these traditions are now rarely practiced, and have been eliminated almost everywhere. Today, we don't bother to *feed the flock* or hear their testimonies and favorite Scripture verses. But we still seek their pledges (absent the "decoration"). This reminds me of the church we now attend in Florida. While we've not formally joined (for personal reasons) and do not receive their official communications, they never miss mailing to us their weekly offering envelopes!

Hudson Taylor Armerding entered this world on the 21st of June 1918 in Albuquerque, New Mexico. His mother, Eva May (Taylor) Armerding was married to Dr. Carl A. Armerding, an itinerant preacher to Native Americans.

Hudson's parents named him after James Hudson Taylor (1832-1905), a famous British missionary to China. Although the missionary, J.

Hudson Taylor, and Hudson Armerding's mother, Eva (Taylor) Armerding, each have a Taylor pedigree traced back into Yorkshire, England, recent research has failed to identify a common ancestor.[2]

Hudson Armerding attended high school at San Diego, California. After graduating in 1935, he worked for two *gap years* on a New Zealand farm before enrolling at Wheaton College in Illinois. There, between 1937 and 1941, Hudson became a friend and classmate of Billy Graham and earned a degree in history (B.A., Wheaton College, 1941). Hudson later earned degrees in international affairs (M.A., Clark University, 1942) and history (Ph.D., University of Chicago, 1948).

Between those two advanced degrees, and during World War Two, Hudson Armerding served three years (1942-1945) as a distinguished naval officer in the Pacific Theater, aboard the USS Wichita and in eleven battles. During a brief leave home, he took a wife on December 26th, 1944: the Wheaton College voice instructor, Miriam Lucille (Bailey).

God blessed Hudson and Miriam (Bailey) Armerding with five children, born 1947-1957:

i. **Carreen A. Armerding**, born 18 Apr. 1947; married Rev. Dr. Paul Raymond Smith.[3]
ii. **Hudson Taylor Armerding II**, born 28 Oct. 1948; married Linda J.[4] (Lower).[5]
iii. **Paul Timothy Armerding**, born 18 Jul. 1953; married Laurel[6] Sue (Carlson).[7]
iv. **Miriam Ruth 'Mimi' Armerding**, born 17 Oct. 1955; married Paul Lowell Swisher.[8]

v. *Jonathan Edwards Armerding*,[9] born 15 Jun. 1957;[10] married Deborah Louise (Means)[11] on 9 Apr. 1983 in El Paso, Tex.[12]

The Armerdings, in 1948, began preparing for missions work in China. But those plans came to an end the next year when Communists took control of that country.

Dr. Armerding next became dean of Gordon College and Seminary in Wenham, Massachusetts (1949–1961), part of that time also filling-in as acting president.

During the 1950s, Hudson Armerding also pastored Trinity Baptist Church, meeting in an old but very well-kept building in downtown Brockton, Massachusetts. This congregation had been founded in 1883 as the Swedish Baptist Church.[13]

Swedish Baptist Church in Brockton, Mass., circa **1912** (later renamed Trinity Baptist Church).
(ebay.com)

This city church's growth was largely due to Dr. Hudson T. Armerding and his preaching. He was a little bit out-of-the-ordinary, a stalwart of a man, with a distinctive voice. At preaching, he was a master of delivery. His sermon messages were very logical and relevant. Even at that time, a well-educated man, such as he was, still needed to be interesting and listenable in order to attract people – especially the younger ones like us!

Trinity Baptist Church later purchased, renovated, and moved across town to 1367 Main Street – in a much-improved neighborhood, and with more ample parking. Brockton Christian School, a ministry of this church, is where my son, Keith Whitaker, graduated from high school in 1983; the ceremony was held in Trinity Baptist Church.

In 1961, Dr. Armerding left Massachusetts to teach history at Wheaton College. In 1962, he became Wheaton's first provost, preparing to succeed then-president Dr. Raymond Edman. Armerding then served seventeen years as Wheaton's president (1965–1982).

While my daughter, Dale Whitaker, attended Wheaton (1973–1975), we visited with President Armerding at his campus office. Hudson and I renewed our *old times*, reminiscing about those days at Trinity Baptist Church in Brockton, Mass.

It was during these years that president Armerding guided this Christian college campus through some turbulent times:

> During the difficult years of the Vietnam War, Dr. Armstrong . . . . worked, despite his military background, to accept with grace those students who protested the war.[14]

It was his sympathetic understanding and leadership that helped students integrate their faith with their learning, while addressing the cultural issues with which society was dealing.

President Armerding promoted stability by positive, effective leadership and was successful when others might have collapsed.

During Hudson Armerding's presidency at Wheaton, new buildings were constructed, one of them dedicated in his honor as Armerding Hall. He also served on boards of numerous Christian organizations, and was president of the National Association of Evangelicals (1970-1972).

Probably Dr. Hudson Armerding's most outstanding contribution occurred when he convinced his old college friend and classmate, Rev. Dr. Billy Graham, to entrust his archival

Billy Graham Center at Wheaton College, Wheaton, Illinois. 29 May 2013

[Christoffer Lukas Müller (https://commons.wikimedia.org/wiki/File:Wheaton_College_Billy_Graham_Center.JPG), „Wheaton College Billy Graham Center", edited by Stephen L. Robbins, <https://creativecommons.org/licenses/by-sa/3.0/legalcode>.]

papers to Wheaton College. In 1980, that large collection was deposited at the Billy Graham Center on campus.

In 2009, having lived for 91 years, Hudson Taylor Armerding passed to his eternal reward, on December 1st at Carol Stream, Illinois. He had been a champion in dedicated Christian service, a progressive educator, an encourager of those who aspired to Christian service, and a preacher *extraordinaire*.

*. . . Not Just Any Preacher,
but An Extraordinary One!*

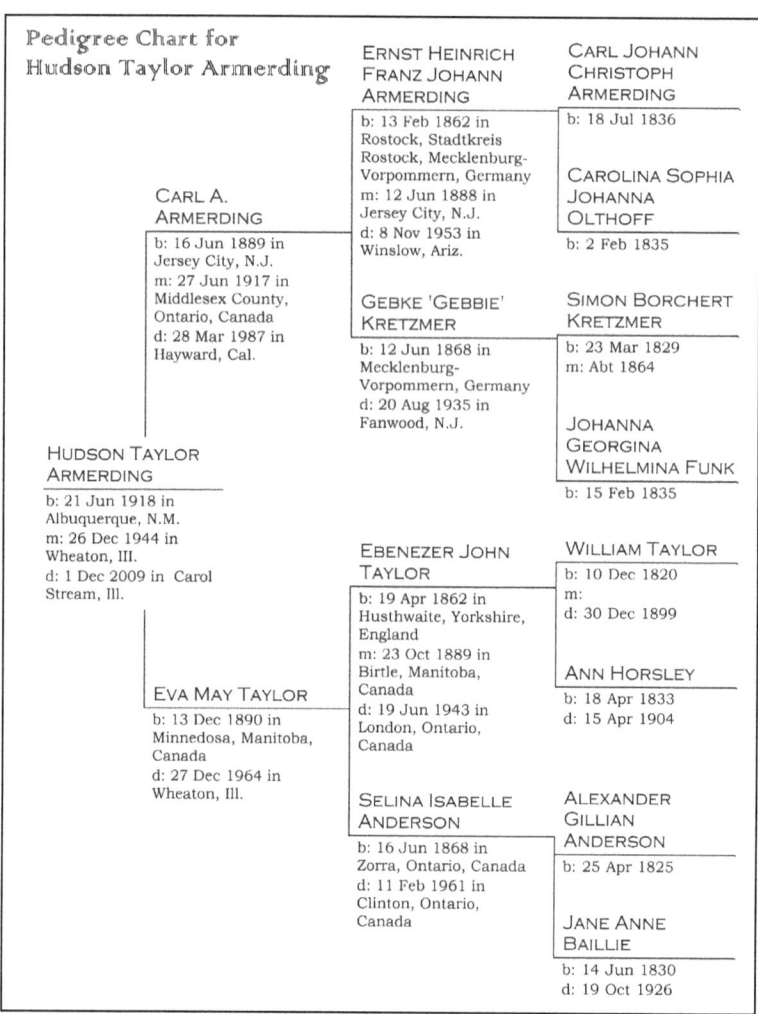

ENDNOTES

[1] Except where otherwise indicated, most of the biographical information about Hudson Armerding has been gleaned from: "Armerding, Hudson T.," *Archives of Wheaton College*, Wheaton College, ©2020. Web: <https://archives.wheaton.edu/agents/people/2671>; accessed 02 Nov. 2020.

[2] Research conducted by the editor, Stephen L. Robbins, using the online resources of FamilySearch.org, MyHeritage.com, and Ancestry.com.

[3] "U.S. Public Records Index" [database], MyHeritage.com. Record for Carreen A Smith ; "Remembering Rev. Dr. Paul R. Smith (HR)," *Seattle Presbytery PC (USA)*, updated 20 July 2020, Seattle Presbytery, ©2020.

⁴ "U.S. Public Records Index" [database], MyHeritage.com. Record for Hudson Taylor Armerding.

⁵ "James Carlton Lower, August 04, 1927 - February 10, 2009" [obituary], *Coyle Funeral and Cremation Services*, Legacy.com, © 2020. Web: <https://www.coylefuneralhome.com/obituaries/James-Lower/#!/Obituary>; accessed 02 Nov. 2020. "He is survived by . . . children Linda Armerding, (Taylor) . . ."

⁶ "U.S. Public Records Index" [database], MyHeritage.com. Record for Paul Timothy Armerding.

⁷ "Texas Birth Index, 1903-1997" [database], *FamilySearch.org*. Web: (https://familysearch.org/ark:/61903/1:1:VDJL-KMW : 5 December 2014), Laurel Sue Carlson in entry for Allison Hannah Armerding, 09 Feb 1981.

⁸ "U.S. Public Records Index" [database], MyHeritage.com. Record for Miriam R Swisher.

⁹ "Miriam B. Armerding" [obituary], *LNP Lancaster Online*, [posted] 4 Jul. 2006, updated 12 Sep. 2013 LNP Media Group Inc., © 2020. Web: <https://lancasteronline.com/obituaries/miriam-b-armerding/article_9240308d-8d54-5dc7-a6dd-2bfea2f8ea8f.html>; accessed 02 Nov. 2020. "Surviving . . . Jonathan Edwards Armerding of Albuquerque, N.M."

¹⁰ "U.S. Public Records Index" [database], MyHeritage.com. Record for Jonathan E Armerding.

¹¹ "Marjorie Ruth (Douglass) Means, 1925-2019" [obituary], *El Paso Times* (El Paso, Tex.), 15 Feb. 2019, Legacy.com, ©2020. Web: <https://www.legacy.com/obituaries/elpasotimes/obituary.aspx?n=marjorie-ruth-means-douglass&pid=191556463&fhid=23300>; accessed 02 Nov. 2020. ". . . four children . . . [including] Deborah Louise Means Armerding ..."

¹² "Texas Marriages and Divorces" [database], MyHeritage.com. Record for Jonathan E Armerding & Deborah L Means.

¹³ "Collection: Trinity Baptist Church (Brockton, Mass.) records," *Past Perfect Collections Database*, Swenson Swedish Immigration Research Center. Web: <https://augustana.pastperfectonline.com/archive/64063386-B4D4-4603-9C91-168321407486>; accessed 02 Nov. 2020.

¹⁴ "Armerding, Hudson T.," *Archives of Wheaton College*, Wheaton College, ©2020. Web: <https://archives.wheaton.edu/agents/people/2671>; accessed 02 Nov. 2020.

**Stan Griffin
Cornerstone Baptist Church, Exeter, Maine, 19 October 2020**

(image credit: Stan Griffin, "Sacrificial Living. Part 2" [videorecording]. Cornerstone Baptist Church [Exeter, Me.], 19 Oct. 2020. Web: <https://youtu.be/tonUzJQDSZc>.)

(below:) **Map of Exeter, Maine from Colby's 1885 Maine Atlas.**[1]

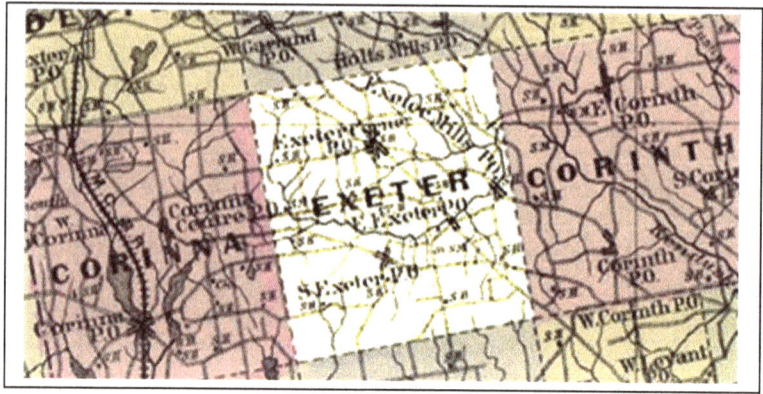

Chapter 14

Pastor STANLEY HARLAND GRIFFIN

There still are ministers dedicated to their *calling* who value advancing the Gospel above any monetary reward, status, or desire to avoid offending anyone.

One such pastor – and, most assuredly, there *are* more like him – ministers in a small, rural potato-growing town. He is Pastor Stan Griffin, the bi-vocational preacher at Cornerstone Baptist Church, Exeter, Maine. One full-time staff assistant helps Pastor Stan with the church's routine ministry.[2] In this

Former Free Will Baptist Church (built 1855). Now Cornerstone Baptist Church.
(courtesy of Stan Griffin)

community of 1092 persons,[3] the weekly worship service attendance is about 400![4]

About 25 years ago, at this town's crossroads, a little white church with a tall steeple (typical for New England) was all-but-abandoned, and no longer of any consequence – except as a picturesque structure nestled among scenic rolling hills.

A local boy, Stan Griffin, went off to college to study for ministry. Then he chose to reopen a closed church and minister in his home area. Details are told on the church's web site:

(above:) **Stan Griffin, Summer 1979.**
(below:) **Lori, Torie, Stan & Philip Griffin, Aug. 1994.** *(photos courtesy of Stan Griffin)*

> Stan Griffin was born and raised in Levant, Maine in a Christian home to Paul & Mary Griffin. Stan attended Hyles-Anderson College, Indiana in 1981. He then transferred to Baptist Bible College East in Massachusetts, then on to

Bangor Baptist College in 1983. That same year, he married his high school sweetheart, Lori White. . . .

Always feeling called to preach, Stan and his family started Cornerstone Baptist Church of Exeter, in April 1994. Married for 18 years, the Lord called Lori home after a three-year battle with cancer, in 2001. In 2002, Stan married Emily Leavitt. . . .[5]

Within a few years, the church built an addition for a larger worship center. Later, the members erected a much larger building

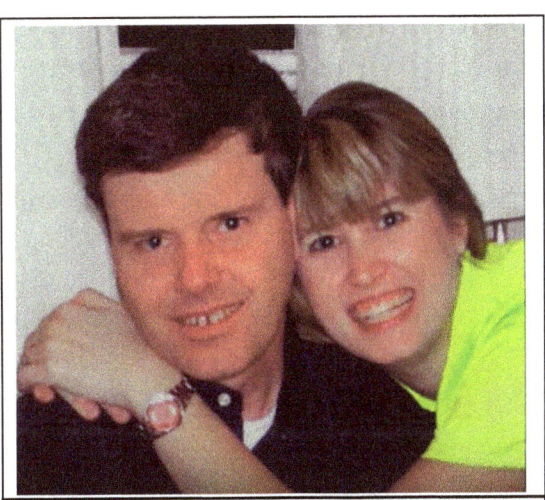

(above:) **Stan and Emily Griffin in 2006.**
(below:) **Cornerstone Baptist Church additions.**
(images courtesy of Stan Griffin)

which seats several hundred persons. This *minister* also became a prosperous local businessman, noticeably applying his business acumen to the functioning of the church.

Today, the Sunday morning worship service is tastefully executed. A worshipful atmosphere is introduced by a piano, an organ, and an older lady playing violin music. The tempo increases when the service actually begins. At that time, a group of *praise singers* renders more contemporary music which is often based upon recognizable hymns. Next, a *praise band* erupts with a lively, upbeat rendition of a more contemporary song; the very inspiring lyrics are projected onto a screen. The congregation's participation is notable. Then it is sermon time; this concludes with a meaningful, directed (but not prolonged) *call* and a benediction.

Grand Opening for the new auditorium – August 28th, 2011
(courtesy of Stan Griffin)

We have worshipped, and also celebrated! The entire service takes place within the space of one hour. This respects a person's *attention span*. And, the fact that one may exit while still awake and alert (and hungry?) is most appreciated.

But more importantly, this *preacher* isn't reticent about speaking against unChristian and unbiblical trends in the local, state and national political arenas. It is also evident that Stan Griffin's business involvement translates well into this church's operation. It is further apparent that he is surrounded by many who enhance the ministry with their distinct capabilities. The positive results are obvious.

It is most comforting to know that there are still people of various vocations who are dedicated to their work, striving for positive results. It is also comforting to realize there are still a few places of worship which champion Bible truths and present them effectively, without apology or compromise.

Back in the 1940s, in a small *down Maine* rural church, I heard the preacher describing a vivid sunset as "looking thru a freshly-butchered pig's carved ribs." I thought to myself, "Only these farm people would *get the picture*." City folk would have no idea what he was talking about!

Now, let's *fast forward* almost sixty years to March of 2020. The global coronavirus pandemic has forced closure of congregate assemblies. We find Stan Griffin, the bi-vocational pastor of Exeter, Maine's Cornerstone Baptist Church, unable to continue the large in-person Wednesday night meetings at the church. So, he has innovatively begun producing a video series of Wednesday night messages, titled "Garage Talk." It began in March 2020 with episode 1, "Garage Talk With Stan,"[6] recorded on March 20th at his home garage in Levant, Maine, then uploaded on

March 25th to *YouTube* (an online video-sharing platform) for all to view safely at their homes, on their computers.

Garage Talk **video series title frame.** *(courtesy of Stan Griffin)*

The pastor's wife, Emily, is the "expert" camera handler and "director." She does so ably on Sundays, and she excels in Wednesday's "Garage Talk" programing.

A panning view inside Stan's building reveals a usual, but neater-than-most, garage-shop. It seems somewhat "cleaned up." Probably even the women viewers would be excited to see the inside of their pastor's garage. Do you suppose they admonished their husbands to *clean up their acts*?

On the walls can be seen tools, hoses, ladders and the like, all properly hung. Tool boxes, snow

Pastor Stan Griffin in *Garage Talk*. *(courtesy of Stan Griffin)*

shovels, benches and other shop accoutrements are generally *on standby* in their assigned places. Then there was a John Deere 425 garden tractor, a Kawasaki 300 four-wheeler, a motorcycle, a Kubota lawn tractor, a large pipe threader, and a vintage automobile. Stan Griffin's garage was not a "Jay Leno's Garage,"[7] but it was almost as interesting!

Bi-vocational Pastor Stan's garage also has a "junk area," mostly of old boiler piping. He

Pastor Stan's junk pile. *(courtesy of Stan Griffin)*

discussed this "junk pile" on one Wednesday evening video,[8] relating it to the mess of junk in some people's lives. Saving "junk" for future repurposing is evidence of Stan Griffin's Yankee thrift, to be sure. But this pile's contents are also a clue to his other vocation.

Pastor Stan is a local businessman in the realm of home heating, ranging from systems installation, service and maintenance, to heating oil deliveries. Stan and his first wife Lori established their business, Griffin Oil, in 1987,[9] after a long association with his father. Stan's Dad,

Paul Griffin, had conducted a gasoline service station at a nearby crossroads corner. During the past several years, though, Stan has sold some of his business interests.[10]

Operating a business from its very basic beginnings, and through its growth into the well-known, vibrant and professional enterprise it is today, gives insight into how Pastor Stan could similarly manage a new church from its humble beginnings to what it has become. His wife's assistance, no doubt, is a contributing factor. In addition, Stan claims that she is the best pie maker he knows!

The "Garage Talk" *YouTube* video series is unique, attention-gaining, timely, appropriate and interesting. This *out-of-the-ordinary* preacher, Stan Griffin, often expresses within his messages some very basic thoughts to illustrate his outline. His use of the vernacular is well-understood by the down-to-earth local parishioners – just as well as those who, about sixty years ago, had understood their pastor's *pig's ribs* reference.

As this book goes to press, "Garage Talk" continues (now at episode 47, titled "Father's Day and dated 16 June 2011").[11]

One week, the topic was "Stewards,"[12]

Stan's restored 1939 Ford sedan in episode 7 of *Garage Talk*: "God's Recycling Program" 6 May 2020

(courtesy of Stan Griffin)

about being *good* stewards – caretakers of what we have, because it all belongs to God.

Another week, the subject was "God's Recycling Plan,"[13] illustrated with a restored 1939 Ford sedan in the garage.

In yet another weekly episode, Pastor Griffin ruminated on the "The East Wind"[14] that seems ever-present. He began this illustration by getting out his ladder and a bundle of shingles, then proceeding up onto the roof. There, he replaced missing shingles and some wind-damaged ones. Preacher Griffin's message is this: Into everyone's life the wind blows; we must be prepared to cope with whatever blows our way.

Stan replaces shingles.
(courtesy of Stan Griffin)

On February 23rd 2020, Pastor Stan Griffin's subject was Psalm 73, as he "preached through" the book of Psalms. He titled this sermon: "Can You Smell What You're Stepping In?"[15] (You might try to correlate this in your own study of Psalm 73). Pastor Griffin's attention-getting note comes after he explains how, for years, he has delivered oil to customers using his oil truck and its hose with a nozzle at the end. From his long experience, he distills this keen observation and wise admonition:

> Why do pets always choose the area of the fill-pipe to conduct their business? . . . . You

understood this when back in the truck, and the heater running, as you headed for your next delivery! . . . . Watch where you step![16]

Preacher Stan Griffin

— not just ANY minister —

but the example of a preacher whose

"steps . . . are ordered by the Lord."
— *Psalm 37:23 (King James Version)*

==

The Stan Griffin Family

STANLEY HARLAND GRIFFIN, born 23 Feb. 1962[17] in Levant, Me.,[18] son of Paul F. & Mary L. (Lufkin) Griffin.

Stan Griffin married (1st) LORI SUE WHITE, 4 Jun. 1983 in Me.[19] Lori was born 12 June 1962 in Bangor, Me.,[20] daughter of Raymond M. & Joyce M. (Williams) White. Lori died 9 Jun. 2001 in Levant, Me.[21]

Children of Stanley H. & Lori S. (White) Griffin:
    i. ***Philip Stanley Griffin,*** born 8 May 1991 in Bangor, Me.[22] He married Meagen Marie (Stubenrod), 3 Jun. 2018 in Exeter, Me.[23]
    ii. ***Victoria ' Tori ' Sue Griffin,*** born 17 Jun. 1994 in Bangor, Me.[24]

Stan Griffin married (2nd) EMILY BROOKE LEAVITT in 2002.[25] Emily was born 11 Oct. 1976,[26] daughter of Robert T. & Pamela Jane (Vanidestine) Leavitt.

Children of Stanley H. & Emily B. (Leavitt) Griffin:
    i. ***Kaitlyn Griffin,*** born Sep. 2008.[27]
    ii. ***Cody Griffin,*** born Oct. 2012.[28]

Pedigree Chart for Stanley Harland Griffin

STANLEY HARLAND GRIFFIN
b: 23 Feb 1962 in Levant, Maine

- **PAUL F GRIFFIN**
  b: 8 Dec 1936 in Maine
  m: 16 Jan 1957 in Maine
  - **ARTHUR STANLEY GRIFFIN • SENIOR**
    b: 2 May 1897 in Levant, Maine
    m: 13 Mar 1919 in Levant, Maine
    d: 12 Dec 1978 in Levant, Maine
    - **STANLEY ROLLINS GRIFFIN**
      b: 13 Jul 1868 in Me.
      m: 3 Jun 1896 in Me.
    - **LOTTIE EDNA JORDAN**
      b: 25 May 1876 in Me.
      d: 5 Jun 1923 in Me.
  - **DORIS LOUISE BATCHELDER**
    b: 13 Mar 1902 in Levant, Maine
    d: Mar 1977 in Levant, Maine
    - **WALTER NELSON BATCHELDER**
      b: 8 May 1868 in Me.
      m: 21 Nov 1891 in Me.
    - **ANNIE RUTH WAUGH**
      b: 13 Dec 1873 in Me.
      d: 3 Mar 1949 in Me.
- **MARY L LUFKIN**
  b: 30 Jun 1941
  - **HARLAND LINWOOD LUFKIN**
    b: 21 Apr 1910 in Norwood, Massachusetts
    m: 18 Sep 1933 in Bangor, Maine
    d: 15 Oct 1957 in Levant, Maine
    - **HARRY GARFIELD LUFKIN**
      b: 23 May 1881 in Me.
      m: 19 Feb 1908 in MA
    - **MARY ELIZABETH HAYNES**
      b: 30 Jun 1882 in Kan.
      d: 26 Apr 1935 in Me.
  - **LOIS JEAN WITHEE**
    b: 11 Oct 1915 in Malone, New York
    d: 5 Jul 1998 in Bangor, Maine
    - **IRVIN ALBERT WITHEE**
      b: Sep 1871 in Me.
      m: 2 Jul 1894 in Me.
    - **EDNA ELLEN WOODBURY**
      b: Dec 1874 in Me.
      d: 3 Jan 1931 in Me.

Stan Griffin: Our *Owner's Manual*, the unchanging *Bible*, can fix problems. (*"Things change,"* Garage Talk, episode 21, 19 Aug 2020; courtesy of Stan Griffin)

Cross and Crown
Detail from a stained-glass window at Vassalboro Methodist Church, Vassalboro, Maine.

(photo by Stephen L. Robbins, June 2018; edited)

[12] **Blessed is the man who remains steadfast under trial, for when he has stood the test he will receive the crown of life, which God has promised to those who love him.**

-- James 1:12 (English Standard Version)

ENDNOTES

[1] Rumsey Collection, and Colby, George N.; George N. Colby & Co. *Map of Penobscot County, Maine*. (1885). [n.d.] [internet resource]. Web: <https://www.davidrumsey.com/luna/servlet/detail/RUMSEY~8~1~331 80~1170549>. Originally a part of: Colby, George N. *Atlas of the State of Maine: Including Statistics and Descriptions of Its History, Educational System, Geology, Rail Roads, Natural Resources, Summer Resorts and Manufacturing Interests* [atlas] (Houlton, Maine: George N. Colby, 1885).

[2] Griffin, Stanley H. to Albert P. Whitaker, Jr., telephone interview, 28 October 2020.

[3] U.S. Census Bureau. *Maine, 2010: Population and Housing Unit Counts*. ([Washington, D.C.]: U.S. Department of Commerce, Economics and Statistics Administration, U.S. Census Bureau, Sept. 2012), p. 16. Web: <https://www.census.gov/prod/cen2010/cph-2-1.pdf>. "Table 8. Population and Housing Units: 1990 to 2010; and Area Measurements and Density: 2010." Population > 2010 > Maine > Penobscot County > Exeter town: 1,092.

[4] Author's estimate.

[5] "Stan Griffin," *Cornerstone Baptist Church*, Cornerstone Baptist Church of Exeter, Maine, ©2020. Web: <https://www.cbcexeter.org/people/pastor-stan-griffin/>.

[6] Griffin, Stanley H., "Garage Talk With Stan" [videorecording], *Cornerstone Baptist Church*, Cornerstone Baptist Church of Exeter, Maine, 25 March 2020. (Garage talk ; episode 1). Web: <https://www.youtube.com/watch?v=k17zSG8qPAI>.

[7] "Jay Leno's Garage" is a popular television series on collecting motor cars. It is hosted by Jay Leno, formerly the host of CNBC's "Tonight Show" until his retirement in 2014—["Jay Leno's Garage," *CNBC*. Web: <https://www.cnbc.com/jay-lenos-garage/>.

[8] Griffin, Stanley H., "God's Recycling Plan" [videorecording], *Cornerstone Baptist Church*, Cornerstone Baptist Church of Exeter, Maine, 6 May 2020. (Garage talk ; episode 7). Web: <https://www.youtube.com/watch?v=xsOdP7EwBYQ>. Summary: "Vintage Car."

[9] "Stan Griffin," *Cornerstone Baptist Church*, op cit. "In 1987, Stan and Lori started Griffin Oil out of their home in Levant."

[10] Griffin, Stanley H. to Albert P. Whitaker, Jr., telephone interview, 28 October 2020.

[11] Griffin, Stanley H., "Father's Day" [videorecording], *Cornerstone Baptist Church*, Cornerstone Baptist Church of Exeter, Maine, 16 June 2021. (Garage talk ; episode 47). Web: <https://www.youtube.com/watch?v=Az7U5ZJ2L50>.

[12] Griffin, Stanley H., "Stewards" [videorecording], *Cornerstone Baptist Church*, Cornerstone Baptist Church of Exeter, Maine, 20 May 2020. (Garage talk ; episode 9). Web: <https://www.youtube.com/watch?v=JyHVJUX0xNY>. Summary: "Being stewards of what God has blessed you with."

[13] Griffin, Stanley H., "God's Recycling Plan," op. cit.

[14] Griffin, Stanley H., "The East Wind" [videorecording], *Cornerstone Baptist Church*, Cornerstone Baptist Church of Exeter, Maine, 13 May 2020. (Garage talk ; episode 8). Web: <https://www.youtube.com/watch?v=RKWToUGK8Q0>. Summary: "Putting shingles back on the roof of the big garage."

[15] Griffin, Stanley H., "Can You Smell What You're Stepping In?" [videoecording], *Cornerstone Baptist Church*, Cornerstone Baptist Church of Exeter, Maine, 23 Feb. 2020. Web: <https://www.youtube.com/watch?v=EGryNdMQ0a8>.

[16] Ibid.

[17] "Stanley Griffin's Reputation Profile," *MyLife*, MyLife,com, ©2020. Web: <https://www.mylife.com/stanley-griffin/e337296360108>.

[18] "Stan Griffin," *Cornerstone Baptist Church*, op cit. "Stan Griffin was born and raised in Levant, Maine in a Christian home to Paul & Mary Griffin."

[19] "Maine, Marriage Index, 1892-1996" [database], ancestry.com.

[20] "Social Security Applications and Claims Index, 1936-2007" [database], ancestry.com.

[21] "Lori S. Griffin" [obituary], *Bangor Daily News* (Bangor, Me.), Mon., 11 Jun. 2001, p. 14. Web [image, newspapers.com].

[22] "New Citizens. At Bangor. Eastern Maine Medical Center, *Bangor Daily News* (Bangor, Me.), Tue., 21 May 1991, p. 18. Web: [image, newspapers.com]. "To Lori and Stanley Griffin of Levant, a son, Philip Stanley, May 8, 1991."

[23] Griffin, Stanley H., "Phil & Meagen Wedding" [videorecording], *Cornerstone Baptist Church*, Cornerstone Baptist Church of Exeter, Maine, 3 June 2018. Web: <https://www.youtube.com/watch?v=LmfcG8Xm1hM>.

[24] "Births. Eastern Maine Medical Center, Bangor" [birth announcement], *Bangor Daily News* (Bangor, Me.), Mon., 11 July 1994, p. 16. Web: [image, newspapers.com]. "To Lori and Stan Griffin, Levant, a daughter, Victoria Sue, June 17, 1994."

[25] "Stan Griffin," *Cornerstone Baptist Church*, op cit. "In 2002, Stan married Emily Leavitt."

[26] "Emily Griffin's Reputation Profile," *MyLife*, MyLife,com, ©2020. Web: <https://www.mylife.com/emily-griffin/e202691253960>.

[27] "Stan Griffin," *Cornerstone Baptist Church*, op cit. ". . . Kaitlyn was born in September 2008 . . ."

[28] "Stan Griffin," *Cornerstone Baptist Church*, op cit. ". . .Cody [was born] in October 2012."

. . . it would need very potent arguments to prove that a man had done his duty who has never preached beyond the walls of his meeting-house – Charles Haddon Spurgeon (<u>Second Series of Lectures to My Students</u> *(London: Passmore and Alabaster, 1877, p. 76-77. Web: <https://archive.org/details/1877secondseries00spur/page/76>)*

If Preacher Spurgeon were here today

(edited images: wikimedia.org, ebay.com, archive.spurgeon.org)

Chapter 15

AMEN!

> "24 **The Lord bless you and keep you;**
> 25 **The Lord make His face shine upon you,
> And be gracious to you**"
> —*Numbers 6:24-25 (New King James Version)*

We cannot read about these dedicated PREACHERS without sensing that they represent a very talented, exciting and interesting segment of society. We are inspired to investigate the reasons and methods that allowed them to emerge as successful and noteworthy servants of God in their world, exhibited in the lives they impacted. In reality, each one's accomplishments and achievements appear to be explained, in a large part, by his *approach* to his profession.

Historically, pastors visited people in their homes, thus befriending them, praying with them, hearing of their successes and struggles, and learning their concerns. These same pastors became involved in the community's activities, sports programs, homeowners' associations, sometimes advocacy groups, the chamber of commerce, and fraternal organizations. They often assisted people in some activity where an extra hand was needed. They were a foundational member of the society to which they came to minister.

In our present world, many clergymen appear as occupying a position not unlike a king – sitting upon a throne, removed from direct contact with most persons, but periodically speaking words they feel their parishoners should hear and heed.

The PREACHERS we've written about have demonstrated lasting rewards following their descent from a ceremonial position to approaching people through INVOLVEMENT. Here, one receives friendship, acceptance, relevance and respect – each an effective encouragement to more regular church attendance, where the Lord could be introduced by a credible, honored and trusted spokesperson. This *approach by involvement* appears to have led to (and could still result in) a more successful ministry.

Who can measure the influence of the pastor's council on local (even national) politics, and moral and ethical decisions, as he mingles with the population beyond just his congregation? The *Reverend* is, or should be, respected for his wisdom, knowledge and spiritual guidance, as a *set apart* authority.

It is with some regret and consternation that, within many circles where they've failed to mingle, pastors may no longer be viewed as credible or worthy of respect. For their part, pastors have a host of excuses to draw upon. Some in ministry are just uninterested in mingling, some think they are too busy, and others believe that separation is mandatory. Absent a pastor's presence, organizations have no moral compass nor guidance; in fact, *religion* gets totally *shelved*. If the church and its leadership are not interested in them, "them" is uninterested in the church.

The exceptional PREACHERS we present prove how pastoral INVOLVEMENT can *make a difference* in positive ways.

In addition to *involvement*, these men have demonstrated positive leadership in other areas. They have approached their *call to full-time Christian service* apart from expectations of financial gain.

For perhaps a majority of laymen today, their career choice is based upon its potential financial rewards, sometimes ignoring their talents, desires, interests, and abilities. Those choosing a ministry occupation, can now find much-improved salary levels and attractively lower work demands; the spiritual condition of the populace may get a dangerously lower priority.

We appreciate pastors who place gospel proclamation above expected financial gain. That said, we still want our pastors to have a "normal" life like ours and enjoy the same material comforts that we do. But, "we get what we work" has to be factored into this equation. Specifically, we note that Dr. Philbrook assumed the pastorate in Randolph at the beginning of, and through, the *Great Depression;* and he somehow managed to do his work despite obvious hardship, "for the cause of Christ."

We admire our preachers' positive approaches throughout long hours accomplishing their tasks – without complaint. As in other professions, the pastors' hard work has realized great rewards. We note that throughout the 1900s, the typical church staff consisted of only its pastor – no associates and possibly no secretary. And this sole pastor accomplished more than an entire church staff does today. Some, like "Bill" Stone, were responsible for literally *keeping the fire burning*. Such dedication has reaped vast rewards; only eternity will reveal their extent.

In larger churches (however they are defined), one now sees an abundance of *pastor associates* (however they may be implemented). It is commendable if their appointments were necessary to lessen the minister's workload and responsibilities. But *associates* seldom reach out beyond their church's walls to involve themselves with the *common folk* in their towns, cities or hamlets. There they could develop credibility for their church – with no more than their friendliness, concern, viability, and interest.

A revised *approach* seems key – something the church and progressive pastor-preachers will need to reconsider. The church should no longer be that building on the hill where a group of misunderstood, isolated, independent thinkers meet for "funny" ideas and practices. A church's interaction with its local community is necessary to dispel its being perceived as a gathering of *strange* and unknown people.

And one more thing! In this day of relaxed thinking and dispelled formality, the church and congregation which still addresses its leader as *Pastor, Preacher,* or *Doctor* (and not by his first name) displays earned and proper respect.

We trust that you have enjoyed reading about the lives and ministries of these unique preachers.

We also hope that you may share the excitement of their ministries. To some we admonish, "Go and do likewise." To others, may you have a new appreciation for the *preacher* you are, or know.

A PREACHER is one who declares God's truth, through a lecture on a Scriptural theme, or an oration on a theological truth, with the intent to arouse hearts, to awaken to God's life-giving glory, and to enthrall those *born again*— (paraphrased from Jonathan Edwards, a dynamic evangelist of the past).

Incidentally, a *pastoralist* is a person who raises livestock!

The act of *benediction* is an anticipated and concluding blessing on a congregation, announced by the preacher, using God-given words from Scripture. It is so much more dignified, reverent and fitting than most of today's *invitations* that a benediction has often been substituted for an invitation.

Hear ye!

20 **Now the God of peace, that brought again from the dead our Lord Jesus, that great shepherd of the sheep, through the blood of the everlasting covenant,**
21 **Make you perfect in every good work to do his will, working in you that which is wellpleasing in his sight, through Jesus Christ; to whom be glory for ever and ever. Amen.**
—*Hebrews 13: 20-21 (King James Version)*

Court is adjourned!

PLEASE BE SEATED!

Amen.

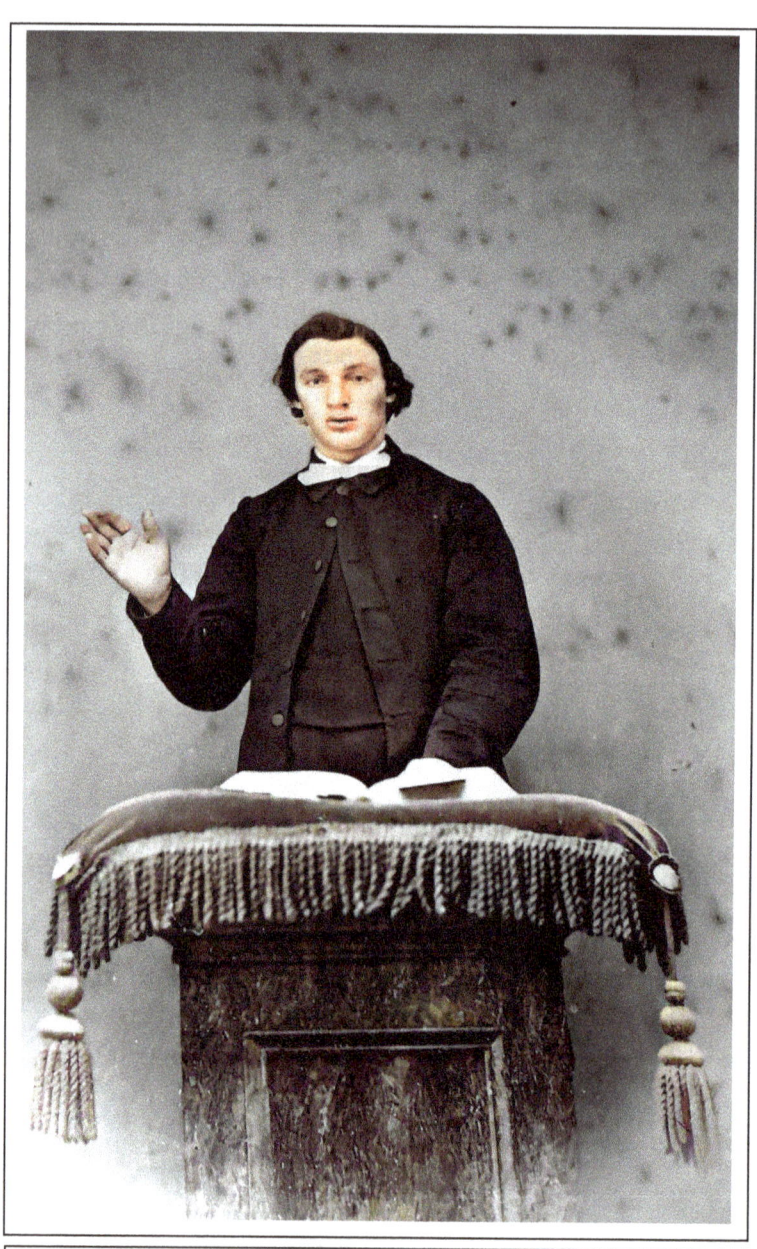

A young preacher of the 1800s *(ebay.com; edited)*

Chapter 16

EPILOG!

> "13 ... **Jesus Christ;** 14 **Who gave himself for us, that he might redeem us from all iniquity, and purify unto himself A PECULIAR PEOPLE, zealous of good works."**
> —*Titus 2:13b-14 (King James Version;* **author's emphasis added**)

In writing this book, I considered including the interesting stories of other PREACHERS with whom I have been associated over many years. Unfortunately, space and time have not permitted each one a chapter in this publication. Regardless, I am forever grateful for so many who not only ministered to me spiritually, but were instrumental in my training for whatever church endeavors I pursued during my lifetime. Although they are not extensively profiled, permit me to briefly mention a few preachers worthy of recognition.

Rev. E. Russell Goodnow was pastor of a small country church in West Bridgewater, Mass. which we attended after moving away from First Baptist Church in Randolph. From him I learned, first hand, some real basics in church operations. In addition to becoming a deacon for the first time, I was responsible for producing the weekly church bulletin, put together in the parsonage attic. Basic tools included a manual typewriter and a hand-cranked mimeograph. Pastor Goodnow later went on to become dean at Providence-Barrington College, until its merger with Gordon College.

Then came our move to First Baptist Church of Rockland, and the pastorate of Rev. Howard Higgins (see chapter 8). Then we moved to Central Baptist Church of Middleboro, where we got to know Rev. Paul West. He pastored there for over twenty-five years. During this time, it was my privilege to assist Dr. Vernon Grounds of Denver Seminary in conferring Dr. West's doctorate degree.

At Middleboro, I became the unofficial *worship leader* and *song leader*. The Sunday night service was generally a full house event, and broadcast live over a local radio station. My abilities for these roles were developed under Dr. Carlton Booth. <u>On The Mountain Top</u>[1] is his autobiography.

Pastor Paul West often enjoyed homemade popovers at our home in Bridgewater, baked by Norma. Many times, the dinner party included the presence of Clifford Jones (see chapter 7).

For a time, W. Glyn Evans was our *interim pastor*, becoming a close Whitaker family friend. He wrote books, including the devotional, <u>Daily With The King</u>.[2] His very unusual preaching style demanded attention and response.

Another *preacher* with whom it was a pleasure to work and learn was Rev. Stuart Taylor. He was truly an excellent Bible expositor and a successful leader. It was my pleasure to drive to Canada with some of the *deacon board* to hear and interview him, before a calling him to Central Baptist Church. Rev. Taylor's first visit to Middleboro is a truly entertaining story, flavored by the author's limousine picking him up at Boston's Logan airport. The drama and remembrances of that event are another story, told in our first book!³

While at Central Baptist, one new attendee was Rev. Walter Dryer. He had pastored a church in Claremont, N.H. but moved to southern Mass. to be *executive director* of Community Chaplains Service, Inc. He succeeded the founder, Rev. David Kimball, who retired for medical reasons. David's wife, Gwen, wrote his biography: <u>"You Say What, Lord?"</u>⁴ This was a fast-growing ministry to nursing home patients, led by many retired ministers. I became a *director* and *chairman of the board* and served with Pastor Dryer for several years. Our fellowship has continued even after Pastor Dryer's retirement to North Carolina.

Many preachers crossed my path, each with a different style and charged personality. Dr. Gordon Anderson, an evangelist-pastor who founded Tele-Missions, International, spoke with authority in his loud and deep Norwegian accent. Indeed, he could PREACH; and once heard, he was remembered! His book, <u>Born To Preach</u>,⁵ written in his 90s, details an exciting life.

When I served on the board of Tele-Missions, International, Dr. Ben Armstrong was a frequent attendee and speaker. Formerly a Presbyterian pastor, he was then *director* of National Religious Broadcasters and a dynamic speaker. Associations with presidents, world leaders and dignitaries were a part of his life. Ben became a dear friend, continuously assisting the Tele-Missions ministry. Norma and Ruth Armstrong (Ben's wife) often spent time together in various cities during meeting sessions, followed by shopping together – mostly for shoes! Ben's book, <u>The Electric Church</u>[6] tells a story worth reading.

For several years, we were associated with Dr. John DeBrine and his radio program, *Songtime*. He was perhaps the first Christian *disc jockey*. John was another dynamic in-the-pulpit expositor who had the power to *move the crowd* in positive ways – and especially for the support of his soul-winning ministry. Dr. John DeBrine recently died, on March 3rd, 2021 at the age of 96 years. His by-line, often heard on the airwaves, was: "Grow in grace, so you won't groan in disgrace."

Relating stories of well-known personalities is interesting. But we need not forget the PREACHERS in so many of our smaller and struggling churches, who give themselves sacrificially to *getting the WORD out* so that people may respond to the Gospel. Pastor John Hooper,[7] my son-in-law makes this list. John is the one *preacher* of them all who most thrills me. Coming out of a less-than-coveted background, Pastor John now has a zeal to make the Lord known to his rural audience. As a *preacher*, he excels with full and deep study, preparation, and delivery of a well-thought-out, logical and convincing sermon – worthy of a greatly expanded audience.

This listing could continue, each *preacher* having a unique influence on me. They were PREACHERS – not just *any* preachers – but extraordinary ones, dedicated to the Lord, and with a zeal for evangelizing anyone they encountered.

Educated expositors, talented leaders, dedicated servants of the Lord, and most of all – my mentors.

H̲ear Ye!

The Parson in Geoffrey Chaucer's *Canterbury Tales*
in Chaucer's **Middle English** and in *Modern English (interlinear)*

He was a shepherde, and noght a mercenarie.

He was a shepherd and not a hired man.

And though he hooly were and vertuous,

And though he holy was, and virtuous,

He was to synful man nat despitous,

He was to sinful men not spiteful,

Ne of his speche daungerous ne digne,

Nor in his speech overbearing nor arrogant,

But in his techyng discreet and benygne.

But in his teaching respectful and warmhearted.

Endnotes

[1] Booth, F. Carlton. *On the Mountain Top*. (Wheaton, Ill: Tyndale House Publishers, 1984).
[2] Evans, W. Glyn (William Glyn). *Daily with the King*. (Chicago: Moody Press, ©1978).
[3] Whitaker, Albert Preston., Jr. with Stephen L. Robbins. *This Is My Story: A Story of the Whitaker Family*. (Brewer, Maine: North Wind Publishing, ©2015), p. 447, 506, 552-553.
[4] Kimball, Gwen Bibber. *"You Say What, Lord?": A Journey into Trust, the Story of Community Chaplain Service*. Pittsburgh: Dorrance Publishing Company, ©1998.

[5] Anderson, Dr. Gordon S., Sr. *Born to Preach: The Amazing Journey and Adventures of an Evangelist-Pastor*. ([United States]: Xulon Press, ©2014).

[6] Armstrong, Ben. *The Electric Church*. Nashville: Thomas Nelson Publishers, ©1979.

[7] John Hooper is pastor of The Maple Street Church, Barnstead, N.H.

Appendices

Appendix A

HOW TO BE KING OF YOUR CASTLE
by Polly Utley

Hey Guys

Would you like to be king of your castle
Where the world becomes your oyster?
Would you like your wife to adore you,
Where your ego she would always bolster?

Would you like her to fancy you handsome
Even though you're average, you know?
Would you like her to say you're a he-man,
With those muscles a-bulging just so?

Would you want her to call you her hero
And say you'd protect her from harm?
Would she say she'd not fear an intruder,
That you'd fight for her life – makes her calm?

Would you want her to tell all her girlfriends
'Bout the way you romance her each day?
Would she say you just thrill her each morning,
With a kiss and a "Love you always"?

'Bout the candy and flowers you send her
On the special of specials – you know?
The birthdays, and heart days, the wedding
That comes 'round every year 'bout now?

Would you like her to say you're a father,
Of excellence, kindness, and fun?
That you help with the kids in the evening,
When she has to be out on the run?

Can she say you help with the housework?
Take your place in the house that's a mess?
Not the chair that's inviting and comfy,
With the TV – to calm your distress!

Is she proud that you split 50-50,
The chores that are waiting to be?
Completed with cheer and no hassle,
When she earns the money – like thee?

Would you like for your home to be Heaven,
Where Christ really reigns so supreme?
Where no squabbles and fusses are present,
Where there's peace and contentment, it seems?

Where the world is shut out of your lifestyle,
And the LORD is the word in your home?
Where you and your spouse pray together,
And you know you are never alone?

I'm fixin' to give you the answer,
To all that I've said here today!
Now listen to all of the wisdom;
You'll be glad, you'll be wise – I pray!

To my husband – I'm queen of the nation.
I'm a princess that's never done wrong.
He treats me like an angel – made out of glass,
I'm fragile, I'm delicate – not strong!

Here's a day in the life of my husband!
In his duties as king of the hill!
No wonder I love him, adore him and such,
When I tell you the truth, then you will!

In getting me off in the morning,
To the job that I have, that's so nice,
He tells me, "Hey Hon, it's time to get up,
But 10 minutes to sleep, will suffice"!

He lays awake for the time that's allotted,
He lets me snooze till the clock is all gone!
Then gently he wakes me, "I'm sorry it's time."
I get up – get all dressed and adorned!

He brings me coffee to the room where I sleep;
And helps me with lunch and my things!
He heats up the car when the weather is cold,
And cleans off the frosting that clings!

We kneel by the bed when the Scripture is read,
To ask for the start of the day.
He takes my hand and kisses it light,
That's the signal to start in to pray.

We pray for the kids, and all of the grands,
For their troubles, their sorrows, and plight.
We pray for their souls, that their day will be nice,
They'll prosper, they'll be happy, not fight!

We pray for the church, and all of you here,
That you'll grow in the Lord all your days.
We pray or the number to increase in our fold,
If we do that – A Building We'll Raise!!!!!!

I come home from school when day's work is done,
I'm met at the door with a kiss!
"Hi Babe! How's your day?", he says with a smile,
As he makes me a cup of hot bliss!

That's tea, or caffeine, or maybe some juice,
But when given with love, it is bliss!
We sit down to talk, and rest for my bones,
He tells me my company he missed!

As I look around, I break out in smiles,
For the house is as neat as can be.
Lest you think he's a saint and never does sin,
The score he will get is a three!!!

Three out of five is a very good grade,
But some things he leaves in the sink.
The floor is all shined, and the rugs are all clean,
But the bathroom, he gives it a wink!!

Ah! Ha! What is that I smell from the ov!
Pot pie with the crust Oh! So brown!
He gets an A for the baking he does,
And the bread is so high – less the crown!!

"Have I told you today that I love you, my dear?",
He says with his lips on my neck.
"Why, no!", say I with a coy little smile,
I hug him – He breaks out in a sweat!

Whoops! Back to the subject we're discussing today,
Of how you can make wives submit!
To your every whim if it's coming from HIM,
Who guides you from that BOOK OF WRIT.

Supper is served and the TV turned on,
We help each other with this.
I get the drinks and maybe the forks,
He does the rest, His heart bless!

The supper is finished, the TV turned off,
He's off to the office to play!
I think he is cute when he punches the keys,
A small boy, a new toy to display!

He gets tired, you know, of doing compute,
And comes to the den to recoup.
He sits by my side, On the couch we abide,
And into his arms I will swoop!!

"Have I told you today that I love you, my dear?",
He says with his lips — now POLLY!!!!!
Stop thinking like that, these guys are all nice,
Their thoughts are all pure, by golly!!!!!!!

Well anyway fellas, you get my drift,
Of how you can make wife adore.
The things that you do, the things that you say
And, generally, S<small>LAVE</small> for you more!!!!

Just treat her as if you are courting her still.
Remember how precious that was?
She did no wrong, she was a delight –
H<small>EY</small>!! She's S<small>TILL</small> great in all that she does!!!!

Appendix B

MEMORIES OF MY CHURCH
by Polly Utley

I remember the day back in '79 . . .
We started a new work, we felt it was time.
First Wednesday we met at Richard and Pat's.
We were excited and knew God agreed with that!

Next came the carport of Shirley and Troy.
We set up the chairs and gathered with joy.
What a wonderful time of singing and fun,
The tie that binds was around everyone!!

We stayed at the Welch's and planned where to seek
To establish a building to meet in each week.
The firehouse was offered, we need search no more,
We worshipped one Sunday & fire closed our doors!!

Well, back to the carport of Shirley and Troy.
We set up the chairs and gathered with joy . . .
What a wonderful time of singing and fun,
The tie that binds still 'round everyone!!

As time went on, we, of course, had to move.
The carport had shrunk, what were we to do??
*The L*ORD *had it worked out, no cause for a fuss.*
The church on the highway? Would it share with us?

They worshipped on Saturday, so Sundays were free!
You think they would let us rent, for a fee??
The men got together with the Seventh-day folk.
"Of course you can use it", that pastor spoke!!

How long did we use those folks' precious things?
'Twas more than a year, if my memory rings!
We grew and we grew till we finally faced,
That we had to get out and find our own place!

We first had to find the most perfect spot,
To build our church, so that it sought,
All the Bridgetown community and welcome it here,
To share lives with ours, and know GOD was near.

You know how the LORD works in mysterious ways?
The chapel appeared not long after we prayed!
Oh, of course, it took work to set up the plan,
To move it from there, to our very own land!!

The memories have flooded my thoughts as I write,
'Bout things that happened both day and night.
In that little church with its innocent charm,
The LORD smiled upon it, wrapped it up in his arms!!

Can you picture it still, with its sweet little rooms?
'Twas not a mansion, but we made it bloom,
With pews made of oak, with its rugs for our feet,
With a piano, a podium, for Rolla to preach!!

Hey! Remember the time the preacher said, "Y'all,
Please pray for our sick, especially my Poll . . .
She is home in bed, just as sick as can be.
Troy is home too, in bed, like she"!!!!!!!!

Remembered we giggled, and guffawed with glee???
The preacher said, "What? Why you laughing at me?
Oh! No!!", he said scolding, "Your mind – it is bent!!
It's there in the gutter – Please! Won't you repent?"

"This is your life, Rolla Utley," we said. . . .
Chris spoke of him, of the life that he led,
How he came to be part of GOD's family,
Then how he came to this place, presently!!

Who was it that had that big bright idea??
To buy him a suit to wear, when he's here??
The suit came from Goodwill, all crumpled and stuff,
They gave it to him with grass in the cuff!!!!!

Oh! My word! I can't stand it – I'm going to cry!
I can't stop my brain as much as I try!
I must get along with this history . . .
Of how our church grew to give us memories!!

The day finally came to raise this first wall. . .
The guys got together to work, one and all. . .
We gals came along to help with the plan,
We cooked for those guys, and errands we ran!!

We cleaned and we polished as each room was done!
We helped with the paint and curtains we hung!
The nursery was ready, right down to the bibs.
We had swings, toys, rockers, and Jenny Lind cribs!!

"We shall not all sleep", said the sign on the wall!
"But we'll all be changed." Get the meaning, you all?
The preacher announced from the pulpit, you see, . . .
"All of you young folks should start a family"!!

We were building the church, one step at a time.
We paid half of this house with our nickels & dimes.
Each time we asked if finances were there,
We were told to go on, L<small>ORD</small> answered our prayers!!!

So many things have happened each year.
Remember the songs, when Christmas came near?
I remember that play – the name I'm remiss. . .
Paul ruined my song with his howling – with Chris!

We had sorrows and woes, and riches untold.
We had wonderful times when we meet.
We had sermons so great, stacked high on our plate,
And of course, great food here to eat!!!!!!

We had school for children when summertime came,
We've had parties for them and for us!
We gals loved to gather for brides or for babes,
We'd shower them all, make a fuss!!!!!

I must tell you more of this story today . . .
Why Bonnie and I sit apart, always!
We cannot behave, no matter we try.
Listen to this, and you will know why!!

You gals in the back with your lips all a chatter,
Please share it with us and say what's the matter.
Bonnie stood up, I slid down in the pew.
"Oh! Sir!," said she, "We would embarrass you!!"

"Tut! Tut!", said the preacher all rigid and stern,
"I've had my say! And now it's your turn."
"Oh dear!", said Bon. I 'LAID' down in the pew.
"Our names, when they're shortened, spell BM????"

"Ahem!", said the preacher, and choked on his spit!
"I'm sorry I asked. Let's just get on with it!!
Come forward, dear wife, and sit by the door!
You will sit there forever; With Bonnie? – no more!!!"

Well, you can see today how the LORD worked it out!
With our prayers & our labor, that's what it's about!
Folks getting together, with love on their minds,
Let's sing it as one – "Blest be the tie that binds!!!!!"

Appendix C

THE SUNDAY STONE [1]
by Rev. Eugene S. Philbrook

In old English coal mines there is sometimes found a very curious and interesting deposit of limestone. When a section of this rock is examined it is found to consist of many "strata," or layers, one above another, with this peculiarity that, after six layers of a smoky or blackish color, there appears with great regularity a layer of pure white. And so it is through the whole formation – six layers of dark and then a stratum of white. "How did it happen?" The answer is easy. Water, highly impregnated with carbonate of lime, trickled through the roof and walls of the mine and left its stony deposit upon the floor. When the men were working, coal dust mingled with the lime water and colored the layer. When the men rested, as all God-fearing and law-abiding people should rest, if possible, one day in seven, the deposit for that day was pure and white. Thus, all unconsciously, those sturdy English colliers left an enduring record of their righteousness as a lesson for others, including ourselves; and the recording stone is appropriately called "the Sunday Stone."

Through all Christian society a similar formation may be traced. Six dusty days of toil and care and one day of rest and worship, this is the law of God and man; but some, not satisfied with coloring the six, would also smutch the remaining one. Let us "remember the Sabbath day to keep it holy," for it is a Divine and venerable institution. When the world was fresh from the hand of the Creator, the Sabbath principle was laid down, and "the Lord blessed the Sabbath day and hallowed it." It is evident that before the Mosaic law was given this day was recognized and observed. At Sinai, amidst the thunders and lightnings of the Mount that burned with the fire of God's presence, the "ten commandments" were given. They are the essence of moral and religious truth and duty, and the embodiment of eternal and universal principles of righteousness. Idolatry and profanity are always and everywhere sinful. Murder, adultery, theft and perjury are universally black and damnable. Dishonor toward parents and covetousness are eternally iniquitous. And now, surrounded by these nine, we discover a tenth, "remember the Sabbath day to keep it holy." It is safe to say that this commandment is violated by thousands of people who would be shocked at the very idea of breaking some of the others. The fourth commandment is just as sacred and binding as the first three or last six. It was not done away by Christ, as some attempt to argue, but remembered and hallowed and spiritualized by Him. Neither was the Divine idea lost when the day was changed from the seventh to the first. Christ arose upon the first day of the week, and appeared to His disciples upon successive Sundays. The Apostles celebrated the Lord's Supper upon the first day of the week, and upon that day religious meetings were held and benevolent offerings were made. Before the death of the Apostle John it was widely observed as the Christian Sabbath and known as "the Lord's Day." Thus sanctioned by apostolic usage, the day was legally recognized by Constantine in 321 and made a law of the church by the Council of Laodicea in 363. The essential idea is one day in seven for rest and worship.

The Christian Sabbath is a human and humane institution. It ministers to the manifold nature and needs of mankind – physical, moral and spiritual. The human structure is built on the seven-day plan. God says, "rest one day in seven." If you overwork, "typhoid fever may get you. Then you will probably get well or die on the seventh, fourteenth or twenty-first day." When the great premier, William E. Gladstone, was asked to speak into a phonograph that a record might be made for use 50 years later, this was what he said, "I owe my life and vigor through a long and busy career, to the Sabbath day with its blessed surcease of toil!" The physical benefits of the day can never be estimated. It has probably done more to conserve health and strength of men than improved sanitation, medical discoveries and the revival of athletic sports all together. Hence the violation of the Sabbath law is always fraught with evil consequences. God Almighty says, "Honor my day," and the person who tramples it under his foot will surely, sooner or later, meet with misfortune. The law of the State also says, "Honor this day"; and if you kill game on Sunday or keep your shop open you are a fit subject for the indignation of the community and the action of the court.

Again, the Christian Sabbath is a blessed and blessing institution. "God blessed the Sabbath day and hallowed it," that is, He set it apart as something sacred and benevolent. The day is an inestimable physical good, but it is a moral and spiritual necessity. It is intended to minister to the higher nature and need of man. We are living in a strenuous and materialistic age, which tends to cramp and imprison the soul. A certain nobleman captured his chief enemy and built him into the wall of his castle, piling the great stones about him and leaving him there to perish. That is about the way many people treat their own souls. Six days in the week they tug and strain to pile up around themselves a mass of "rocks," and the seventh they use to cement the wall with Godless pleasure. "The Manufacturing Jeweler," a trade journal, is responsible for the statement that more than two million dollars' worth of jewels are lost every season at American summer resorts. It is a notable fact also, as Dr. Banks says, that "more people lose the priceless jewels of character in their hours of amusement and recreation than while engaged in the serious work of life." The lesson is evident.

"The Sunday Stone" is itself "a gem of purest ray serene," which should be polished and guarded with the utmost care. King Edward received as a Christmas gift the largest diamond in the world. The rough stone was discovered by chance in the debris of the Premier mine, near Pretoria. It weighed over one pound and six ounces, and was named "the Cullinan," from the president of the mining company. The gem was split, cut and polished in Amsterdam by the most skillful experts, four of whom worked a whole year from seven in the morning till nine at night, in a special locked and guarded room, putting the finishing touches on the King's jewels. Every night the stones were conveyed by the manager, guarded by ten fully armed men, to a room with walls of iron and cement, where they were placed in a safe in a secret vault having nine locks. Today the great Cullinan diamond graces the crown jewels of England. There is a jewel even more precious which should be most jealously guarded from theft and pollution for the King of Heaven – it is the Christian Sabbath.

ENDNOTES

[1] Published in: *Sanford Tribune* (Sanford, Maine), Friday, 15 January 1909, page 4. Online: <https://springvale.advantage-preservation.com/> ; accessed 09 June 2020.

Appendix D

OUR PASTOR
A Tribute to Dr. Eugene S. Philbrook

by Mrs. Edwin Stetson[1]

He walks with God.
O truth divine that God and man may thus entwine.
And we with eyes of faith may see
Through veil of flesh, Thee, only Thee.

He leads his flock like Him of old,
In paths unseen, through pastures green.
In quiet prayer he awaits His will,
And draws all men within the fold,
And if he loves to linger where
The brooks and hills hide treasures rare,
We know he finds nature's Creator there –
      He walks with God.

This patient, saintly man ordained
To carry on the work and plan of Him
Who knows so well the thoughts and ways of man,
And on this servant His burden laid;
The way is so often hard beset with many secret fears.
The years exact their toll of sacrifice and tears,
Still on he goes, his Master's business must be done.
Night falls, and man's race will soon be run –
      He walks with God

None knock in vain at his door for help,
The marriage rite, or funeral bier, the hospital call,
The sick that wait, calmly as he goes, his duty clear.
The widow and orphan feel the unseen Presence
Revealed by kindly smile and deed, by symbol of a holy zeal –
      He walks with God.

And, if man's selfishness and greed bite deep,
Within his soul a holy vigil keeps
And, Enoch-like, he walks with God,
This noble man in intent, thought and plan
Lives but to serve God and his fellowman.
And, walking thus, through day and hour,
Men see and feel the secret of his power –
        He walks with God.

ENDNOTES

[1] An attempt was made to contact some of Mrs. Stetson's descendants, for permission to include her poem here. The response was positive, and there are no known copyright restrictions.

    A "reading by Mrs. Linda Whittemore, an original poem, 'Our Pastor,' by Mrs. Edwin Stetson" was read 16 May 1940 at a surprise party in celebration of Rev. Eugene S. Philbrook's 20th anniversary as a pastor at First Baptist Church in Randolph, Mass.—["Rev. E.S. Philbrook Honored By Friends and Parishoners," _Patriot Ledger_ (Quincy, Mass.), Fri., 17 May 1940 , p. 18 (image, genealogybank.com); no poem text.].

    The text of the poem was printed in the church bulletin for Rev. Philbrook's funeral service.

Appendix E

Plus Ultra

. . . of making many books, there is no end
—Ecclesiastes 12:12 (King James Version)

by Albert P. Whitaker, Junior

The pastor of my church during my "growing up" years was the Reverend Doctor Eugene Philbrook, a long-time pastor of the First Baptist Church of Randolph, Massachusetts. He was a mentor to me, especially in my years at Boston University. Many early evening visits with him in his study, at his parsonage between the Church and our house, broadened my horizons. And his help in formulating theses and papers will always be remembered and much appreciated. Among other things, he often advised both Harvey Cossaboom and myself in public Scripture reading, the art of sermon preparation and delivery.

Frequently, he would usher us into the church sanctuary to practice Bible reading, or message delivery at the pulpit, while he sat in the last row and coached us in proper elocution and reading. I can still hear him, in his quiet professional demeanor, give encouragement to read slowly, with careful enunciation and distinct sounds, never dropping the last word or syllable, effectively projecting our God-given ability and voice strength. There were no microphones or sound systems then, just the acoustics of the room and voice power. Over and over again, we practiced until Doctor Philbrook felt we had mastered the lesson. The skills learned here were often proven extremely useful in my lifetime of speaking opportunities, including representing the Gideons. How much the majority of our young people today need to develop these skills!

When Doctor Philbrook went "home" to Heaven, his wife Bessie gave to Harvey and me a file cabinet of his sermon notes. These were in the form of letter-size paper, folded halfway, and with various newspaper or magazine clippings or other notes folded into a neat package. On the face appeared the sermon title, often a Scripture reference, and then the places and dates where he had used this material. These outlines were written in ink pen in an older type of script, and underlined as emphasis was warranted. Harvey and I went through these files and divided them according to our own interests. Over many years, I have often used at least some of these topics and the written score, and have even used some of the unique illustrations that have been timeless.

I often think of a time when we, as young people, attended another church in the next town on some Sunday evenings. The pastor divulged to me that he had just preached the seventh message in a series, and that he had preached the same series the seven weeks prior, but with one exception: he changed his illustrations. He was surprised that no one had noticed. (At least no one had said anything!). Doctor Philbrook's unusual and unique titles (which I subsequently used) would have quickly identified our emphasis, possibly more readily.

My interest and curiosity were elevated by one cover sheet of Doctor Philbrook's many sets of sermon notes. In heavy red ink were the words, in quotation marks, "PLUS ULTRA" and a subtitle, "Sail On." And even more interesting was the date and location of his presentation: "Paterson, New Jersey" and "March 25, 1928." I have no idea why or where he was preaching in Paterson, New Jersey. However, additional dates had been added: "Everett, Mass., April 14, 1929 – Exchange[1] with Rev. A. Judson Hughes." Other dates appear: June 23, 1941 at North Reading State Sanatorium; Randolph, Massachusetts, October 12, 1941; Columbus Day, Randolph, Massachusetts, October 12, 1947. Obviously this was a popular sermon of the Reverend Doctor Philbrook. And, do you know what? It became a favorite sermon of mine as well. I often enjoyed using a message title that would catch one's eye and imagination, and usually it was more effective. On one occasion, but for a reason I do not recall, I was asked by the pastor of the church we were attending, the First Baptist Church of Rockland, Massachusetts, to deliver the morning message. I chose this title, "Plus Ultra," and I think it got the attention of the Pastor, Reverend Howard Higgins. As I remember, he was obviously excited by my delivery, and even asked if I would share my notes with him! Bingo!

I was reminded recently, by one of that church's members then accompanying me, that I had costumed up to appear like Christopher Columbus on that date. And I entered the pulpit, just in time to speak, by proceeding down the center aisle, complete with a three-cornered hat and buckled shoes! I can assure you that my flair for getting attention did just that!

As the conclusion of this book, I want to incorporate some of this message as my challenge to succeeding generations: that what transpires after me should be written as a continuation of this treatise. The book of Revelation, the last book of the Bible, cautions that no one should add anything to the Scripture without severe consequences.[2] Further, warning is issued to not take away anything.[3] I do not make any such threats, in the genuine desire that additions should be made from time to time to update and continue the family record. Deletions, where any further research uncovers any change or alterations to correct the record, and make it more accurate, should be undertaken. And no special period attire is necessary!

Now to the lesson: In your best imagination, travel with me today, back into history, to Spain and the year 1492 (That's over 523 years ago!). A poor man with gray hair, disheartened and dejected, rode out from Granada on his mule. Ever since he was a boy, he had been haunted with the idea that the earth is round. He believed that there were lands beyond the seas horizon. The spark that glowed in the soul of this poor Genoese lad became the flame that illuminated a new world!

But this day it appears Columbus had failed in

his efforts to explore his idea further. His last hope of obtaining royal aid to prove his point is gone! He rides his lowly beast – deserting friends call him crazy. Wise men ridicule his theory that the earth is round. How can men walk with their feet up and their heads hanging down? How can trees grow with their roots in the air? Why, it is evident that the water would fall out of the rivers and ponds, and seas. The earth is flat! It is rank heresy to say the earth is round!

Now, Christopher Columbus has waited seven years. His wife is now dead. He draws maps to keep himself from starving. His last interview with King Ferdinand has failed to get his support, either in funds or experimental encouragement. Hope and ambition have fled. His life has failed!

But wait a moment! He is called back. Isabella, wife of the King, has become interested and curious, and possibly decided his efforts would be worth the risk. She offered to pledge her jewels to raise the needed money for Columbus to pursue his experiment.

And so it came to pass that three small vessels sailed out of the harbor of Palos – the sheltered waters -- out into the unknown, untried, western sea. The crews were distracted, almost mutinous. They believed they were sailing to certain extinction. If they did not drop off the edge of the world they would be cooked in a boiling sea!

"Sail On!" ordered Columbus. The compass no longer points directly to the North. SAIL ON, MORE, MUCH MORE BEYOND! Two thousand three hundred miles from land!

A bush floating in the sea. A bush with wild berries. A piece of carved wood – SAIL ON! A light – at 2:00 o'clock in the morning, October 12, from the mast of the PINTA, Roderigo de Friana on the watch, shouts "Land, Land, Land! Sailors are wild with joy. They throw themselves on their knees before Columbus crying out for forgiveness. Reaching shore, the hero of the world's greatest expedition of discovery unfolds the flag of Spain and takes possession of a "New World."

At the same time of this great historical event, a Spanish coin was in circulation. Stamped upon this coin there was a representation of the Pillars of Hercules standing upon either side of the narrow Strait of Gibraltar. On one side is the mighty rock – towering 1400 feet above the sea, key to the Mediterranean. On the reverse side is the uppermost point of Africa. On this ancient Spanish coin, above the Pillars of Hercules, was the motto – in Latin – NE PLUS ULTRA, i.e. "Nothing More Beyond." The Atlantic was a wild waste of forbidding waters – Woe betide the daring mariner who sailed his ship too far and dropped off the rim of the earth into nothingness! Men looked out through the Pillars of Hercules and saw the sun drop beyond the Atlantic and they shuddered and cried NE PLUS ULTRA – Nothing More Beyond!

But Columbus changed all that. Now the motto must be changed! It must now read, simply and grandly, PLUS ULTRA, More Beyond! But even Columbus did not know how much more. He died in ignorance of the vast new world he had discovered.

Obviously there is much more that could be said to build a complete sermon. The applications are obvious and our purpose is not to pursue that avenue here. Suffice it to be known that I recognize there is much more to come and be added to this book, until the return of Jesus. To end this Whitaker history by believing that NE PLUS ULTRA, there is no more beyond, would be futile. There IS more beyond. PLUS ULTRA!

Will you take up the cause and record the next events? You will need Columbus' drive and persistence, and time will prove its worth. A friend of mine, now with the Lord, founder of a very successful business that was born in the depression years, put it this way – "Keep Sawing Wood." (Or, as Dr. Philbrook said, "Plus Ultra!").

There is "More Beyond" to the "born again."[4] Who among those that have died of physical death before us have experienced a brief moment of interruption from earth to a real heaven and are continuing in the enjoyment of their endowment of "eternal life"? It is our hope that many among our predecessors will be there.

ENDNOTES

[1] Pulpit exchange between Baptist Churches was a tradition in those days.
[2] Revelation 22:18.
[3] Revelation 22:19.
[4] Jesus said, **Marvel not that I said unto thee, Ye must be born again**.-- John 3:7 (King James Version).

Appendix F

THE UPPERTAKER

Written by Polly Utley

I'm not looking for the undertaker
I'm looking for the uppertaker
I'm not looking for that sly old faker
I'm looking towards my heavenly maker

I've had a lifetime of walking with Him
I've not regretted a day since that life did begin!!
How precious the walk my path did take
Each step He directed was for the Kingdom's sake.

To study the Word and pass it along
To teach and preach and maybe sing praise songs
To marry and bury and comfort the grieved
What a change in my life since the day I believed!

I want you to know I am ready to shout
When I'm talking to God – that's what I'm about
To guide one to Heaven is my greatest thrill
To tell that He died for you upon Calvary's Hill!

To show you how to live for Him, no matter what it takes
It took my pain of cancer, an example He did make.
His children aren't spared the trials of life that flood
They are cleansed from all sin by His very precious blood!!

Do you know He took your place by hanging on that tree?
Your sin was laid upon Him to save you and me.
Won't you take His hand and let Him have your heart?
My friends, you'll not regret it and He never will depart!

I guess I've said it all, so your choice is yes or no.
I will tell you one last thing before I let you go.
I don't fear Satan, that evil undertaker.
For I am now with Jesus Christ, the glorious uppertaker!!!

See you soon

Love you all
Barry

Appendix G

TRIBUTE TO BARRY GRAHL

by Dr. Christopher Berchelmann

I wanted to say a few words regarding a person to whom I had the privilege of acting as their physician.

I met Mr. Barry Grahl in January of 2007 when he and Mrs. Ann Grahl came to me as patients. In that 9-year period I saw them both periodically, and rarely for anything serious.

Mr. Grahl would come to the office twice a year for a checkup and I cannot recall (and including my office notes) of ever hearing any serious complaints. He was always happy. He was always fun to have as a patient, and we would invariably end up in philosophical conversations regarding or faith. I am sure everyone knows that Mr. Grahl was a retired Baptist minister and never missed an opportunity to share his faith, discuss religion and praise God. He was one of those people I would see on my appointment list that I look at in the morning to see which patients are coming in, and I was very happy to see Barry Grahl's name on my list. And, believe me, I don't always feel that way about every single patient. In this case it was always a joy to see them coming in. Mr. Grahl always reassured me of faith, of my own faith, and made me a better person and think deeper about Jesus.

It was always fun to have Mr. and Mrs. Grahl in the office (most of the time they would come in together) and to see the obvious pride that Barry took in Ann, and the pride Ann took in Barry to have him as her husband. They seemed to compliment each other so well, and their mutual love was so apparent.

He frequently spoke of his family and took pride in his children as well.

I always felt energized at the end of our conversation, especially in my faith of God.

Ann and Barry are such a joy to be around and he will definitely be missed at our office.

My staff also wished to convey their condolences to Mrs. Grahl and the Grahl family, as they think so highly of them as well.

I also would like to make note of the fact that Mr. Grahl, for all the years I knew him, has basically never had a complaint, including these last few months, even. After he was diagnosed with a lymphoma he never complained. He accepted the situation as it was and showed remarkable bravery, never doubting what the future would be.

To close, I thought of Mr. Barry Grahl as a man of character, of honesty, intense loyalty to his family, to his wife, and to God.

I respect him greatly. I looked up to him and, as I said earlier, he made me a better person.

He will be sincerely missed.

Thank you.

Appendix H

TRIBUTE TO ROLLA UTLEY

by Albert P. Whitaker, Jr.

13 Greater love has no one than this, that someone lay down his life for his friends. 14 You are my friends if you do what I command you. 15 No longer do I call you servants, for the servant does not know what his master is doing; but I have called you friends, for all that I have heard from my Father I have made known to you.
--John 15:13-15 (English Standard Version)

Someone has said, "Friendship is the hardest thing in the world to explain."[1] One must actually experience it. To experience it, the person must be one you *Have fun with*
Have confidence in
Spend time with
Have similar beliefs and interests
Are willing to help each other
And trust one another.

Rolla Lee Utley, Jr., and I were close and dear friends.

He began life in the middle of the Depression years, in a little hamlet just outside Hannibal, Missouri, near the home of Samuel Langhorne Clemens, better known as Mark Twain. Life expectancy was 56 years. While not a friend of Mark Twain, Rolla was my friend. We experienced true friendship.

Rolla's mother passed away when he was thirteen years old and, because his father could not support the family, the children were moved into an orphanage nearby.

Rolla believed the world was much larger than the [orphanage's] confines, discipline and fortress walls. Attired in only bibbed overalls that reached barely to just below his knees, and in bare feet, he walked away from this "home," seeking a better life. Romans 10:15b notes,

> "... 'How beautiful are the feet of those who bring good news'."
> --Romans 10:15b (New International Version)

And Rolla was destined to bring *good news* to many.

Soon after leaving the orphanage, he joined the Navy and participated in the excitement of seven major Pacific-area battles.

After discharge, he joined a prominent lumber company and, over many years, rose to a management position. He remained a faithful and respected businessman for many years.

While so engaged, he felt the calling of the Lord on his life. He began a second and concurrent vocation, pastoring in area churches. Later, he assumed full-time pastorates and remained full-time at the business. And, if this was not demanding enough, he attended seminary full-time, and raised a family!

His marriage to Polly, an ambitious schoolteacher from the State of Maine, with flaming red hair, no doubt spurred him on!

But preaching was in his loins. He accepted a call to pastor two churches along the rugged coast of Maine!

But, as they grew older, real retirement seemed the better part of wisdom, so they sold out and moved to Dover, Florida – joining their daughter and [her] husband, recently returned from military duty in Germany.

Dover First Baptist Church was within walking distance, a real convenience and possibly of the Lord's direction.

But did we say "retirement?"

Soon, Rolla joined the staff of the church as *associate pastor* and [was] responsible for senior adults and the visitation ministry. He did this with zeal, and including the daily *Prayer Line* and many funerals that came as a result of his wide visitation. On his 90th birthday, Rolla preached and quoted the entire 39 verses of Romans 8 from memory.

During this time, another retired pastor, Rev. Barry Grahl, came into the area and joined the Dover church. At the same time, we, Norma and I, recently retiring from the staff of a sister church, began [to] fellowship at Dover as well.

Most Sunday mornings, the three families sat together in the same pew. We became very close friends; we worshipped together, shared life's experiences together, prayed together, ate together, socialized and vacationed together, sharing our cares and concerns – truly friends.

Some Sunday mornings, Rolla would be late to sit in the seat we reserved for him and, despite Polly's always looking back for him, he would arrive during the opening music, from an encounter where he comforted, counseled, advised, and/or encouraged someone before the worship service.

We came to appreciate Rolla's prayer – calming, assuring and reverent, as though we were in the very presence [of], and surrounded with the awe of, his majestic Lord.

Rolla would address me: "Good morning, Brother Whitaker" – with the Memphis accent on my name. I would respond by: "Good morning, Right Reverend."

We will no longer exchange that greeting, but I anticipate Rolla's greeting me in Heaven with the same "Good morning, Brother Whitaker," and we can continue the fellowship we once enjoyed here on Earth.

ENDNOTE

[1] Muhammad Ali.

About the Authors

Albert Preston Whitaker, Jr. is a graduate of Boston University with degrees of A.A. in Education and B.S. in Business Administration. After a brief time in the banking field, he was an organizing principal of A. P. Whitaker & Sons, Inc., a major Massachusetts contractor and construction management firm, which is still operating in its fourth generation. After retirement, he was a full-time church business administrator for a large Southern Baptist Church in Florida. In 2015, he published a documented family history, *This Is My Story: A Story of the Whitaker Family*, with his son-in-law Stephen Robbins. In retirement, he resides in Plant City, Florida and summers in Newport, Maine, along with his wife Norma. They have twenty-two grandchildren and many great-grandchildren.

Stephen L. Robbins is a graduate of the University of Maine with degrees of A.A. in Liberal Studies and B.A. in History. He also has a degree from the University of Rhode Island – Master of Library and Information Studies. He ministered as a professional librarian at Lancaster Bible College, at Toccoa Falls College, and at Grace College and Theological Seminary. Now retired, he resides in Warsaw, Indiana with his wife Dr. Dale E. Robbins, DNP (daughter of author Albert P. Whitaker, Jr.). They have two sons and one grandson.

CPSIA information can be obtained
at www.ICGtesting.com
Printed in the USA
FSHW021339080721
82911FS